The Cornerstone on College Hill

The Cornerstone on College Hill

An Illustrated History of the University of Alaska Fairbanks

TERRENCE COLE

University of Alaska Press
Fairbanks, 1994

Library of Congress Cataloging-in-Publication Data

Cole, Terrence, 1953-
    The cornerstone on College Hill : an illustrated history of the
University of Alaska Fairbanks / Terrence Cole.
      p. cm.
    Includes bibliographical references and index.
    ISBN 0-912006-57-9
    1. University of Alaska, Fairbanks--History--Pictorial works.
I. Title.
LD91.A492C65   1994
378.798'6--dc20   93-40545
                                 CIP

Printed in the United States of America by BookCrafters, Inc.

This publication was printed on acid-free paper that meets the minimum requirements for the
American National Standard for Information Science—Permanence of Paper for Printed Library
Materials ANSI Z39.48-1984.

Publication coordination by Pamela Odom with assistance from Deborah Van Stone.
Book and cover design by Dixon Jones, IMPACT Graphics, Elmer E. Rasmuson Library.

End sheet photograph of Mt. McKinley by Bradford Washburn.
Frontispiece photograph of the Alaska Agricultural College and School of Mines, 1929, courtesy of
the Historical Photograph Collection, Rasmuson Library.
Unless otherwise noted, the photographs in this book are from the collections of the Alaska and
Polar Regions department of the Elmer E. Rasmuson Library, University of Alaska Fairbanks.

Publication support was generously provided by:

Elmer E. Rasmuson Library
Kenneth A. Murray, Kenneth H. Murray and Alastair Murray
Walt Schlotfeldt, Petro Star Inc.
Ken and Olga Carson, CULFABCO, Inc.
Earl H. Beistline
Dick and Marionette Stock
Syun-Ichi and Emiko Akasofu
Don Weldon, VISTA Travel
Merritt Helfferich
Dan and Helga Wilm

*This project is supported in part by a grant from the Alaska Humanities Forum
and the National Endowment for the Humanities, a federal agency.*

To my father,

WILLIAM P. COLE,

and to

ELMER E. RASMUSON,

loyal friend and patron of the
University of Alaska Fairbanks.

CONTENTS

No college campus in America has a wilder or more magnificent natural setting than that of the University of Alaska Fairbanks. Four miles from the center of Fairbanks, Alaska, the campus sits atop a steep ridge of ancient rock one hundred feet above the floodplain of the Tanana Valley. About one hundred miles to the south the peaks of the Alaska Range stand out against the sky, towering above the vast uninhabited expanse of the Tanana Valley and thousands of square miles of subarctic forests. Visible farther in the distance to the southwest is Denali (Mount McKinley), the tallest peak in North America, whose summit stands nearly four miles high.

Since the establishment of the University of Alaska as a small college, Denali has been its symbol. Etched on the university seal is a view of Denali from the north face, and "Ad Summum" (To the Highest Point) is the school's motto. One of my favorite views of UAF is from the north on Farmer's Loop Road; when the light is just right, the ghostly shadow of Denali looms above the university as if the campus lay directly at the foot of the mountain. In 1988, *Outside* magazine called the University of Alaska Fairbanks the "ultimate adventure school," and claimed that the eighth floor of Moore Hall had the best view from any college dormitory anywhere.

Three thousand years ago, on the crest of what was to become College Hill, Athabaskan Indians camped to look for game and to spot approaching enemies. Today, that ancient Indian campsite with the panoramic view is the home of Alaska's oldest institution of higher education, the University of Alaska Fairbanks, a place that has helped expand the horizons of students and faculty for four generations.[1]

This history of UAF commemorates the colorful past of one of America's most unusual educational institutions. The school was incorporated during the First World War in 1917 as the Alaska Agricultural College and School of Mines, and its growth since then reflects the development of Alaska itself. UAF was the last traditional land grant college established in the United States; in 1991, it became one of only a few universities in America to be designated a space grant institution by the National Aeronautics and Space Administration. What began in September 1922 as a small mining town's tiny college (with only six students, six professors, a secretary, a maintenance man, and an administrator) has grown into a modern state university with an enrollment of about 9,000 students. It is recognized for its excellence in research and teaching, and is the cornerstone of the University of Alaska Statewide System.

What the frontier college may have lacked in the way of ivy-covered walls and distinguished scholars, it made up for in greater personal attention to students and greater individual freedom. Throughout its history, Alaska—and its oldest university—have attracted fortune hunters, adventure seekers, oddballs and restless souls who could not or would not fit in elsewhere. Probably in no other university could one regularly find moose meat hanging up to dry in the college dorm (a practice that continued through the 1950s), or students building their own log cabins in the woods near campus, a continuing tradition that dates back to the college's first student-homesteader-graduate, Jack Shanly, the lone member of the class of 1923.

The freedom of the frontier has always been the freedom for people to try to reinvent themselves without the shackles of the past, to become something greater than they were before, to draw upon talents that they never knew existed. Freedom of opportunity has made education at UAF a unique adventure for thousands of men and women in all walks of life.

Traditionally, the small size of the UAF student body has almost forced students to participate in numerous activities, while small classes have required them to get to know their professors personally. "I was in some classes that I was the only student," said mining engineer Patrick O'Neill, a 1941 graduate, "and believe me, I had to be prepared when I went to class."[2]

UAF alumni have gone on to distinguished careers in politics, commerce, mining, agriculture, academia, finance, and government. Many might echo 1955 graduate George B. Schaller, winner of the 1973 National Book Award for *The Serengeti Lion*, and the man whom the *New York Times* called "the most famous field biologist in the world today." Schaller told the *New York Times* that his years at UAF changed his entire life. "I've never been interested in anything but the outdoors," Schaller said, "but it wasn't until I got to the university that I discovered you could make a living out of your hobby."[3]

A few other former students include: United States Senator E. L. "Bob" Bartlett; Alaska Governor Jay S. Hammond; outspoken conservationist and defender of wilderness, Margaret Murie; businessmen Bruce Kennedy and Ron Cosgrave, who made Alaska Airlines into one of the best regional carriers in the world; long-time state senators such as Jay Kerttula of Palmer and Steve Frank of Fairbanks; Roger Markle, former president of Quaker State Motor Oil; journalist George Polk, a pioneer broadcaster with CBS News, for whom one of the premier awards in investigative journalism is named; former *Alaska Magazine* and *Milepost* publisher Robert A. Henning; author and teacher Emily Ivanoff Brown; mining engineers Lonnie Heiner and Joe Usibelli; mathematician Ronald Graham of Bell Laboratories; geophysicist Pierre Saint-Amand, one of the leaders in the field of weather modification; and geophysicists T. Neil Davis and Syun-Ichi Akasofu, pioneers in the investigation of the aurora borealis.

Most UAF alumni would probably agree with the wisdom that Texas historian C. L. Sonnichsen once shared with a graduating class of the University of Texas at El Paso. Sonnichsen told the students never to feel intimidated by those who boast that they come from more elite schools with greater prestige. He said a student's education is a highly individual matter that has nothing to do with the size of a university's endowment or the weight of its reputation. "Ask yourself if you had one teacher who changed your life and turned you on," Sonnichsen said. "If you had one—just one—then this has been a great school for you. If you found him and he found you, you don't have to apologize for your university or worry too much about its deficiencies in things that can be counted."[4]

This book is an effort to tell in words and pictures just a small part of how the University of Alaska Fairbanks has changed the lives of thousands of people over the past seventy-five years. Since 1922 the cumulative enrollment at UAF has totaled more than 125,000; students from all fifty states and from many nations around the globe have come to a northern environment unlike any other in American higher education. It has been a daunting challenge to select from among the tens of thousands of photographs in the University Archives, and to choose from the almost infinite number of stories that can be told.

My own trail to UAF began when three muggers in downtown Philadelphia clobbered my brother Patrick with a metal pipe in the fall of 1969. At the time he was a sophomore at Temple University, but his bad headache and his four-day hospital stay convinced him that there had to be a better place to finish his last two years of college. As Patrick tells the story, after his discharge from the hospital he went to the library to investigate other educational opportunities in the United States as far as possible from center city Philadelphia. The college catalogs were filed alphabetically by state. He ruled out Alabama. Next in line was Alaska. He and I drove an old pickup truck 5,000 miles from Pennsylvania to Fairbanks that summer, and to me the UAF campus has felt like home ever since. Among my six brothers and sisters, five have attended UAF, and four of us have earned our undergraduate degrees in Fairbanks.

There are numerous faculty members, staff and alumni whose experience at UAF goes back decades. My father likes to tell an old joke about a man who went to heaven, eager to entertain the saints with his well-worn rendition of the Johnstown Flood, until reminded that Noah was the long-haired fellow sitting in the front row. Like the man from Johnstown, I realize that there are hundreds of people beginning with Dorothy (Roth) Loftus and her brother-in-law Ted Loftus, two of the original students enrolled in 1922, who know far more than I do about their days on College Hill. Yet whatever the vintage of one's experience at UAF, whether it's from the class of 1932 or 1992, I hope that this book will rekindle a memory or two of the way things used to be.

Many people assisted in the preparation of this volume. Numerous UAF alumni, faculty, staff, friends of the University, and Fairbanks residents gave a helping hand, including Gail Adams, Syun-Ichi and Emiko Akasofu, Sharon and George Bell, Earl H. Beistline, Walter Benesch, Jack Bernet, Clarke and Donna Billings, Art Buswell, Ken and Olga Carson, Debbie Carter, Patrick Cole, Dermot Cole, Douglas Colp, Cora Cook, Jack Distad, Glen Franklin, Al George, Bruce Gordon, Major Terrance Hall, Merritt Helfferich, Gordon and Marilyn Herreid, Clare Hill, Betty Hoch, Mary K. Hughes, William R. Hunt, Rachel Ammons Jones, Charles Keim, Ron Keyes, Ken Kollodge, Niilo Koponen, Michael Krauss, Audrey and Ted Loftus, George "Bill" McGee, Ralph Mathews, Francine Mears, Nancy and Bill Mendenhall, Jim Moody, Terris Moore, Lael Morgan, Susan McInnes, Alastair A. Murray, Kenneth A. Murray, Kenneth H. Murray, Danny Nielsen, Dan O'Neill, Stan Patty, Cam Pollock, Brian Rogers, Lee Salisbury, Walt Schlotfeldt, William Schneider, Jo Scott, Mike Sfraga, Joe Sitton, Ed Skellings, Dick and Marionette Stock, Bill and Sandra Stringer, Al Svenningson, Bruce Thomas, Dorothy and Lane Thompson, Lola Tilly, Ann and Joe Tremarello, Mark Van Rhyn, Joan Wadlow, Ann Walsh, Don Weldon, Dan and Helga Wilm, and William R. Wood.

Anyone who writes about the history of the University of Alaska is in debt to the late William R. Cashen, the great raconteur about the early days on College Hill, whose 1972 book *Farthest North College President* is a spirited account of the presidency of Charles Bunnell. Cashen's book, and his many personal reminiscences in "Cashen's Corner" (his column in back issues of the *Alaska Alumnus*) I found invaluable. Similarly, T. Neil Davis, former acting director of the Geophysical Institute, has written a detailed narrative on the presidency of Terris Moore, *The College Hill Chronicles*, which captures the mood of that transitional era.

Dozens of UAF faculty and staff members have made teaching at UAF and compiling this history a real joy, especially former UAF Chancellor Patrick J. O'Rourke, former Dean Anne Shinkwin, Acting Dean Gerald McBeath and Professor Claus-M. Naske.

Professors Naske and Shinkwin were among the many excellent teachers I was lucky to have while I was a student at the university from 1972 to 1978. A few of the other professors whose hard work and dedication helped inspire this book are John Bernet, Norma Bowkett, and Robert Allen, all formerly of the English department; Donald Lynch and the late Herbert Rasche of geography; and Herman Slotnick and William R. Hunt in history.

My friend and research assistant Jane Haigh took time out from her graduate studies to help select photographs. The able staff of the Elmer E. Rasmuson Library, including Bert Fowler, David Hales, Marge Heath, Gretchen Lake, Mary Larson, Anna Poe, Rose Speranza, Ji Yum, and director Paul McCarthy, made it a pleasure as always to prowl through the university archives. People from various departments on campus helped locate other photographs, including Don Borchert of the Institute of Arctic Biology, Shea Burgess of the history department, Roger Powers of the anthropology department, Wayne Fralick of Wood Center, Helen Stockholm of the Institute of Marine Science, Merritt Helfferich of the Geophysical Institute, Calvin White of University Relations, Bill Hauer of the Large Animal Research Station, and Jim Kowalsky of the Rural Alaska Honors Institute.

Photographer Richard Veazey and his staff at the Rasmuson Library did their usual excellent job of reproducing hundreds of photographs, and designer Dixon Jones created a handsome-looking book. Suzanne Bishop of University Relations and Althea St. Martin, formerly of Alumni Relations, provided much support. Carla Helfferich, Pam Odom and Debbie Van Stone of the University of Alaska Press put in many hours to bring the book together. My wife and editor Marjorie Kowalski Cole provided invaluable suggestions and assistance, while Henry and Desmond Cole put up with a dad who was even more distracted than usual during the year and a half it took to write this book.

Finally, I would like to thank my father, William P. Cole, and Elmer E. Rasmuson, to whom this book is dedicated.

TERRENCE M. COLE
ASSOCIATE PROFESSOR AND CHAIR,
DEPARTMENT OF HISTORY,
UNIVERSITY OF ALASKA FAIRBANKS

The Cornerstone on College Hill

AN ILLINOIS FARM BOY
Judge James Wickersham, the Fairbanks pioneer
who conceived the idea of establishing the Alaska
Agricultural College and School of Mines.

Mary Whalen Collection, Rasmuson Library

ONE

The Cornerstone on College Hill

Near the center of the University of Alaska Fairbanks campus is a weathered block of cement cast in 1915, the original cornerstone of the Alaska Agricultural College and School of Mines. Chipped and worn with age, this relic from the past is a monument to the power of a dream. Every day hundreds of students and faculty walk by the old cornerstone, but few realize that there probably would not have been a University of Alaska Fairbanks if not for this four-foot block of concrete.

The man who laid the college cornerstone—and paid for it out of his own pocket—was Alaska's delegate to Congress, James Wickersham, who conceived the idea of founding the first college in Alaska and pursued the goal with the same determination that made him the most successful and controversial politician in territorial Alaska. An Illinois farm boy born in 1857 who never went past the eighth grade, he appreciated education as only those who earn it the hard way can. Despite his lack of formal schooling, he proved to be a man of many talents: a teacher in a one-room school, lawyer, judge, scholar, amateur ethnologist, book collector, bibliographer, historian, and sportsman. A brilliant and stubbornly independent jurist and politician who sat on the Alaska

district court bench for eight years, he was elected as the territory's delegate to Congress in 1908 and served for fourteen years as the voice of Alaska in Washington, D.C. One party label could not contain him; during Wickersham's career he ran as a Republican, a Roosevelt Republican, a Renegade Republican, a Bull Moose, a Woodrow Wilson Progressive Democrat, and an Independent. When it came to politics in those years, Alaskans were divided into two camps: for and against Wickersham. His legislative efforts led to the establishment by law of the Alaska territorial legislature in 1912, the Alaska Railroad in 1914, the Alaska Agricultural College and School of Mines (now the University of Alaska Fairbanks) in 1915, and Mt. McKinley National Park in 1917.[1]

According to legend, Wickersham's inspiration for an Alaskan land grant college came from a law book he used as a doorstop in his Capitol Hill office during the hot summer months in Washington, D.C. The story goes that one day, while working on legislation to withdraw lands for the creation of a public school system in Alaska, the delegate picked the book off the floor and opened it by chance to the section on land grant colleges. His eye caught the provision that promised such institutions a regular annual appropriation of $50,000 from the federal government.[2] Never one to pass up the chance to get

more money for Alaska, Wickersham submitted legislation that would permit establishment of a land grant college in the Tanana Valley near his home town of Fairbanks.

Judge Wickersham always had a tender place in his heart for Fairbanks and the Tanana Valley. In fact it was Wickersham who literally put Fairbanks on the map—on Judge Wickersham's recommendation trader E. T. Barnette had named the community for Sen. Charles W. Fairbanks of Indiana. One of the judge's political mentors, Senator Fairbanks had helped Wickersham receive his appointment as Alaska district court judge in 1900. After Felix Pedro's 1902 gold strike in the hills to the north, Fairbanks became a

roaring gold rush boom town. Wickersham arrived in the spring of 1903 and quickly enshrined two more political allies with street names in Barnette's town: Cushman Street, in honor of Rep. Francis Cushman from Washington, and Lacey Street, in honor of Rep. John F. Lacey of Iowa.[3] Wickersham ensured the survival of the town he had named when he designated Fairbanks as the new headquarters for his district court in 1904, choosing it over the rival town of Chena, about ten miles below Fairbanks at the mouth of the Chena Slough on the Tanana River. Ever since, the judge had considered Fairbanks his home.

But reasons other than sentiment dictated that Fairbanks should be the location of a school for

A field of stumps surround the few buildings of the Fairbanks Agricultural Experiment Station in about 1909. The ridge in the distance is Ester Dome. The farm, established to "test the practicability of real farming in *the Tanana Valley," later became the nucleus of the Alaska Agricultural College and School of Mines.*

Agricultural Experiment Station Collection, Rasmuson Library

mining and agriculture. The Fairbanks mining district was the richest placer gold region in Alaska. In the previous dozen years gold production from Fairbanks had totaled about sixty-three million dollars, far more than any other district in the territory.[4] Furthermore, the Tanana Valley promised to become the breadbasket of Alaska and the center of agricultural production in the far north.

In the summer of 1905, federal agricultural agents C. C. Georgeson and Fred Rader had surveyed the Fairbanks area to find a suitable location for a U.S. Department of Agriculture Experiment Station.[5] After three days of exploring on horseback they chose about fourteen hundred acres halfway between Chena and Fairbanks along the Tanana Mines Railway, the narrow gauge railroad that connected the two cities with the mining camps in the hills to the north. The railroad's builder and owner, Falcon Joslin, had suggested the site for the government farm. Georgeson thought the gently sloping, south-facing ridge covered with spruce and birch trees was an "admirable tract of land for an experiment station," especially because of its proximity to the railroad.[6]

Agents cleared the first ten acres at the Fairbanks Experiment Station in 1907, and field work began the next year, with the planting of turnips, cabbages, thirty-two varieties of potatoes, and various strains of barley, oats, and rye.[7] Long-range plans called for five hundred acres to be cleared for farming. "This will give an opportunity to test the practicability of real farming in the Tanana Valley," Georgeson wrote in his 1909 annual report. ". . . The chief object of the work at this station is to determine whether or not farming can be made to pay."[8]

By 1915 few members of Congress were convinced that Alaskan agriculture would ever pay. When Wickersham introduced a bill that year to create the Alaska Agricultural College and School of Mines, the delegate said he was "openly derided" by his congressional colleagues. Wickersham claimed that skeptical congressmen "grew merry" at his proposal to reserve about 2,250 acres surrounding the Fairbanks Agricultural Experiment Station for a college campus. According to Wickersham's measure the experiment station land would be transferred to the college if and when the federal government ceased operation of the agricultural station.[9]

Several congressmen ridiculed the very idea of establishing a college in Alaska. Opponents objected most strongly to the specification that the school be placed in Fairbanks. They claimed that the Alaska territorial legislature, not the U.S. Congress, should decide where the college should be located. Wickersham then produced a telegram signed by Alaska Governor J. F. A. Strong and nineteen members of the territorial legislature urging approval of the Fairbanks college.[10]

A congressional supporter of Wickersham pointed out that a college anywhere else in Alaska *but* Fairbanks would be a "joke," though he added that only time would tell if a college in Fairbanks would or would not be a laughing matter as well. Furthermore, by locating the college at Fairbanks, the federal government would eventually be able to rid itself of the costly Fairbanks Experiment Station by turning it over to the college.[11]

In spite of his sarcastic opponents, Wickersham doggedly persevered. As a Fairbanks newspaper later reported his battle, "The members of Congress joked

5

A land grant college
without the land

The original 1915 Alaska land grant legislation reserved about 2,250 acres for a campus site around the Agricultural Experiment Station in Fairbanks. The 1915 law also authorized the federal government to give Alaska's land grant college more than a quarter of a million acres of revenue land in the Tanana Valley, proceeds from the sale and development of which would help finance the operation of the college. Under the terms of the measure written by Delegate James Wickersham, the college was to receive every surveyed and unclaimed Section 33 in an area of about 14,000 square miles from Fairbanks to the foothills of the Alaska Range.

However, this large Tanana Valley land grant never materialized. For decades almost all of the land in the Tanana Valley (like the rest of Alaska) remained unsurveyed and therefore unavailable. As a result the college received only a fraction of its initial grant, about 12,000 acres.

To remedy the situation, in 1929 Congress granted to the college an additional 100,000 acres that could be selected anywhere in Alaska. Even so, the total was less than half of the original acreage authorized in 1915. The coming of Alaska statehood in 1959 extinguished the university's legal rights to further land under the 1915 grant, leaving the university of the largest state in the union with nearly the smallest land grant in the country.

---

him about his proposed bill, not taking it seriously; they thought it ridiculous that such a school should be established away off up here, where nobody lives and the dogs bark at strangers, but they were willing to carry the joke on and they voted for the Wickersham bill, which was all HE wanted."[12] At about four o'clock in the morning on March 4, 1915, the last bill to pass in the last hour of the last day of the Sixty-third Congress was Wickersham's measure reserving a three and a half square mile tract of land for a campus in Fairbanks and about 250,000 acres in the Tanana Valley for the support of the agricultural college.

With the promise of a land grant, Wickersham next had to convince the territorial legislature to fund the construction of a college that could officially accept the gift of land. But first he had to get Alas-

kans to stop laughing long enough to hear his proposal out.

Objections raised in Washington, D.C.—Alaska had too few people and too little money, Fairbanks was too cold and too far away—would also be heard in the legislature in Juneau. Then, too, politicians from other parts of Alaska might support a college, but only if it was located in their districts. Even in Fairbanks many residents thought the notion of establishing a local college was a joke.[13] In 1915 Fairbanks was still a frontier mining camp of log cabins and dirt streets without a single concrete structure. Population and gold production were both declining, and some people feared that Fairbanks was destined to disappear the way so many other mining camps had.

To dampen the humor of his critics and to give an aura of reality to the whole enterprise, Wickersham planned a ceremonial dedication of a college cornerstone, with full Masonic rites, for July 4, 1915. He had no legal right to dedicate anything, since the college did not yet exist. Until the territorial legislature had a chance to meet and pass legislation formally incorporating it, the Alaska Agricultural College and School of Mines would be nothing more than Wickersham's personal obsession.

"At work preparing a tentative list of officials for a bold bluff organization of the Alaska Agri. College and School of Mines," Wickersham wrote in his diary on June 21, 1915. ". . . I intend to 'keep going' until we get the College built and opened. It must not be allowed to stop and the interest of the people not be permitted to lag. So I am pushing forward the organization, though without authority of law . . . ."[14]

Later that week Mr. and Mrs. Wickersham, Fairbanks Episcopal minister Rev. Hope Lumpkin, Harriet Hess, and Fairbanks Mayor Andrew Nerland crowded into the automobile of J. H. Groves and drove four and a half miles out of town on the rugged road to the Fairbanks Experiment Station. They hoped to find a site for the cornerstone somewhere on the parcel around the experiment station reserved for the college campus. East of the farm on the crest of a tree-covered ridge—then known locally as Birch Hill—Wickersham and his companions found an ideal setting. The Athabaskan Indian name for the site was Troth Yeddha' or "Indian Potato Ridge," after the common name of *Hedysarum alpinum*, the small pink flowers that grew profusely on the hillside.[15] It would soon become popularly known as "College Hill." Judge Wickersham asked Mrs. Hess to pick the exact point on the ground for the cornerstone. She broke a small tree and tied a handkerchief to mark the spot among the paper birches.[16]

Best of all, the site offered a majestic view of Denali (Mount McKinley) and the Alaska Range. Ever since James Wickersham had first seen the Alaska Range from Fairbanks in April 1903, he had been irresistibly drawn to the high peaks of southern Alaska. ". . . the view across the fifty-mile valley of the Tanana . . . makes the blood race in one's veins," he wrote.[17] Clearly visible from the spot he picked for the college was the 12,339 foot peak the judge had named in honor of his wife, Mount Deborah. Wickersham himself had made the first serious attempt to climb Denali in 1903; in the 1940s, renowned photographer and climber Bradford Washburn would name the 9,000-foot cliff by which Wickersham had tried his ascent "Wickersham Wall."[18]

With the profile of Denali in the distance, Wickersham and a handful of friends inspired by his vision of the future college hurriedly worked to prepare for the grand celebration. In the hot days of late June 1915—with the temperature climbing to ninety-four degrees in the shade and 115 degrees in the sun—they cut a narrow trail from the Tanana Valley Railway up through the trees to the top of the hill, cleared the land, and poured the cement for the cornerstone. A few people helped, but the judge did much of the work himself. "Am getting very little assistance," he complained in his diary, "but it is because—I suppose—I am doing it without asking much assistance." He also personally paid the bills for the project; the total cost of laying the cornerstone was about $125, of which he paid all but $20 out of his own pocket.[19]

"... WHICH WE ARE THIS DAY DEDICATING...."
Wickersham delivers the main address at the ceremonial laying of the Alaska Agricultural College cornerstone on July 4, 1915.

Wickersham Collection, Alaska State Library

So all would be sure to know what the concrete block in the woods represented, Wickersham planned to spell out the word "CORNERSTONE" on top of the inscription. When the wood frame was removed, however, some of the letters broke and Wickersham covered the entire word with mortar. According to

William R. Cashen, a student and professor closely associated with the University of Alaska for nearly fifty years, Wickersham was alleged to have said: "If they're smart enough to come to college they'll be smart enough to *know* this is a cornerstone!"[20] The inscription that remained read:

The first historian of the University of Alaska

No history of the University of Alaska could be complete without a special tribute to its first historian, William R. Cashen, shown here in 1957 when he was dean of students. For nearly fifty years, from the 1930s to the 1970s, the University of Alaska was his home, and Cashen loved to tell tales about the early days on College Hill. He started on campus as a student in the mid-1930s, during which time he was editor of the *Collegian* and President Bunnell's chauffeur. Five years after graduation he returned as a mathematics instructor. Over the next three decades he held numerous positions, including mathematics department head, dean of men, dean of students, director of summer sessions, head of alumni services,

and marshal of the university. His biography of Charles Bunnell, *Farthest North College President*, was published in 1970. Cashen died in 1981 at the age of sixty-six.

A. A. C. - S. M.
July 4, 1915
L.D. 5915

Thus Wickersham decided the college should be born on the 4th of July and would be called the "Alaska Agricultural College and School of Mines." He added the Masonic year at the bottom to lay claim to yet another historic tradition upon which he was building. The judge's decision to choose the trappings of a Masonic ritual for launching the college so angered Father Francis Monroe, local pastor of the Immaculate Conception Catholic Church, that Monroe refused to have anything to do with the dedication of the stone.[21]

On the afternoon of July 4, 1915, an enthusiastic crowd of about 300 climbed aboard an excursion train of the Tanana Valley Railroad in Fairbanks and rode out toward the clearing in the woods on College Hill. The crowd gathered under bright sunny skies to witness Wickersham's elaborate ceremony and to listen to several speeches, including a few remarks by Superintendent J. W. Neal, manager of the Experiment Station, and the main address by Wickersham. No future professor of the college he was founding could have out-talked the judge. Wickersham was known as a rousing stump speaker with great endurance. He once made a five and a half hour nonstop speech in Congress, one of the longest on record, and had written in his diary the next day, "I feel like a woman who has had a baby—very proud, but damned sore."[22] His nearly 5,000-word address on the laying of the cornerstone was not quite so lengthy. He gave a detailed history of how he had engineered passage of the congressional bill reserving land for the college. Even more important, he related what remained to be done to make the college a reality.

Mining and agriculture would be the foundation of the school he wanted to see on the hillside, but he also foresaw a broader range of study. "While the college which we are this day dedicating will give special prominence to the study of scientific methods of agriculture and mining," he told the assembled crowd, "it will also support a university course and become a fountainhead for the general diffusion of knowledge among the people of Alaska." Wickersham said Congress had given the people of the territory "the most beautiful site in Alaska for the establishment of such a school," as well as a grant of about 250,000 acres in the Tanana Valley to provide continuing income for the school, and the promise of an annual appropriation of $50,000 cash "in perpetuity" for the support and maintenance of the college. He announced that he had formed a committee of a dozen leading Fairbanks residents to lobby the legislature to "provide ways and means for constructing buildings, employing teachers and organizing the work of the college," otherwise both the "free" land grant and the "free" $50,000 annual appropriation would never materialize, and neither would the A.A.C. & S.M.

Judge Wickersham closed his oration with a rousing 4th of July cry to remember Bunker Hill, Saratoga, Trenton, Yorktown and the Alaska Agricultural College and School of Mines. ". . . We who are gathered here today do most solemnly dedicate these grounds and this cornerstone to the everlasting support of the principles of free government, free speech, and free schools for which our forefathers fought."[23]

The crowd went home with Wickersham's oratorical fireworks ringing in their ears, but for two years the lonely cornerstone in the birch trees was all there was to the Alaska Agricultural College and School of Mines. At times it seemed that a small block of concrete with writing on one side was all the college would ever be. Many Alaskans either opposed the whole idea of wasting money on a college located in Alaska, or more specifically opposed the idea of wasting money on a college located in Fairbanks. Opening the institution would cost the territorial treasury $50,000 or more up front in construction costs, or about ten percent of the territory's total annual revenue.[24]

Some people, however, did share the judge's vision that a college—and perhaps eventually a university—would be built on Wickersham's cornerstone. "The University of Alaska is not an idle dream," one Wickersham supporter wrote in November 1915. "It is not a weird fantasy of the brain. It is a truth which each month brings nearer a realization. It is a glimpse of a future of a frontier empire so vast and large that whole states could be lost in it unnoticed."[25]

College supporters found other Alaskans to be skeptical about the wisdom of investing in higher education in part due to Alaska's rapidly declining economic fortunes. Production from Alaska's gold mines, which directly or indirectly supported sixty percent of Alaska's population, had been declining for almost a decade because many of the richest pockets of placer gold were exhausted. By 1914, gold output had fallen nearly thirty percent from the peak year of 1906. Alaskan miners were painfully adjusting to the fact that their richest creeks were running dry and that they needed to mine lower grade deposits of gold more efficiently. Wartime inflation had tripled the cost of gold mining in Alaska, while the price of gold remained frozen by law at about twenty dollars an ounce. The precipitous decline in Alaska's mining industry dealt a "staggering blow to the prosperity of the Territory." As a result, between 1916 and 1918 mining employment in Alaska fell by forty percent and gold production declined by about fifty percent.[26]

"Practically every outgoing steamer is loaded to capacity," Governor Thomas Riggs stated in his 1918 annual report, "and when the seasonal industries of fishing, placer mining and railroad construction are finished for the year the exodus will be almost in the nature of a stampede." The Native population remained relatively stable, as the majority of Native residents lived a subsistence life style in the bush, but the white population of the territory plummeted by an estimated thirty to fifty percent between 1916 and 1918. In 1918 Governor Riggs warned that unless the government actively encouraged settlers and investors, "the Territory will practically become depopulated."[27]

Under the worsening economic conditions in 1917, many people naturally believed that starting a college in an isolated spot like Fairbanks was an ill-conceived scheme that could not succeed. Proponents of the college believed that scientific methods of mining and agriculture could stabilize the economy. They argued that research benefiting farmers and prospectors at an agricultural and mining school was the very solution to the territory's dilemma. "If we are to develop the agricultural and mining resources of this great Territory," the Fairbanks Commercial Club pleaded with the legislature, "what (could be) more reasonable than to here train the rising generation (to learn) the best method of meeting the emergencies and overcoming the difficulties."[28]

When the Alaska legislature convened in Juneau in March 1917, Rep. Andrew Nerland of Fairbanks, who had assisted the judge in laying the cornerstone, and Wickersham's close associate Sen. Dan Sutherland, who would replace Wickersham as delegate in 1921, introduced legislation in both the House and the Senate for the creation of the Alaska Agricultural College and School of Mines in Fairbanks. It was a bitter political battle, inflamed by regional rivalries and jealousies. The editor of the *Anchorage Times* condemned the college in Fairbanks as a "criminal" extravagance that would "serve no useful purpose" and "loot the limited funds of the territorial treasury."[29] Sen. John Ronan from Anchorage supported the idea of an Alaskan college, but he argued that it should be established in the Matanuska Valley, not in a "temporary placer camp" like Fairbanks.[30]

Near the closing days of the session, the bill to establish and appropriate $60,000 for the Alaska Agricultural College and School of Mines came up for a final vote in the house; after two hours of hot debate, during which the opponents "did everything possible to kill the measure," it passed by a single vote.[31] Governor J. F. A. Strong reluctantly signed the bill on May 3, 1917. Thus, one month after the United States entered the war to end all wars, the Alaska Agricultural College and School of Mines was officially born.

The establishment of the A.A.C. & S.M. was one of the sweetest accomplishments of Wickersham's career. Two days after the legislature approved the college bill, the *Fairbanks Daily News-Miner* praised his efforts: "ALL the credit for this benefit is James Wickersham's ALONE." The editor noted that "there is a good deal of the bulldog in Jim's makeup," and that he had ignored those who had laughed at his plans. "If there were any way to attach the name of Wickersham to the title of the Fairbanks college, the *News-Miner* would work to see it done, but name or no name, the college will forever stand as a monument to the achievements of James Wickersham."[32]

In August 1917, the governor named the first eight members of the board of trustees who would be responsible for the organization and opening of the A.A.C. & S.M. They included L. Frank Shaw of Anchorage, Louis Keller of Skagway, Philip Ernst of Nome, and five residents of Fairbanks: Henry Parkin, Tony Nordale, Albert Heilig, R. C. Wood, and Harriet Hess. The lone woman on the board, Hess had marked the site for the cornerstone with her handkerchief in 1915. She would serve on the board for thirty-four years, longer than anyone else in the history of the school.

The trustees from Fairbanks assumed primary responsibility for the college from the beginning. Due to the high cost and slow speed of travel in the years before scheduled air service, the out-of-town trustees never came to any of the thirty-one formal meetings held during the first year. By 1921 the trustees from Nome, Anchorage, and Skagway had been replaced by Fairbanksans, and for the first time the full board was present at a meeting.[33]

Among the problems they faced was where to locate the first college building. There were no funds to build a dormitory, and some Fairbanks residents thought the site Wickersham had selected was so far out of town that it was unrealistic to expect students to walk four and a half miles one way every day to go to school. They suggested instead that the first college building be located closer to Fairbanks, perhaps on the homestead of Paul Rickert (near the current intersection of Cushman Street and Airport Road). But Wickersham's original plan prevailed when one trustee predicted that as Fairbanks grew, College Hill might not seem quite so far away.[34]

Judge Wickersham recommended that the trustees should exhibit long-range vision by building on College Hill the first concrete structure in interior Alaska. Skeptics thought a concrete building might crumble at subarctic winter temperatures of fifty or sixty degrees below zero, but Wickersham believed a permanent building would be a strong symbol of the college's future. Though concrete would cost more than a wood frame building, Wickersham explained to Trustee Harriet Hess that he would "rather have the plans for a large and sufficient building prepared and build one story every two years than to build a balloon frame and have it burn . . . ."[35] Due to the high costs of construction and limited funds, the trustees decided on a two-story wood frame building that could be enlarged with the addition of wings on either end as the need arose.

Construction began on the "Main College Building" in the summer of 1918. Wickersham's cornerstone was found to be too close to the edge of the hill, so it was not used as part of the foundation. Instead the cornerstone was left standing by itself as a monument to the founding of the A.A.C. & S.M, with the Main Building placed across the hill about eighty feet to the north.[36]

Though the shell of the Main Building was structurally complete by the time the Great War ended in November 1918, the wartime shortage of construction materials and steep inflation left the trustees with no money to equip the building or hire a staff. They returned to the legislature in 1919 to ask for more funds, but with the crash of Alaska's economy and the decline of its population during the Great War, the trustees received a cool reception. "The fight over the Fairbanks Agricultural College," a Juneau newspaper explained in May 1919, "has been one of the hardest fought battles ever witnessed in an Alaska Legislature."[37] Despite the trustees' solemn promise not to ask future legislatures for more than $16,000 a year, the college received absolutely no funds at all for the coming biennium. As a result, the trustees boarded up the Main Building on College Hill, and it remained empty for the next two years.

Some politicians hoped that the Alaska Agricultural College and School of Mines was dead, but it struggled back to life in 1921, when the legislature finally granted an emergency appropriation to finish construction of the Main Building, procure equipment, hire a staff, and build a house for the president. Unfunded, the college had already lost two years; now its recovery and survival depended on strong leadership and stability. The man who would nurse the A.A.C. & S.M. back to health—and the first man the trustees hired—was the president, forty-three-year-old Charles E. Bunnell.

During the twenty-eight years Charles Bunnell would serve as chief executive, he did whatever was necessary to keep the college alive, from lobbying the legislature to sweeping the floors, from teaching classes to chopping wood, from recruiting students to cleaning out the coal bin. More than any other single individual, Bunnell was responsible for saving—again and again—the school Judge James Wickersham had established. Ironi-

cally, Bunnell was one of Wickersham's most bitter enemies and the feud between the two men lasted as long as they lived.

Though twenty-one years younger than Wickersham, Bunnell had much in common with his older rival. Both had been federal district court judges in Alaska and were not afraid to make tough decisions; both had sentenced men to death. Judge Wickersham and Judge Bunnell could be unbelievably stubborn; when convinced they were right on an issue, neither man was willing to compromise his honor. Both were disciplined workers, ready to give all of themselves to the task at hand. The two judges also shared a love of books, scholarship, and learning. They both wrote poetry and on occasion might inflict it upon a captive audience.

Their educational backgrounds, however, were quite different. Wickersham came from an older generation, and was largely self-taught; his formal schooling finished in the eighth grade. Bunnell was a prep-school boy and university man with a graduate degree. Bunnell grew up on a small farm in northeastern Pennsylvania. After completing high school he worked his way through two years of prep school and four years of college at Bucknell University, where he majored in classical studies—Latin and Greek—with the goal of becoming a teacher. He was a brilliant student and earned A's in sixty-one of sixty-five college classes, though he naturally found some courses more enthralling than others. One day while sitting in geology class he wrote his sister, "These lectures are dryer than dust, and so I just thought I might write to you a note at this time. I suppose the Prof. thinks that I am very industrious taking so many notes."[38]

CHARLES E. BUNNELL

Democratic Nominee for

DELEGATE TO CONGRESS

Election Nov. 3, 1914

Bunnell's extracurricular activities would fill a college yearbook. He tried to take advantage of everything Bucknell had to offer, all the while working as a waiter to pay his bills: freshman Declamation Team; junior and senior class poet; member of the Cornet Band; staff of the college yearbook; assistant editor of the college paper; and graduation commencement speaker on "The Distinctive Characteristics of Anglo-Saxon Poetry."

In addition to all of the above, Bunnell was shortstop on the baseball team and quarterback of the varsity football team. The fullback to whom he handed-off the football was Christy Mathewson, who would become a Hall of Fame pitcher with the New York Giants by throwing the famous "fadeaway" or screwball that big league batters found nearly impossible to hit.

In 1900, the year Mathewson made his debut with the New York Giants, Bunnell's debut in his chosen career was not so spectacular. "My first day of school was somewhat different than I had anticipated in my college days," the former honor student in Latin and Greek wrote in 1901, "for I had always hoped to make my first appearance before a class in some school of much higher grade than the Public School of Alaska." Hired by the U.S. Bureau of Education as a teacher at Wood Island, near Kodiak, Alaska, for eighty dollars a month, Bunnell found himself in a classroom of Native students, many of whom could not speak English. "I must confess that

I felt for once that I had a problem before me which the X and Y of Algebra could not solve."[39]

Bunnell persevered—and no doubt so did the students. After one year at Wood Island he returned briefly to Pennsylvania, where he married his college classmate Mary Ann Kline. The newlyweds both taught for two years in the Kodiak city public school, during which time Bunnell earned his Master of Arts degree from Bucknell with a thesis on banking, economics, and the law. In 1903 the Bunnells moved to Valdez where he became school principal at $125 a month.

After four years of running the school in Valdez, Bunnell quit to pursue what he thought would be a more lucrative career as a banker, taking the post of assistant cashier in the Reynolds-Alaska Development Company Bank. Unfortunately, bank owner H. D. Reynolds turned out to be a masterful con artist, and his bank failed only nine days after Bunnell was on the job. In desperate need of employment, Bunnell took up the study of law. Through correspondence lessons and independent study in the office of a local attorney, he passed the bar exam in 1908 and joined a successful law practice.

The promising young Valdez attorney was a loyal Democrat active in party politics. He applauded the 1912 election of Dr. Woodrow Wilson, former president of Princeton University, as president of the United States. When it came time in 1914 for Alaskan Democrats to pick a challenger to run against incumbent Delegate James Wickersham, the remains of a badly split Democratic party (half of which had endorsed Wickersham) selected Charles Bunnell as its standard bearer after all of the stronger candidates spurned the dubious opportunity.

Almost no one gave Bunnell, age thirty-six, a chance against Wickersham, the immensely popular head of the territory's most formidable political machine. Bunnell was a young man barely known by anyone outside his home town, and he obviously did not have the stature or the political skills of the veteran judge from Fairbanks. "Some claim that the Democrats are plainly trying to elect Wickersham again," a Juneau newspaper wrote, "and have chosen Mr. Bunnell for the slaughter."[40] Bunnell campaigned on the slogan "A vote for Bunnell is a vote for Wilson," but not even the president of the United States could get Charles Bunnell elected in 1914. Wickersham won by a landslide with almost sixty percent of the vote.[41]

One month after being trounced by Wickersham in the 1914 election, the Democratic administration rewarded Bunnell with an appointment to a seat on the Alaska District Court. Wickersham, never one to rejoice at the success of his opponents, found Bunnell's judgeship hard to take. He grew to hate the young jurist after the contested elections of 1916 and 1918, when Wickersham thought Bunnell was conspiring with other Democrats to steal his congressional seat from him. The House of Representatives upheld Wickersham's narrow victories in both the 1916 and 1918 elections, and the delegate vowed vengeance. When Bunnell's four-year term as judge expired, Wickersham blocked Senate confirmation of Bunnell's reappointment for two years, forcing Bunnell to serve on recess appointments until President Warren G. Harding's Republican administration won election in 1920, removing any hope of reappointment for a Democrat like Bunnell.

On August 1, 1921, the Harding administration announced Bunnell was to be replaced as federal

15

judge pending confirmation of his successor, Cecil R. Clegg. Ten days later, while he was still trying to decide what to do with the rest of his life—perhaps going to graduate school for a Ph.D. at the University of Chicago, perhaps returning to Pennsylvania to practice law—the board of trustees offered Bunnell the position as president of the Alaska Agricultural College and School of Mines. Wickersham, furious that a political hack intellectually unfit (in his opinion) for the job of president would take over the school that he had fathered, lobbied madly behind the scenes to have Bunnell fired. With a Republican majority on the board of trustees, and the support of the new Republican Governor Scott C. Bone, Wickersham believed he had the votes to throw out Bunnell. However, at the meeting of the board of trustees on December 5, 1921, the motion to remove Bunnell from office "for the best interests of the College" failed by a vote of five to three, when two of the five Republicans sided with Bunnell.[42]

Wickersham resigned himself for the time being to the fact that Bunnell had taken control of the Alaska Agricultural College and School of Mines, but he never forgave him. Bunnell claimed that until the day James Wickersham died in 1939, the old judge never failed "to deal me as much misery and opposition as he could conveniently command."[43]

With the vote of approval from the board of trustees in December 1921, Bunnell rapidly pushed ahead with all that needed to be done to open the school: ordering books and laboratory equipment, buying desks and chairs, hiring faculty and staff, choosing a program of study, devising a curriculum, and advertising for students. In September 1922, nine and a half months after Bunnell officially started work, the A.A.C. & S.M. was ready for its grand dedication.

On the afternoon of September 13, 1922, a parade of twenty-four automobiles carrying local residents and special guests drove slowly along the road from Fairbanks to College Hill, where they were met by a trainload of school children. At the College Gate an imposing sign over the road read:

Dedicated Sept. 13, 1922
ALASKA AGRICULTURAL COLLEGE
AND SCHOOL OF MINES

The procession of cars drove under the archway while the children and their teachers, and a few of the college's six faculty members wearing academic robes, lined the edge of the road. As the day wore on, the festivities drew hundreds of people and dozens of cars to the college—causing the first traffic jam in campus history. An impromptu five-piece band made up of local youngsters (who had practiced together only once) provided musical entertainment. The formal ceremonies were held on a stage constructed in front of the Main Building. Alaska Territorial Governor Scott C. Bone was the main speaker of the day.[44]

"The opening of this institution . . . is a potent sign of the times," Bone said. "It speaks progress. It tells the world that Alaska is going ahead. It proclaims, in its name, the fact that agriculture and mining are twin resources of this rich domain. It gives denial to the popular fiction that Alaska is a forbidding, frozen upheaval of ice and snow. It emphasizes the real

Alaska." Governor Bone stressed the importance of the college's unique location. "Away off here near the top of the world," he said, "the institution dedicated to-day occupies a unique position. It has no counterpart. It will command universal interest. It stands out in bright token of Alaska's high aspiration. It will grow as Alaska is surely destined to grow."[45]

The *Fairbanks Daily News-Miner* said afterwards that the A.A.C. & S.M. had "opened in a blaze of glory."[46] But missing from the stage that afternoon was James Wickersham. Everyone in Alaska knew that he had created the school with his quixotic vision, his 1915 land grant bill in Congress, and a four-foot block of concrete. Now, indisposed by politics and pride, Wickersham was obliged to stand aside as the new president, along with the first students, faculty and staff, assumed responsibility for the Alaska Agricultural College and School of Mines.

Portfolio
1903–1922

DEDICATION DAY AT THE ALASKA
*Agricultural College and School
of Mines, September 13, 1922.*

JAMES WICKERSHAM WAS ONE OF ALASKA'S MOST *gifted and popular politicians. He served as Alaska's delegate to Congress for fourteen years. This Wickersham rally in the mining camp of Fox, about ten miles north of Fairbanks, greeted the candidate in his 1910 campaign for delegate.*

Wickersham Collection, Alaska State Library

(OPPOSITE) E. T. BARNETTE'S TRADING POST—WHICH *became the city of Fairbanks—as it looked about the time that Judge James Wickersham first saw it in 1903. Wickersham, on whose suggestion the town was named Fairbanks, located his courthouse here and thus ensured the community's survival. The photographer was standing near what became the center of downtown Fairbanks, at approximately the corner of Second and Cushman Streets. Only a dozen years after this photo was taken, Wickersham proposed that Fairbanks be the home of the first college in Alaska.*

Wickersham Collection, Alaska State Library

GOLD MINERS WORKING UNDERGROUND
*on a creek in the Fairbanks mining
district. As the center of the richest
placer gold mining region in Alaska,
Fairbanks seemed to be an ideal location
for a mining school.*

Archie Lewis Collection, Rasmuson Library

ESTER STATION ON THE
*narrow gauge Tanana
Valley Railway, which
linked the communities of
Fairbanks and Chena
with the gold mines in the
hills to the north. Left of
the tracks was a
1,400–acre Agricultural
Experiment Station
established by the U.S.
Government in 1905.*

Author's collection

BESIDES PRODUCING
*millions of dollars in gold
every year, the Tanana
Valley was also one of
the most productive
agricultural regions in
Alaska, as shown by
this exhibit at the
Tanana Valley fair in
September 1909.*

Author's collection

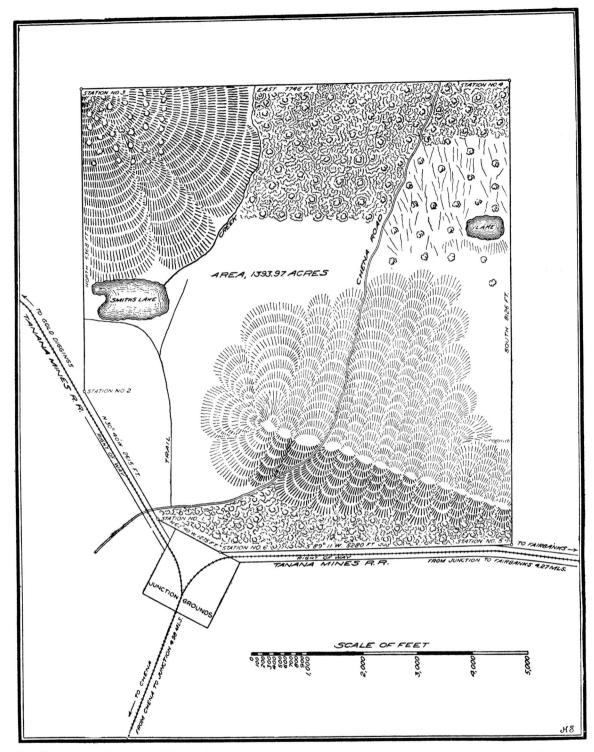

FIG. 1.—Map of proposed United States reservation for experiment station purposes between Fairbanks and Chena, Alaska.

A 1905 MAP OF THE U.S. AGRICULTURAL EXPERIMENT Station alongside the tracks of the Tanana Mines Railroad near Fairbanks. The experiment station became the nucleus of the Alaska Agricultural College and School of Mines.

Rasmuson Library

23

AFTER THE STUMPS WERE PULLED, THE SOUTH
*facing slope of the experimental farm proved to be
ideal for raising grain. On the left is the base of Chena
Ridge and in the background on the right is the
shoulder of Ester Dome.*

Agricultural Experiment Station Collection, Rasmuson Library

J. W. NEAL, APPOINTED *superintendent of the Fairbanks Agricultural Experiment Station in 1908, stands with his wife and daughter in front of the station cabin in 1917.*

Agricultural Experiment Station Collection, Rasmuson Library

THRASHING WHEAT EXPERIMENTAL FARM FAIRBANKS AAA

THRASHING WHEAT *at the Fairbanks Experiment Station.*

Agricultural Experiment Station Collection, Rasmuson Library

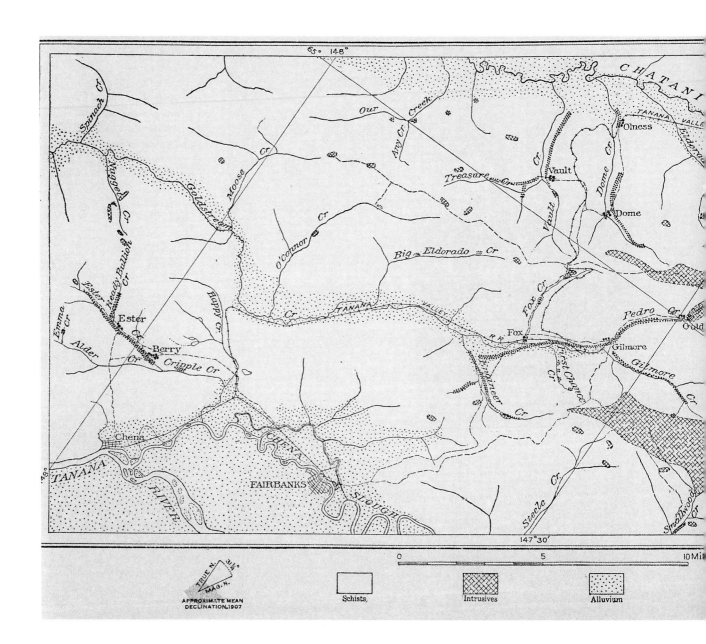

A MAP OF THE FAIRBANKS MINING DISTRICT
published in 1911. The site Wickersham chose for the
Alaska Agricultural College and School of Mines in
1915 was near the junction of the narrow gauge
Tanana Valley Railroad from Chena and Fairbanks.

U.S. Geological Survey

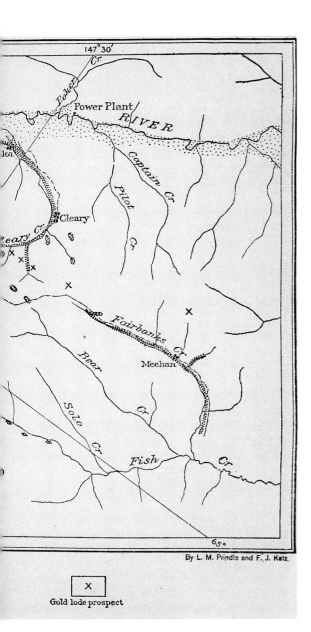

By L. M. Prindle and F. J. Katz.

☒
Gold lode prospect

Mike Yankovich on his homestead northwest of College.

AMONG THE DOZENS OF FARMERS WHO HOME-
steaded in the Tanana Valley, several farmed land
near the Agricultural Experiment Station and the
Alaska Agricultural College, including Hampton
Ballaine, for whom Ballaine Lake is named, and Mike
Yankovich (shown above). Yankovich's farm is today
part of UAF's Large Animal Research Station,
popularly known as the Musk Ox Farm.

Agricultural Experiment Station Collection, Rasmuson Library

JAMES WICKERSHAM AND HIS WIFE DEBORAH AT
*their home in Fairbanks. Wickersham named Mount
Deborah in the Alaska Range, clearly visible from the
ridge on which he located the college, in honor
of his wife.*

Wickersham Collection, Alaska State Library

THE CITY OF FAIRBANKS AS IT LOOKED IN ABOUT
*1915, when James Wickersham suggested a ridge
four miles from town to be the site of the Alaska
Agricultural College and School of Mines.*

Erskine Collection, Rasmuson Library

IN MARCH 1915, WICKERSHAM CONVINCED
*Congress to reserve up to 250,000 acres in the Tanana
Valley for support of a land grant college in Alaska.
Many Alaskans were still skeptical about establishing
a college in a mining camp, so in order to get local
Fairbanks residents to take his plans seriously
Wickersham staged a cornerstone dedication with full
Masonic rites on July 4, 1915. Originally above the
initials A.A.C.-S.M. he had written the word
"CORNERSTONE," but some of the letters broke and
he filled in the word with mortar. Wickersham
allegedly said, "If they're smart enough to come to
college, they'll be smart enough to know that this is a
cornerstone."*

Historical Photograph Collection, Rasmuson Library

FAIRBANKS YOUNGSTERS *dressed in their best clothes stand attentively to watch Judge Wickersham's cornerstone dedication ceremony on July 4, 1915. Standing in the center of the second row is the judge's wife, Deborah Wickersham.*

Wickersham Collection, Alaska State Library

FOLLOWING THE INCORPORATION OF *the Alaska Agricultural College and School of Mines by the territorial legislature in 1917, the "Main Building" was constructed on College Hill in 1918. Due to the failure of the 1919 legislature to appropriate any funds for the college in the 1919–1921 biennium, it sat boarded up and empty until the next legislative session, two years later.*

Historical Photograph Collection, Rasmuson Library

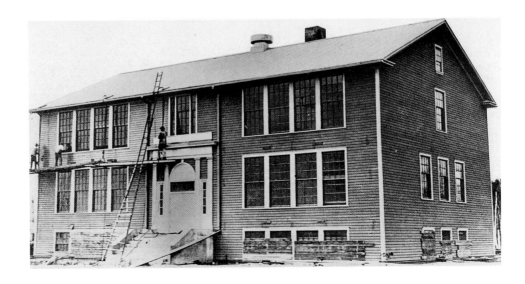

FOR THE THANKLESS TASK OF RUNNING AGAINST
*Wickersham in the November 1914 election for
delegate, the Democratic administration rewarded
Charles E. Bunnell one month later with a judgeship
on the Alaska District Court. Judge Bunnell is shown
here in his chambers in Fairbanks. When Bunnell lost
his seat on the bench after the 1920 election of
Republican Warren G. Harding, he accepted the
position of president of the Alaska Agricultural
College and School of Mines in 1921.*

Charles E. Bunnell Collection, Rasmuson Library

A HASTILY ASSEMBLED BAND OF FAIRBANKS *musicians—which had practiced together only once— played for the visiting guests and dignitaries present for the dedication of the college in September 1922.*

Charles E. Bunnell Collection, Rasmuson Library

AT THE COLLEGE'S DEDICATION DAY CEREMONIES ON *September 13, 1922, Louise and Louis Gillette stand on the cornerstone to assist two members of the Signal Corps with the raising of the Alaska flag.*

Dorothy Loftus Collection, Rasmuson Library

WITH THE GUESTS AND FACULTY SEATED ON A *platform in front of the Main Building, the crowd standing in the hayfield that served as the campus green watches the dedication day ceremonies on September 13, 1922.*

Rasmuson Library

(OPPOSITE) THE FRONT PAGE OF THE Fairbanks Daily News-Miner *the day after the dedication of the Alaska Agricultural College and School of Mines.*

Rasmuson Library

WHY NOT STUDY MINING & MINING ENGINEERING IN A MINING COUNTRY AT THE ALASKA AGRICULTURAL COLLEGE AND SCHOOL OF MINES?

DON'T CRITICISE THOSE WHO LIVE ELSEWHERE. PITY THEM.

Fairbanks Daily News-Miner

AIN'T GOD GOOD TO FAIRBANKS? AIN'T HE, THO!!!

TWENTYTH YEAR—NO. 238 | FAIRBANKS, ALASKA THURSDAY, SEPT. 14, 1922 | WHOLE NUMBER—6050

A NEW HOPE FOR STRIKE SETTLEMENT

CHICAGO, Sept. 14.—(AP)—President Jewell announced that the striking shop crafts policy committee of ninety had authorized him to negotiate individual peace agreements with the railroads of the country, based upon the terms of a general settlement plan adopted by the committee.

Declaring that the settlement of the railroad shopmen's strike could be predicted, possibly late during the day, the general policy committee of the Federated Shopcrafts went into session at 10:30 yesterday morning. "We hope to reach decision today, and I can predict nothing further than that, "President Jewell said when opening the session.

NEAR SETTLEMENT ANNOUNCED BY DAVIS

WASHINGTON, Sept. 14.—(AP)—A virtual settlement of the rail strikes on about forty per cent of the roads was announced by Secretary of Labor Davis yesterday, who based his opinion on reports of the meeting at Chicago of the General Policy committee of the Shopcrafts unions.

LABOR WILL HAVE PARTY

ATLANTIC CITY, N. J., Sept. 14.—(AP)—With the arrival of James O'Connor, chairman o fthe American Federation of Labor Non-Partisan Political Commission, the executive council of the Federation is prepared to devise a program of political activity, with its purposes to enter local, state and the national polls at the forthcoming elections.

The council members predict that labor will designate at least fifty non-partisan candidates for seats now occupied by national senators and representatives who are declared to be opposed to the aims of the Federation.

An attempt will be made at affiliation wth the farmers' vote, and a presidential campaign in 1924 is a foregone conclusion among labor chiefs.

Alice E. Miller is registered at the Pioneer from Boise, Idaho.

Juluis Monson is a new arrival at the Pioneer Hotel.

FIRE LOSS

TERRE HAUTE, Sept. 14.—A fire early yesterday practically destroyed the plant of the American Hominy company here. The damage is estimated at nearly $1,000,000.

LITTLE HOPE FOR MINERS

JACKSON, Calif., Sept. 14.—(AP)—"We will break into the Argonaut mine Friday and will find some of the miners alive," Clarence I. Jarvis, member of the Board of Control and Governor Stephens' representative, said yesterday after a preliminary survey of conditions surrounding the disaster.

The prospects of breaking thru the underground levels of the Argonaut mine early Friday are not promising, as the workers on the thirty-six hundred foot level met another disheartening set back when they ran into an old ore chute breaking into a stope. The release brought a large quantity of muck into the drift, which must now be shovelled out.

KLAN HAS AUXILIARY

FORT WORTH, Sept. 14.—(AP)—Mrs. I. C. Tutum, of stop number six on the Dallas interurban, who was decoyed from her home late last Tuesday night and given one hundred lashes with a cat-o'nine-tails by four men, is in a serious condition.

The whipping was given by "a commission of four" of the "Ladies of the Invisible Eye," a communication addressed to newspapers stated, for the alleged "ruining of a daughter."

Walter Fiher, who is with the drills at Chatanika returned this morning.

MURDERS OWN

KANSAS CITY, Sept. 14.—Tony Dinoto, whose two two daughters disappeared recently, confessed that he killed both and threw their bodies in the Missouri river.

DEDICATION OF THE FARTHEST NORTH COLLEGE NICELY CELEBRATED

God IS good to Fairbanks, and you know it.

Opening of its own accord on the 13th day of the month, with a 23 combination of officials and dignitaries on the platform and steps of the College, with Jupiter Pluvius emptying his waterwagon all over the country until within an hour of the start of the procession, the Alaska Agricultural College and School of Mines opened in a blaze of glory, God sent an avalanche of sunshine, and there wasn't a hitch or the lack of a thrill in every moment of the celebration from the time the auto procession reached the College Gate until they had left the College grounds at the close of the exercises.

AT THE START TO THE COLLEGE

The Committee started work at 5 a. m., on opening day. There was a lot of unfinished business to attend to that morning. At 8 o'clock the flags were delivered at the College, before the train reached there with the College Faculty, the Janitor was working his head off with straightening up the place for the day, and the movie man was with the Committee to "vision" the pictures he would take there later in the day. The hills were covered with fog, and it looked like no pictures and a misty bedraggled procession, so the Three-in-One, for protection, with nobody but the Janitor there to help, held a little doormat of a dedication on the front steps and grounds for fear it would get no further than that because of the weather. After the faculty arrived, the Committee after delivering the flags and rehearsing again with President Bunnell hit it up for home, exceeding the speed limits. Half way to town the sun came thru the clouds and bathed the golden grainfields of the outlying farms in splendor, but after taking one look at the speeders retired from sight and the rain started falling, and kept doing it. BUT, before sun played its two minute engagement for us, a little rainbow "showed," and that settled it. The Driver didn't look to do any further driving that day, but intended to chain his wheels the minute he reached town. The Cameraman couldn't see a hope of being able to "get" a picture that day or the chance to air his camera. Only "Potlach Bill" knew there would be sunshine when needed. "You are like the late Herman Barthel," said Charley, "You know the sun will shine, but YOU CAN'T BELIEVE YOURSELF!" But, the sun DID shine, just when needed, and all was well. Faith will move mountain, (if assisted by dynamite and steam shovel.)

THE GREATEST ARE THE LITTLER ONES

At 12:30 the school children and teachers, headed by the band, broke into Cushman street and began to register in the camera's eye. During the the week they had begun tearing up Cushman street for sewer purposes, and that did not help the picture. Then here and there an auto would butt in, between the children and the camera. The dear little tads, earnest and enthusiastic, have been taught to march in close formation, and the children's procession which could have stretched two blocks didn't, but, it was beautiful, and solemn for that. As they came to the bridge the Governor and party saluted them from the reviewing Stand, and they passed over the bridge to their special train registering every foot of the way in the camera. Their train beat the auto procession to the College, and they stood for an hour at the College gate waiting to receive the auto procession. It must have been a little hard on them, but they were Soldiers of Education and they never deserted their posts. The delay was caused by the fact that the leading guests were hungry and had to have lunch before following the children.

AUTO PROCESSION SOMEHOW GOOD

After luncheon the auto procession started for the College, headed by the Humphrey's auto carrying the Governor and his party, and followed by the carriages containing the regents and the people who formed the procession. Do as we could, only 24 autos would register for the occasion and it looked bad for the auto procession from the Stagemanager's standpoint. At the finish as the autos arrived at the College and followed the move of the Stagmanager's wand (cane) in parking, they kept coming until they had filed all the parking space and were still coming when the Stagemanager "beat it" to the front of the College to get out of sight of arriving autos which he didn't know what to do with or where to place. If his estimate can be taken for the right one, there were no less than a million autos in the procession. And, they were all filed.

EDUCATION GATE ENTRANCE TO COLLEGE ROAD

As the procession reached the Education Gate at the end of the Noyes bridge, they found a reception there. At each side of the gate stood a Signal Corps man at salute, at his feet Native Son Gillette or Native Daughter Gillette, thru the gate to the turn of the road the Boy Scouts, left arm on their bikes, right hand at salute as the procession passed. Then the beautiful ride to the College over autoroads which were a surprise even to the local autoists who had traveled them only the night before, and a greater surprise to the Governor and the Coast visitors who never saw such fine auto roads elsewhere in Alaska.

AT THE COLLEGE GATE

As the procession came to the College Gate (the camerman at the corner of the road from which he had already "taken" the Gate and the rows of welcomers behind it, awaiting them) they found Professor Bruce, Professor of Chemistry and Physics and Prof. Morgan, Professor of Agriculture and Military Science, one on either side of the gate, with Native Son Gilletter or Native Daughter Gillette with them, behind the gate the long row of school children and teachers lining the approach to the College on either side of which (but not in front) the autos parked and their occupants left them and gathered on the campus in front of the College for the dedicatory exercises.

THE EXERCISES OF THE DAY

Explaining the seeming activities of the Stagemanager at the exercises. The dedicators must come out the College at the right moment; the flag must be raised at the right moment; the band must play the Star Spangled Banner at the right moment, and the exercises must proceed as exercises must do, and without delay or a hitch. THEN comes the PICTURE. A movie camera only works one way at a time—it doesn't take pictures from both ends of the camera at the same moment. The cameraman had to get the dedicators on their exit from the College doors to the platform; then turn and "get" the FLAG. The flagraisers were experienced Signal Corps men of long service, Pvts. Paul Krepps and Lionel Edwardes, and, according to Army rules they couldn't "break" their flag until the Star Spangled Banner started to "break" —that was their signal. So the dedicators had to be brought out the moment the camera was ready to register them; the camera then had to turn to catch the flag-raising, and the cameraman had to signal to the Stagemanager the moment to start the band playing. The dedicators were all ready to "go," the flagraisers were ready at any moment, and the band was full of wind and rarin' to play. That's how came it so, and there wasn't a break in the affair, but the Stagemanager was a busy boy for a few moments—it would have been his fault had there been a flaw in the start.

EXERCISES AT THE COLLEGE

An inspiring scene was presented as the Governor and his party, guests of the occasion, regents and members of the faculty took their places on the speakers' stand, which had been erected about the main entrance to the College building. The hundreds who had come from town by automobile or by train were grouped on the campus immediately before the speakers.

When all had taken their places on the stand the band struck up The Star Spangled Banner, and the American flag, having as a back ground the broad expanse of the Tanana Valley, dotted with homes, farms and outstanding grain fields and painted in autumn's colors was unfurled over the campus. All stood with bowed head as the Rev. Frederick G. Scherer delivered the invocation.

The introductory speaker, Morton E. Stevens, president of the Board of Regents of the Alaska Agricultural College and School of Mines, explained the founding of land grant colleges and dwelt on the history and scope of the Alaska institution, concluding with the introduction of the Honorable Scott C. Bone, Governor of Alaska. The Governor, as he arose to address the assemblage was greeted with prolonged applause. His address follows:

(Continued on page 4)

THIRTY DROWN

GIBRALTAR, Sept. 14.—Thirty women and children were drowned when the German passenger steamer Hammonia sank last Saturday, according to advices received here.

TARIFF ON FINAL ROAD

WASHINGTON, Sept. 14.—(AP)—The action of the Republican conferees in writing back into the Tariff bill the disembargo provision was denounced yesterday in the House by Representative Fish,, as "the worst example of the working of invisible government that had ever been seen." The statement was greeted with vigorous applause, both by Republicans and Democrats.

WASHINGTON, Sept. 14.—(AP)—Among the important rates in the Administration tariff bill, as agreed upon in conference, is included "fresh or frozen salmon, mackeral and halibut 2 cents per pound; herring and mackerel, pickled or salted, one cent per pound.

YESTERDAY'S REPORT ON TARIFF

WASHINGTON, Sept. 13.—(AP)—The Administration tariff bill was finally perfected in the conference and presented to the House to be called up Thursday with the expectation that it would be disposed of not later than the Thursday following, altho action in the Senate may be delayed a week or more.

Experts say the Level bill is slightly under the Payne-Aldrich, but considerably above the Underwood law.

Joe Bristow, who has been in the Circle district during the summer, arrived in Fairbanks on Tuesday' train.

Mrs. Helen M. Lynch of Anchorage arrived in Fairbanks on Tuesday evening and expects to spend some time here.

SEATTLE CROWDED

SEATTLE, Sept. 14.—The influx of Alaskans is filling the local hotels with cannerymen, fox farmers, hunters and oil locators.

RELIEF FOR THE GREEKS

CONSTANTINOPLE, Sept. 14.—(AP)—The United States destroyer Edsall left here for Smyrna last Tuesday, with supplies from the Near East Relief for the starving refugees stranded there.

THEIR WIRES ARE CROSSED

CONSTANTINOPLE, Sept. 14.—(AP)—The Greeks say that they expect to remove to home ports thousands of disarmed Greek soldiers who still remain on the peninsula west of Smyrna, betwen the Gulf of Smyrna and the Gulf of Scalanopa, according to the Greek Military Mission here; but these disarmed Greek soldies are described as an adequate armed force protecting the seven mile wide isthmus separating the peninsula from the mainland.

The Turkish Nationalists have taken but few prisoners, the Greeks claim, but they admit that many are unaccounted for and are probably wandering the region betwen Smyrna and Aivalik, sixty miles north.

RED CROSS WILL RUSH TO RELIEF

WASHINGTON, Sept. 14.—(AP)—An appropriation of $25,0000 for relief for the suffering thousands of refugees in Smyrna, as a result of the defeat of the Greek armies was made yesterday by the American Red Cross.

HEARING ON INJUNCTION

CHICAGO, Sept. 14.—(AP)—Efforts of the attorneys for the striking shopcrafts leaders to forestall the reading of additional hundreds of the twenty thousand affidavits of violence, produced by the government in support o the injunction, failed again yesterday.

The government rejected all overtures for speeding up the case and eliminating, or classifying, the affidavits.

Judge Wilkerson sustained the government's quotations of right to the broadest latitude in its effort to show a chain of nation-wide outbreaks and its claims of a concerted conspiracy to destroy interstate traffic and the intimidation of railway employees.

Dan Leach is a business visitor in Fairbanks this week.

A "VERY PLAIN TWO-AND-A-HALF-STORY FRAME BUILDING"
*The "Old Main" building, seen through the birch trees on
College Hill.*

LarVern Keys Collection, Rasmuson Library

TWO

Farthest North College 1922–1935

When the bill to create the Alaska Agricultural College and School of Mines came before the legislature in 1917, the Fairbanks Commercial Club and the Fairbanks School Board boasted that 150 students were ready to enroll on opening day. Governor J. F. A. Strong thought if only half that number showed up for the first day of classes, the college would still be a success.[1] When opening day finally arrived on September 18, 1922, only six students—five of whom were from Fairbanks—signed up to register.

The first to enroll was Roden Davis, followed by Earl Foster, Donald Morgan, Ethel Bailey, Art Loftus and Dorothy Roth. All were from Fairbanks except Loftus, a resident of Tomahawk, Wisconsin. "Their names will live in college history of the Northland when they are gone . . .," the *Fairbanks News-Miner* predicted. With a registration fee of two dollars a head (tuition was free for everyone), the college netted a grand total of twelve dollars which was placed in the "safe," one of President Bunnell's empty cigar boxes.[2]

The four men and two women who registered for classes that day posed for a class picture around the college cornerstone. As they started their college careers they were all certain to receive plenty of individual attention, since the faculty, including President Bunnell, outnumbered the study body seven to six. The catalog offered five major fields of study—Agriculture, Home Economics, General Science, Civil Engineering, and Mining Engineering—and during the first semester alone a total of sixteen different courses from which to select:

English I
Inorganic Chemistry I
Live Stock Production I
Botany I
Physiology
Military Science
Foods I
Design
Physics of the Home
Physical Education
Trigonometry
Current History
Engineering Drawing I
Engineering Problems I
Plane Surveying
Mechanical Drawing

Bunnell had recruited the faculty during the previous spring and summer with the idea that each instructor would teach two subjects—preferably more. He had hoped to find one person to teach not only math and civil engineering, but Spanish and French as well. He claimed such a mathematician could be found, though admittedly not "at every turn." Bunnell had even higher expectations for his presidential secretary (the only other member of the administration besides himself), who was to be the secretary, the registrar, the college librarian, and a teacher of "Stenography, Typewriting, Bookkeeping and Commercial Arithmetic."[3]

The five men and one woman who agreed to accept Bunnell's challenge of teaching at a new college in frontier Alaska ranged in age from twenty-four to thirty-five. Half of the new faculty were graduates of the University of Washington in

Seattle: Archie Truesdell, professor of mathematics and civil engineering; Earl Pilgrim, professor of mining engineering and metallurgy; and Ernest Patty, professor of geology and mineralogy. At Kansas State Agricultural College, the alma mater of Milton Snodgrass and George Gasser of the Fairbanks Experiment Station, Bunnell found Clinton Morgan, professor of agriculture and instructor in military science, and Elizabeth Kirkpatrick, professor of home economics and English. Herbert Bruce, professor of chemistry and physics, came from Lafayette College in Easton, Pennsylvania. Of the six professors, three had earned bachelor of science degrees and three had master of science degrees.[4]

For years the college faculty were virtually private tutors since many classes contained only one student. There was always time to answer questions, and to discuss any number of topics not necessarily in the lesson plan. Margaret Thomas (Murie), the lone member of the graduating class of 1924, remembered an episode one day in a one-on-one banking and finance class taught by President Bunnell. "I don't remember why, but for some reason we were talking about Edgar Allan Poe. He (Bunnell) asked me if I had ever read *The Cask of Amontillado*. I said no so he turned around and took down a book and read me the story. And that was the banking and finance class for that morning." Ladessa Hall (Nordale), the first professor of business administration, arrived in 1923 to find only one student registered in a class. When she asked Bunnell if the class should be cancelled he said, "Oh no. You'll teach that class if there's just half a student."[5]

Bunnell hired LarVern Borell from Idaho as his secretary. Her first visit to the Alaska Agricultural College was unforgettable. "The President was watching me closely to see how I responded to the situation," she recalled. "It was so very different from the colleges I had known." On top of the hill there were no trees or shrubs. "The campus," she said, "was a hayfield."[6]

Bunnell had planted wheat and clover around the Main Building as the most practical and profitable method of landscaping. The president and the trustees complained when stray cows from the Experiment Station trampled the campus "green" in the summer of 1922. As historian Bill Cashen commented, like most land grant schools the A.A.C. would be dubbed a "cow college," but the name did not have to be literally true.[7]

Besides the president's small house, the only other structure was the Main Building, which Borell described as a "very plain two and a half story frame building." Bunnell led her on the grand tour of the facilities. The basement contained the heating and electric plant, two laboratories, and two rooms for domestic science. There were ten small classrooms, four on the first floor and six on the second, each with new student desks and chairs in a jumbled pile waiting for instructors to arrange them. Her challenge was the organization of the library, which was supposed to occupy two rooms on the first floor.

". . . I found books everywhere," she wrote, "piled in the halls, in the men's room, along with sawdust in the carpenter shop; well, about everywhere except in the two rooms designated Library. In those two rooms—no books, no tables, no shelves! . . . Many of the books had been gifts from personal libraries and were not really college material but they were books and would help fill the shelves—when there were shelves!"[8] Among the donated books was a complete set of former President Woodrow Wilson's ten-volume *History of the American People*, personally autographed and dedicated to the Alaska Agricultural College and School of Mines. On September 28, 1922, the first book accessioned in the library was officially put on the shelf: a volume entitled *Alaska—its Meaning to the World*.[9]

In addition to serving as the college librarian, presidential secretary, accountant, bookstore manager, and bell ringer to mark the start of each class, Borell was also the registrar. Though only six students enrolled on opening day, by the time registration for the first semester closed about three weeks later, the student body had doubled in size from six to twelve. The six new collegians were: Jack Hosler from Anchorage; Jack Shanly from Long Island, New York; Jule and Ted Loftus (brothers of Art) from Wisconsin; and John and Robert McCombe, twin brothers from Quebec. Thus among the first twelve students were three Loftus brothers and two McCombe brothers, and they comprised the starting five of the college's first basketball team: Ted Loftus played center, Art and Jule Loftus were forwards, and John and Robert McCombe were the guards. President Bunnell called them the "Full House Squad—three of a kind and a pair."[10]

All six of the latecomers were men, resulting in a lopsided male-female ratio of ten men and two women; the relative scarcity of college women in Fairbanks would long be a complaint of local college men. At least one romance blossomed among that first batch of students. Art Loftus and Dorothy Roth were the fifth and sixth students respectively to enroll. Dorothy had just graduated from Fairbanks High School and had no money to go to college Outside. Her father was Rhinehart F. Roth, a former U.S. District Attorney and an old friend and colleague of Bunnell while he was on the bench. On opening day Dorothy's boyfriend, Art Loftus, drove her out to the Alaska Agricultural College and School of Mines in his Model T. Like many other future students, Art's decision to enroll with her at the Fairbanks college that September was inspired by the climate. The coming months "looked long and cold," Dorothy recalls, and Art "decided that he might just as well attend college that winter." After Dorothy graduated in 1927, she and Art were happily married for fifty-five years until Art's death in 1982.[11]

By February 1923, three additional students from Fairbanks had registered for the second semester, raising to fifteen the final enrollment for the college's first year in credit courses. One of the three

second semester students was Thelma Bruce, wife of chemistry professor Herbert Bruce. A student of botany, she was the college's first graduate student. She was also the first in a long line of scientists associated with the land grant college whose research focused on the practical application of scientific knowledge to the problems of Alaskan agriculture. Bruce experimented with the "hybridization" of the Alaskan blueberry, trying to determine methods of increasing the size of the berries and raising the yield per acre.[12]

Among the first dozen students, the oldest was Jack Shanly, who, at age twenty-eight, was the same age or older than several of the faculty members. Shanly had already completed three years of college at Cornell, making him the only upperclassman and the only member of the "senior class." He was naturally elected president of the first student association.

Shanly would become the first graduate of the Alaska Agricultural College and School of Mines in 1923. Bunnell had convinced Shanly to return to school and complete his college education because the president wanted the distinction of honoring a graduating class every year from the beginning of the school's existence.

The college's first graduate, like thousands who would follow in his footsteps at the Fairbanks school, was hardly a typical college student. Older than the "traditional" student, Shanly was a dropout who had been around the world by the time he enrolled in his first course in Fairbanks. Shanly had quit Cornell in 1917 to drive an ambulance for the French Army during the First World War. When the United States entered the war, Shanly returned to the States by ship to San Francisco, catching a ride part way on a British troop transport to India. When the war ended he was in naval flight school in Florida.

After the war Shanly planned to stake a homestead in the Peace River country of Alberta, but during a stint in a logging camp in the Pacific Northwest he learned of the high wages and free transportation to Alaska offered to workers on the Alaska Railroad, then under construction from Seward to Fairbanks. Shanly arrived in Fairbanks in 1922 and became the first homesteader to settle in what is now called the community of College, Alaska, on the southeast corner of the campus at the foot of College Hill. The story goes that Shanly met President Bunnell while filing his homestead papers at the Federal Building in Fairbanks, and the president convinced him to return to school so that he could earn his college degree in agriculture and "prove up on a homestead at the same time." Shanly built two cabins; one for himself and one that he rented out to the McCombe brothers.[13]

In the spring Shanly put on a memorable dinner party for the faculty. Home Economics instructor Elizabeth Kirkpatrick and secretary LarVern Borell arrived to find Shanly had nothing prepared. "Shanly was no help at all," Borell said. "The principle thing I remember was he wanted to string decorative lanterns out to the road. We got him to peeling potatoes." When Ernest Patty arrived, he said Kirkpatrick had just discovered that Shanly had forgotten to get the main dish of the evening. Shanly quickly dashed outside and returned a few minutes later with four frozen rabbits he had snared around his cabin. Patty said he and all the other young professors looked the other way while at Shanly's

house. Prohibition was the law of the land, but "quite obviously Jack had a brew of homemade beer going in one corner of the kitchen."[14]

Shanly was not the only student homesteader to stake his claim on the flats close to the college. South of campus and across the railroad tracks (near what is now called Loftus Road) the three Loftus brothers located three adjoining homesteads, and Jule, Art, and Ted shared a 20' x 22' cabin among the "tall spruces and cottonwoods" along the banks of the Jennie M. or Deadman Slough. They called the cabin their homestead "frat house," where they could enjoy the jolly life of fraternity men "without the bother of Greek letters on the door."

At the "last of the land grant colleges," Art Loftus wrote, the availability of free land, which had made the land grant college system possible, offered the unique feature of homesteads or personal "land grants" to individual students like the Loftus brothers, who otherwise might not have had the money to go to school. The three brothers dipped their drinking water from the slough, cut their firewood right on their doorstep, and subsisted on white rabbits, spruce hens and grouse. Art Loftus wrote that after "a strenuous day of wrestling with the college work," it was a pleasure to come home to the cabin they had built with their own hands, "that might from its appearance, be a thousand miles from college or from civilization."

"What more would a student want," Loftus wrote, "than to take a homestead beside the campus for one verse of a song, and live within a few minutes' walk of a first class mining college . . . ? Here are the

"FRAT HOUSE"
Exterior and interior views of the Loftus brothers' cabin on the flats below College Hill. Numerous students staked homesteads in the woods near the campus, where they slept, studied, and shivered in tiny lumber shacks and log cabins.

Dorothy Loftus Collection, Rasmuson Library

advantages of civilization, combined with the lure of the wilderness."[15]

One advantage of civilization that the Loftus boys often did without was bread. Dorothy Roth told Bill Cashen years later that the so-called sandwiches which the brothers brought to school for lunch "often consisted of left over sourdough hotcakes filled with whatever would add flavor—beans, sauerkraut or catsup."[16]

One later bachelor-student moved into a wood chopper's dugout in the trees north of the campus clearing (near where the Fine Arts complex is now located) that was barely four feet wide and seven feet long. His little hut was described politely as "dingy and deserted, damp, ill-chinked and low-ceilinged" and "as uninviting as a dilapidated root cellar." He remodeled it with "box material," and equipped it with "a bookcase and study table, a Yukon stove, a cot, and a partition which separates the realm of the stomach from the realm of the mind."

In the 1920s and 1930s students who camped in the small shacks and cabins without electricity or running water on the flats below campus were jokingly known as residents of "Yertchville." The name was derived from the word "yurt," the nomadic skin tent common in Siberia. In the 1940s some called the area "Vulture Flats." But whatever the era in which they attended school, the college nomads who enjoyed the freedom of the flats—a freedom not found at any other institution of higher education in America—went to school on the cheap, sleeping, studying, and shivering in tiny scrap lumber shacks, sod huts, and log cabins of their own design.[17]

Until 1925 there were no dormitories at the college, and except for President Bunnell and the hardy individualists in their cabins near the campus, all faculty and students lived in Fairbanks. Few students or instructors had automobiles, and those who had vehicles did not generally run them in the winter. Fortunately the college was adjacent to the Alaska Railroad, which had purchased and rehabilitated the old Tanana Valley Railroad in 1917, adding a third rail to accommodate both standard gauge and the original narrow gauge equipment. Throughout the 1920s, the Alaska Railroad provided transportation to and from the college. A small, self-propelled, narrow gauge rail car with a gasoline engine made the trip three times a day (morning, noon, and evening) six days a week. Round-trip fare on the "Toonerville Trolley" (nicknamed after a newspaper cartoon) was twenty-five cents. And anyone who missed the last trip of the day had to walk four and a half miles back to Fairbanks along the railroad tracks.[18]

At the foot of College Hill the railroad built a small passenger shelter with the word "College" on a sign on the roof; henceforth the stop became known as College Station. When Bunnell applied for a post office at the school in 1925, the name he requested was College, Alaska. The president thought by emphasizing the existence of such a distinct place, politicians from other regions would realize the Alaska College belonged to the entire territory and was not merely a Fairbanks institution.[19]

The independent community of College, Alaska (of which Bunnell was officially postmaster for twenty-two years, though students performed the actual work) symbolized the self-reliant spirit of the college and its president. For more than a quarter of a century, President Bunnell ran the college as if he were the proprietor of a small family business. If an issue didn't cross the president's desk, it didn't concern the college. He made it his business to become personally involved in every aspect of college life, from the most trivial of details to matters of great importance. His word was law; faculty members served at his pleasure, without tenure, and there was never any question about who was in charge.

The president's normal work day began at about 7:00 A.M., and he sometimes would not quit until midnight. Woe to instructors who arrived on campus late, for they could be sure to find Bunnell standing quietly in the hallway looking at his watch. He was surprised when others did not always want to work fourteen hours a day, seven days a week. Seldom did visitors find him without his shirt sleeves rolled up. Tourists who saw the president weeding the pansy beds or sweeping a classroom floor often mistook him for the janitor, to his great amusement.[20] One day, while digging the basement for a small cabin that became the first faculty and staff housing on campus (other than his own cottage), Bunnell put down his shovel to greet a visiting Austrian nobleman who was shocked that a college president in America would have to work like a peasant.[21]

One of the great joys of building a new institution was the rare opportunity to create the traditions of the future. "Instead of following traditions," Bunnell told the students, "it is your privilege to make them." The president worked to establish a distinctive school spirit and to cultivate the genuine college atmosphere and opportunities he had enjoyed as a student at Bucknell.

During the college's first semester Bunnell pushed the establishment of "The Student Association of the Alaska Agricultural College and School of Mines," whose primary purpose was "to foster a spirit of loyalty and devotion to our College . . . ."[22] Bunnell expected all students, as he explained in the catalog, to "be punctual in attendance and to conduct themselves as ladies and gentlemen," both on and off the college grounds. The college's code of honor was strict. Dishonoring the college or failing "to make proper use of the opportunities the College offers" would be "sufficient reasons for requesting . . . withdrawal from the institution."[23]

The first annual freshman bonfire, symbolizing the passing of the torch of knowledge, and the initiation of the new freshman class, was held in the fall of 1923. Over the following decades the bonfire would become the college's most honored ceremony and tradition. Each fall entering students were required to build a skyscraper of scrap wood up to fifty or sixty feet high, and the lighting of the huge bonfire by President Bunnell signaled that a new school year had begun.[24]

A former shortstop and quarterback, President Bunnell believed that organized sports instilled discipline and aided the development of mind and body. The college introduced the game of ice hockey to Fairbanks in the fall of 1925. Bob and John McCombe, who had played the game while growing up in Quebec, were key figures in the formation of the Fairbanks Hockey Association which remodeled an old Fairbanks roller rink on Fourth Avenue into an ice rink. The McCombe twins taught hockey to four of their classmates, none of whom had ever played before, to make up the college's first hockey team: Clarence Burglin (in the goal), George King, John Luss, and Donald Morgan. With no substitutes on the bench, the six students played every minute of every game. Nevertheless, the college team won the first ever Crosby Keen Trophy for 1926, taking three out of four games against Fairbanks, including the final game by a score of 21–4. After the championship game Bob McCombe predicted that hockey would "before long . . . take its place as the leading winter sport" in Fairbanks.[25]

Despite the enthusiasm of the McCombes, hockey never approached the popularity of basketball, the leading sport on campus. Having grown up in Canada, the McCombes were unfamiliar with the hardwood game. They played basketball as if it were ice hockey. Mining professor Earl Pilgrim, the college's first basketball coach, put together the "Full House squad" comprising the McCombe twins and the three Loftus brothers. He said when the McCombes were guarding an opponent they liked to "administer a few body blows, which would weaken him for the rest of the game."[26] The starting five were a formidable line-up. "The physique of these boys would gladden the heart of any varsity coach," the *Collegian* reported. When they played a visiting team from Anchorage High School, the *Collegian* called it "most exciting game ever played in the North." Both sides "fought like demons," but the game was still scoreless after eighteen minutes. By the end of the first half, Anchorage had scored one point and the "Full House" had scored four. The final score was College 11—Anchorage 8.[27]

Like many college administrators, President Bunnell saw sports as a fine mechanism for the promotion of his school. A.A.C. basketball teams be-

gan to tour the territory in 1926. When the team arrived in Ketchikan, the editor of the local paper said that seeing the squad on the floor made the college "a real live institution, something tangible" to Ketchikan residents for the first time. Previously, he thought, the college had "not been easy to visualize, but when it leaves its classrooms and laboratories and comes to the people of the territory with an athletic team, the curtain is pulled back and a dynamic factor in college life faces the public."[28]

Not that most of the small high school basketball teams throughout the territory looked forward to being the next victim on a goodwill tour of the college globetrotters. For example the 1927–1928 college team went undefeated, winning seventeen games in a row on the road. The powerful 1933–1934 team, coached by James Ryan, covered an estimated 3,000 miles and demolished the high school teams at Seward, Cordova, Juneau, Sitka, Ketchikan, Petersburg and Skagway by a combined score of 328–79, winning by scores such as 54–6 and 50–4. Their only two losses came at the hands of the Metlakatla Town team and the Juneau firemen.[29]

Just as he tried to use basketball to advertise the college, Bunnell capitalized on the A.A.C.'s greatest distinction: the world's "Farthest North College." He boasted that the exact "center of our College building" lay at a latitude of 64 degrees, 51 minutes and 21 seconds north.[30] To send the message of the farthest north college out to the world, Bunnell started publication of the *Farthest-North Collegian* in February 1923. The magazine later evolved into a monthly newspaper managed and staffed by students under close faculty supervision;

ROCK POKER
The winter short course for miners and prospectors was one of the most popular offerings at the college. Dean Ernest Patty (seated on the far left) invented the game of "rock poker" to help the men learn the identification of minerals.

Charles E. Bunnell Collection, Rasmuson Library

the *Collegian* served as the official organ of the college and the university for more than three decades.

As remarkable as the college's high northern latitude was its majestic view of the Alaska Range. Judge Bunnell, like Judge Wickersham, thought the view of Denali or Mount McKinley from the front steps of the Main Building would serve as a constant inspiration for students and teachers, and the symbol of all they hoped to achieve in their little building on College Hill. "One could not wish for a grander or more majestic sight," Bunnell wrote. The president created an official seal for the Alaska Agricultural College and School of Mines showing "the outline of Mount McKinley as seen from the College steps," or at least as seen through a high-powered telescope mounted on the steps. As a scholar of the classics, President Bunnell thought the college motto suggested by Mrs. Bunnell, "Ad Summum," was perfect. "'To the highest point'," he wrote, "is our ambition in scholarship, honor and citizenship. We do not ask to have our efforts estimated by any other measure."[31] In the 1950s Bunnell wrote a poem entitled "Ad Summum." Set to music for a performance by the University of Alaska Chorus, he hoped it would become a new official university song. It read in part:

AD SUMMUM means for you and me
Our best, not once, but every day.
Together we will gain the heights,
The motto of the U. of A.[32]

Bunnell attached great importance to the fact that the mountain he adopted as the college symbol—Mount McKinley—had been named by William A. Dickey, a Princeton graduate and a prospector. In Bunnell's mind, Dickey represented the ideal scholar and man of achievement. "College men have nothing to lose by becoming prospectors and miners," Bunnell wrote, "and prospectors and miners can well afford to become college men."[33]

The challenge of teaching prospectors to be students and students to be prospectors was a natural goal for a land grant institution. In the mid-nineteenth century the land grant college movement had revolutionized higher education in America. Previously, attending a college or university had been the privilege of an elite upper class, but grants of millions of acres of land from the public domain provided for the endowment and support in each state or territory of colleges teaching "agriculture and the mechanic arts," and the doors of higher education swung open for the first time to working class Americans. The mission of land grant schools was to "promote the liberal and practical education of the industrial classes."[34]

Offerings at the Alaska Agricultural College and School of Mines, especially the noncredit short courses in mining, agriculture, and home economics, focused on the applied "practical" benefits of higher education. From the beginning Bunnell targeted working prospectors, farmers, and housewives, as potential students, teaching them subjects as diverse as Feeds and Feeding, Farm Crops, Dairying, Child Care and Training, Handicrafts, Geology, and Ore Dressing. The only requirement for entry into the short courses was that "the candidate be able to read and write the English language well enough for ordinary use."[35]

No more colorful a collection of students ever entered the halls of higher education than the ten week "short course miners." Veterans of the Klondike stampede, hard rock drillers, beach miners from Nome, prospectors from out of the hills, all signed up to see what the college boys could teach them. Ernest Patty, one of the first six professors hired by Bunnell in 1922 and Bunnell's right hand man (Patty became both the first college dean and the head of the School of Mines) invented the game of "rock poker" to teach old-timers the rudiments of scientific geology.

"I did not think that men from the hills would feel any great enthusiasm sitting in a lecture hall," Patty wrote, "while a professor held up a rock and said, 'This is granite. Observe the typical coarse-grained appearance.'" He figured all miners had "a working knowledge of poker," however, and designed a game in which each player was dealt a hand of numbered rocks and minerals instead of cards. If a man "opened with a granite," the others all had to either see him one granite, or else lay down another rock or mineral and name it. The winner received a free dinner. Patty remembered that shortly after he

first introduced the game, one hand almost ended in a brawl when a player nearly slugged another who claimed to have a diorite wild card. On the whole, "rock poker" proved to be so popular that Patty eventually included the game in the regular college curriculum.[36]

By assisting miners and farmers in building the industrial base of the territory, Bunnell hoped to make the practical value of higher education plain to all Alaskans. Yet it was always an uphill struggle. He fought constantly with the territorial legislature for sufficient funds to keep the doors of the college open. The annual federal land grant college appropriation of $50,000, which Wickersham had used as the bait to procure initial support for the establishment of the college, was increased to $77,000 a year by the mid-1930s. Nevertheless, federal funds provided only about half of the school's expenses, leaving the fate of the college in the hands of territorial legislators.

From one biennium to the next (the legislature met only in odd-numbered years) the survival of the institution always hung in the balance. Every two years Bunnell would have to justify the college's existence, usually winning a meager territorial appropriation that served only as a stay of execution until the next legislative session. Many politicians from regions outside of Fairbanks believed the college was a colossal waste of money which the territory could ill afford, and never relented in their efforts to cut funding of what one called Bunnell's "$50,000 woodshed" on College Hill.[37]

With money always tight, the college was on a perpetual austerity budget. If necessary, the president would draw on his own personal bank account to buy an essential piece of college equipment or to loan money to a needy student. In fact, he spent every dollar of the college's budget as if it had come out of his own pocket. All of the employees on campus, except for the president, the professors, the chief engineer and the cooks, were students. Among the facilities run by student staff were the college post office, the college barber shop, and the college newspaper.

The student editor of the *Collegian* was also entrusted with the task of chauffeuring the president around in Bunnell's 1926 two-door Buick sedan. President Bunnell was a man of many accomplishments, but one thing he never learned to do was drive a car. Driving the judge was not an easy assignment. According to his driver in the mid-1930s, William Cashen, Bunnell may not have known how to drive, but he was nevertheless a world champion back seat driver with "an amazing collection of driving tips and suggestions at his command," who "maintained a rather constant discourse on the subject of safe and sane driving." The president preferred speeds of twenty-five miles an hour or less.[38]

Students worked as painters and groundskeepers, clerical assistants and janitors, dining room attendants and library clerks, coal haulers, assistant engineers, and faculty research assistants. By hiring students to do everything except teach Bunnell gave practical experience to most of the student body, and subsidized the education of individuals who could not otherwise afford to stay in school. Furthermore, he made every dollar of the college's appropriation go twice as far since the money paid out in student wages usually came back in college fees.[39]

Nothing at the A.A.C. escaped the scrutiny of its thrifty president. When home economics professor Lola Cremeans (Tilly) arrived on campus in 1929, she gave her boss a list of vegetables she needed to purchase for the classroom. Bunnell returned a few hours later, wearing his work clothes and carrying a cardboard box full of vegetables he had dug out of his own garden.[40] Dean Ernest Patty recalled that one year the power plant shut down on the last day of school to cut costs, and anyone living on campus in the summer months, such as he and his family, had water, light and heat only once a week on Saturday mornings. The "Dean's House"—so called because Dean Patty lived in it for ten years, and his successor Dean William Elmhirst Duckering lived in it for fifteen—had originally been the home of the maintenance man, and was briefly the women's dormitory before it was taken over by the deans. Though it stood on campus for more than forty years, for a long time the Dean's House did not officially exist. Bunnell and the janitor had built it themselves out of scrap lumber left over from the construction of the Main Building and the president's cottage. "Rumor had it that there wasn't a board in the structure over four feet long," Bill Cashen once said, "but that was an exaggeration. I spotted at least three."[41]

With the college's financial picture so bleak, planning for the future was a precarious exercise. Nevertheless, Bunnell did the best selling job he could and the results were clearly evident in the growth of the College Hill campus. From an enrollment of fifteen credit course students in 1922–1923, the college more than tripled in size by its second year to fifty-two students. Thereafter, the growth of the student body was slow but steady. The first four graduating classes comprised a total of only four individuals from four different disciplines over four years:

1923—Jack Shanly, agriculture
1924—Margaret Thomas (Murie),
              business administration
1925—Jamie Cameron, home economics
1926—Donald Morgan, mining engineering

In 1927, the first multiple graduation class in college history, two women and five men received their degrees—Florence Roth (Thompson), Dorothy Roth (Loftus), Ted Loftus, George Lingo, Bill McCarty, John McCombe, and Clifford Smith—nearly tripling in one year the total number of students with diplomas from the Alaska Agricultural College and School of Mines.

A dramatic increase in enrollment came with the start of the Great Depression. Though Alaska did not suffer as much as some other regions of the country during the 1930s, Alaskans knew the horror of vanishing jobs and shrinking paychecks. Haunted by the fear of unemployment, students seeking admission turned up at the college door in unprecedented numbers. Between 1929 and 1930 the number of students working for degrees at the college jumped from 86 to 131, a rise of more than fifty percent, and by 1934–1935 the student body had grown another twenty-five percent to 164 students.[42]

During the depression, the Alaska College not only offered training for the future, but thanks to Bunnell's policy of hiring student labor, the college could generally provide employment to all students who needed it. Enrollment also increased due to the relative strength of Alaskan gold mining, an industry which the college advertised as "depression proof." About one-third of the college's graduates between 1923 and 1935 earned their livelihood by either digging for gold themselves or working for a gold mining company. Gold mining had begun to revive from its World War I depression in the 1920s when the U.S. Smelting, Refining and Mining Co. of Boston began large scale dredging of the placers at Fairbanks and Nome. In 1934 President Franklin D. Roosevelt's New Deal boosted the official price of gold by seventy percent to thirty-five dollars an ounce, starting the first Alaskan gold rush in almost a generation.[43]

The growth of the college's facilities never kept pace with the increasing enrollment. In 1922, two small buildings stood in the middle of a hay field on College Hill. Twelve years later, there was a true college campus. The first two dormitories opened in 1925 and 1927 (later known respectively as "Club Dorm" and "Main Dorm") providing on-campus student housing for a total of eighty-five men and women. The dorms offered clean beds and steam-heated rooms

FIGURE 1

FIGURE 2

FIGURE 3

How old is the University of Alaska?

Satchel Paige, the great baseball pitcher, once asked, "How old would you be if you didn't know how old you was?" The same question has often troubled administrators at the University of Alaska Fairbanks. Since 1965 the university has celebrated 1917, the year of the incorporation of the Alaska Agricultural College and School of Mines by the Territorial Legislature, as the official year of its birth. However, for decades a sometimes acrimonious debate raged over the actual age of the institution. In this case age, like beauty, was in the eye of the beholder, principally the university president at the time. Each of the university's first four presidents changed the year on the official seal at least once.

When President Bunnell created the institution's first seal (Figure 1 above), he picked 1922 as the year on the seal, since that was the year when the first students enrolled. Thirteen years later, in 1935, the Alaska Agricultural College and School of Mines became the University of Alaska, and both the name and the date were changed to reflect the birth of the new university (Figure 2). President Bunnell, however, upset about the loss of the college's first thirteen years, subsequently modified the seal to include both years (Figure 3).

William Cashen recalled that Bunnell asked the engravers in Seattle to separate the two dates with a star, i.e. 1922 ✸ 1935, but by mistake the seal came back with the years separated instead by a dash, i.e. 1922–1935. For years this caused interminable confusion. From the inclusive dates, one might have assumed that the university was born in 1922 and died in 1935—and that its motto should have been "In Memoriam" instead of "Ad Summum."

In 1949, Terris Moore, the university's second president, moved at the request of alumni to end the confusion. After considering several different dates, including 1915, 1917, 1918, 1921, and 1922, he

for ten dollars a month, with board available for an additional forty-five dollars a month in the college dining room, located in the basement of the women's residence hall.

Construction of an east wing on the Main Building in 1923 and a west wing in 1925 had tripled the size of the college's central structure. The east wing housed the School of Mines. On the top floor of the west wing, in a high-ceilinged room "braced with steel girders," was the college's first athletic facility, described at the time as "the finest gymnasium in the Interior, regulation size for basketball and ideal for dances, assemblies and other all-college affairs."[44]

Yet as fine as it was in 1925, the gym in the Main Building was totally inadequate only five years later. Bunnell explained in his biennial report in 1929–1931 that when physical education classes were in session, everyone in the entire structure knew it. The

FIGURE 4

FIGURE 5

FIGURE 6

adopted 1917 upon the recommendation of the Association of Land Grant Colleges and Universities (Figure 4).

Many alumni and faculty, including President Emeritus Bunnell, were angered by the change. In fact the issue was so controversial that some university publications preferred leaving the year off the seal completely (Figure 5). After Moore left office in 1953, the new president, Ernest Patty, changed the year on the seal back to 1922 (Figure 6). And thus it remained until 1965, when the fourth university president, William R. Wood, changed the date back to 1917. It was claimed he did so not only because 1917 seemed the most appropriate date, but also because the fiftieth anniversary of the university in 1967 would therefore coincide with the 1967 centennial celebration of the U.S. purchase of Alaska (Figure 7).

The history of the changing dates on the university seal inspired William Cashen to predict in 1969 that someday in the "year 2000 or thereabouts

FIGURE 7

a new University president is going to pause in front of our Cornerstone." Cashen warned that when the future president's "eyes light up at the startling discovery that the date thereon is July 4, 1915," the official age of the university will probably change again.

pounding on the gym floor, he wrote, "is racking the building considerably and rendering classroom use of the rooms below for a portion of the day very disagreeable . . . ."[45]

In 1930 Bunnell requested $45,000 from the legislature to construct a new combination gymnasium-library-museum of reinforced concrete. This time he realized that the gym should be on the ground floor of the building, with the library and museum above it. When Bunnell only received about half of the required appropriation, he built the first floor to house the gym, and covered it with a temporary sheet metal roof until further funding would be available to add the upstairs library. The gymnasium (today known as "Signers' Hall") was the first concrete structure on the campus, and the first of six proposed "permanent," fireproof structures that Bunnell envisioned on the hill.[46]

THE "ARCTIC LINDBERGH"
Pilot Carl Ben Eielson, for whom the Eielson Memorial Building is named.

Charles E. Bunnell Collection,
Rasmuson Library

Construction of the second concrete structure on campus began in 1934, with the groundbreaking for the first story of the Eielson Memorial Building, dedicated in memory of Fairbanks aviator Carl Ben Eielson, the Charles Lindbergh of polar aviation. Eielson, whose accomplishments included the first air mail flight in Alaska, the first crossing of the Arctic Ocean by airplane, and the first flight over Antarctica, crashed and died in 1929 at a remote site in northeastern Siberia. In his honor, the Fairbanks chapter of the American Legion decided to raise funds for construction of a $100,000 "Colonel Carl Ben Eielson Building of Aeronautical Engineering" at the Alaska Agricultural College and School of Mines.

Establishing an aeronautical school at the college made perfect sense. Aviation was one of Alaska's fastest growing industries in the 1930s, and Fairbanks was its center. Charles Bunnell (who personally was a white-knuckle flier who hated to see his employees fly) thought Fairbanks an ideal base for aerial transportation between North America and Asia on the "World's Great Northern Highway" of the air. "Fairbanks certainly faces a brilliant future," the

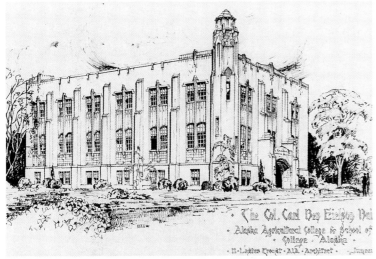

THE DREAM AND THE REALITY
The original ornate plans for the Eielson Memorial Building (top), contrasted with the first floor as actually constructed in 1934.

Charles E. Bunnell Collection,
Rasmuson Library

Fairbanks Daily News-Miner predicted in 1934. "Aside from . . . mining activities our city will soon be known all over the world as the center of aviation when contemplated air routes to Europe and Asia are established." Furthermore, the paper argued, Fairbanks was the most logical place in Alaska for a northern military air base then under discussion in Congress.[47]

In 1930, plans originally called for the three-story Eielson Building to be the west wing of the college's central core, and one of several identical concrete structures on campus decorated with a "frieze of white

quartz . . . at the juncture of the first and second stories." The architect's drawings pictured the Eielson Building as a handsome edifice crowned like a castle with a small tower on its southwest corner. The proposed building was intended to house a complete school of aeronautical engineering equipped with a "specially constructed wind tunnel, with apparatus for testing air currents and all atmospheric conditions."[48]

Due to the depression, only a fraction of the necessary funds for the Eielson Memorial were ever donated, forcing drastic cuts to the building plans and necessitating the elimination of the aeronautical school. The first floor of the Eielson Building was built in 1934 and covered with a temporary roof; the building—which at one time or another would house virtually every department on campus from the post office to the president's office—was not completed until 1950.

Appropriately, the man who turned the first shovelful of dirt to break ground on the Eielson Building in May 1934 was James Wickersham. Ever since he had failed in his attempt to have Bunnell fired in 1921, the old judge officially had nothing to do with the college. On a brief visit back to Fairbanks in 1922 (he had moved to Juneau after leaving office in 1920) Wickersham said he found that many of his old adversaries were pleasant and friendly, but not the college president. "Also met Bunnell," Wickersham wrote in his diary, "who grunted when I spoke to him."[49] Their feud had mellowed somewhat over the years. In 1927, the territorial legislature had appropriated $5,000 for the college to publish Wickersham's *Bibliography of Alaskan Literature, 1724–1924*, a magnificent work of scholarship which had taken him almost two decades to complete. The college published Wickersham's bibliography in 1928 as Vol. 1, No. 1. of the *Miscellaneous Publications of the Alaska Agricultural College and School of Mines*. The volume, still unsurpassed for the era it covers, listed 10,380 separate items, including every article, book, newspaper, and government report that Wickersham and the staff of the Library of Congress could find published on Alaska in the previous two hundred years.

In 1933, over the judge's initial objections, his second wife, Grace Wickersham, accepted an ap-pointment from the governor to the college's board of trustees.[50] Some months later, Wickersham received a personal invitation from Bunnell to break the ground for the new Eielson Building and to deliver the commencement address at the 1934 graduation ceremony.

Judge Wickersham, now almost seventy-seven years old, was thrilled to get the opportunity to speak to the twenty members of the class of 1934, the largest graduating class in the history of the institution he had established. The judge treated the restless graduates and their relatives to a lengthy, scholarly dissertation entitled "The Asia-American Migration Route," which filled several entire pages in the next day's newspaper. Wickersham enjoyed the recognition. He wrote in his diary, "a glorious day—fine view across the Tanana Valley—from the beautiful white birch tree campus" marked by "the great concrete cornerstone which I dedicated on July 4, 1915."[51]

Though Bunnell was glad to give Wickersham credit for all he deserved, the president was careful not to overdo the acclaim. Bill Cashen, the newly appointed editor of the *Collegian* in 1934, recalled Bunnell's obvious displeasure when the president read over Cashen's first draft of a long editorial praising Wickersham's selection as commencement speaker. On the president's strong "suggestion," Cashen condensed the editorial into six sentences.[52] Bunnell and the trustees paid greater tribute to the college's founding father the following year, when Wickersham was given the first and only honorary doctor of laws degree ever granted by the Alaska Agricultural College and School of Mines. (The college had granted its first honorary doctor of science degree in 1932 to James Gordon Steese, pioneer Alaskan road builder.) Wickersham admitted in his diary that he was nervous at the 1935 ceremony. "President Bunnell in answer to my inquiry as to what I shall do or say in the function of receiving the degree of Doctor of Laws answered: Keep still and look wise—we will do the balance."[53]

When he had laid the college cornerstone twenty years earlier, Wickersham had believed that the site would one day be the home of a genuine university. Thanks to the hard work of President Bunnell and his staff, the dream had become a reality. Official recognition of the college's progress came in 1934, when the Northwest Association of Secondary Schools, Colleges and Universities granted full accreditation to the Alaska Agricultural College and School of Mines as a four-year institution.[54]

Just two months before Judge Wickersham received his honorary degree in 1935, the Alaska legislature had passed a bill introduced by George A. Lingo, the first Alaska College graduate to win a seat in the legislature, officially changing the name of the A.A.C. & S.M. to the University of Alaska, effective July 1, 1935.[55] Thus, almost twenty years to the day after Wickersham laid the cornerstone of the Alaska Agricultural College and School of Mines on College Hill, the college which had graduated ninety-three students over thirteen years was officially reborn as the University of Alaska.

Photo by N. Wien

Portfolio
1922–1935

THE FIRST AERIAL PHOTOGRAPH OF THE CAMPUS, *taken by pioneer aviator Noel Wien in 1925. In the background on the left, construction is underway on the first dormitory (later called "Club Dorm") and also on the west wing of the Main Building. The Collegian reported in December 1925 that Wien had to let go of his controls at 500 feet, "and while the plane shot downwards he used both hands to snap the picture, righting the ship as it dived close above the roof of the main building."*

Historical Photograph Collection, Rasmuson Library

STUDENTS WERE IN SHORT SUPPLY
*when the college first opened in 1922. President
Bunnell personally recruited members of the
Fairbanks High School graduating class of 1922
(shown above) to consider attending the Alaska
Agricultural College and School of Mines. Four of the
dozen students who registered during the college's
first semester in 1922 were from this class. Within two
years nearly all of these 11 Fairbanks high school
graduates had enrolled at the college, including E. L.
"Bob" Bartlett (middle of the back row), who later
became Alaska's Delegate to Congress and a United
States Senator, and his future wife Vide Gaustad
(directly in front of him). From left to right front row:
Donald Morgan, Jack Hosler, Roden Davis, Hugh
Smith; 2nd row: Dorothy Roth, Thelma Blaker,
Dorothy Billson, Vide Gaustad; 3rd row: Clifford
Smith, Bob Bartlett, Clarence Burglin.*

Dorothy Loftus Collection, Rasmuson Library

"THE CAMPUS WAS A HAYFIELD," *said LarVern Borell when she first saw the Alaska Agricultural College in 1922. Bunnell planted wheat on the "campus green" because he thought it the most practical and profitable method of landscaping.*

Charles E. Bunnell Collection, Rasmuson Library

MARGARET (THOMAS) MURIE, THE FIRST WOMAN *graduate of the Alaska Agricultural College and School of Mines in 1924, and her husband Olaus (left), visit with Jess Rust, an old family friend from Fairbanks.*

Otto Geist Collection, Rasmuson Library

(ABOVE) A VIEW OF THE CAMPUS IN THE 1920S
from the agricultural experimental station,
with the Main Building in the distance.

Agricultural Experiment Station Collection, Rasmuson Library

(BELOW) A WINTER VIEW
of the "upper campus" in the 1920s.

Alumni Services Collection, Rasmuson Library

Alaska Agriculture College Fairbanks A.A.A.   Sept 21-1929.

"Photo By" Marier Bros.

THIS AERIAL VIEW OF THE CAMPUS IN 1929
*shows the dramatic growth of the college in the
previous few years. Campus facilities include a mine
shop building and stamp mill on the far right at the
foot of the hill between the road and the railroad*
*tracks. President Bunnell's six-room cottage stands by
itself near the "College Gate" on the road leading to
the campus.*

Bob Johnston

JACK SHANLY, THE FIRST GRADUATE
*of the Alaska Agricultural College and School
of Mines, had dropped out of Cornell during
the First World War to drive an ambulance
for the French Army. He returned to school at
the A.A.C. & S. M. in 1922 to pursue his
degree and prove up on a homestead at the
same time. He graduated from the Fairbanks
college in 1923 with a bachelor's degree in
agriculture, and a homestead at the foot of
College Hill.*

LarVern Keys Collection, Rasmuson Library

(BELOW) THE MCCOMBE TWINS, JOHN AND
*Robert—two of the 12 students who enrolled
for the first semester in 1922—with their pet
bear cubs.*

Dorothy Loftus Collection, Rasmuson Library

HALF A DOZEN OF THE FIRST
*students in the college library
in the Main Building.*

Historical Photograph Collection,
Rasmuson Library

AN AERIAL VIEW
of the "flats" below
College Hill in the 1930s.

LarVern Keys Collection,
Rasmuson Library

WAITING FOR A TRAIN
Early transportation to and from the college was via the Alaska Railroad. The one-room College Station was located at the foot of College Hill.

Dorothy Loftus Collection,
Rasmuson Library

FOR EIGHT YEARS THE ALASKA RAILROAD
operated a small, self-propelled narrow gauge trolley between the college and the Fairbanks station four miles away. Driven by conductor Art Marsh, the "Toonerville Trolley" was an old Beach electric car saved from the scrap heap and remodeled with a gasoline engine. It ceased operation after regular bus service to the college began in 1931.

Charles E. Bunnell Collection, Rasmuson Library

AN ALASKA RAILROAD STANDARD
gauge train leaving College in the spring of 1930. The middle rail was for the "Toonerville Trolley," the narrow gauge gasoline car shown at left. The third rail was torn up in 1931.

Fran Christy Collection, Rasmuson Library

PRESIDENT BUNNELL WAS ALWAYS AMUSED WHEN
*visitors mistook him for the campus janitor, since he
was as likely to be found sweeping the floor as pushing
papers behind his desk. He is shown here standing in
front of an 80 horsepower Ames fire tube boiler being
installed at the power plant in 1925.*

LarVern Keys collection, Rasmuson Library

RELAXING OUTSIDE A CABIN AT BIRCH LAKE ON THE *Richardson Highway south of Fairbanks. From left to right: Larry Gasser, President Bunnell, Mrs. Hutchins, Mrs. Bunnell, Mr. Hutchins.*

Charles E. Bunnell Collection, Rasmuson Library

PRESIDENT BUNNELL
picking berries.

Alumni Services Collection,
Rasmuson Library

BEGINNING IN THE FALL OF 1923, THE ANNUAL
*freshman bonfire was one of the highlights of every
academic year. The lighting by President Bunnell of
the skyscraper of scrap wood (opposite page)—some
years reaching as high as 50-60 feet—marked the
inauguration of a new school year and the passing of
the "torch of knowledge" to entering freshmen.
(Above) Students and faculty enjoy one of the early
freshmen bonfires. President Bunnell stands at the far
right.*

Above: Dorothy Loftus Collection, Rasmuson Library
Opposite page: Charles E. Bunnell Collection, Rasmuson Library

Bunnell did his best to advertise the college *all across Alaska. Ernest Patty, professor of geology and mineralogy, arranged this mineral and paleontology display for the September 1924 Western Alaskan Fair in Anchorage.*

Otto Geist Collection, Rasmuson Library

The college's first basketball team, *the "Full House" squad of 1922–1923, so named by President Bunnell because the starting five (back row) consisted of "three of a kind and a pair," the three Loftus brothers and the McCombe twins. In one game the "Full House" beat Anchorage High School by a score of 11 to 8. Back row from left to right: Earl Pilgrim (the coach and first professor of mining engineering), Robert McCombe, Art Loftus, Ted Loftus, Jule Loftus, and John McCombe; in front: Roden Davis and Jack Hosler.*

Charles E. Bunnell Collection, Rasmuson Library

THE WOMEN'S BASKETBALL TEAM OF 1924–1925 *sported fashionable "Roaring Twenties" headbands emblazoned with their college letters. On their trip to Anchorage in January 1925 they defeated the Anchorage women by scores of 12 to 7 and 10 to 9.*

From left to right kneeling: Genevieve Parker, forward; Lucy Buteau, substitute; Florence Roth, forward; standing: Albina Miller, guard; Alta Herzer, center; and Thelma Blaker, captain.

Dorothy Loftus Collection, Rasmuson Library

72

THE WOMEN'S BASKETBALL TEAM OF 1931–1932
*Front row left to right: Bettie Scheffler, Audrey Steel
and Ruby Olsen; standing: Jean Hunter, Helen Linck,
Clair Weller and Violet Lundell.*

George
Karabelnikoff

Robert
Henning

John
O'Shea

Woodrow
Johansen

Harry
Lundell

Glen
Franklin

Coach
James Ryan

William
O'Neill

Harry
Brandt

1933-34

83-1

UNDER COACH JAMES RYAN, THE MEN'S BASKETBALL
team of 1933–1934 traveled almost 3,000 miles across the
territory, beating the high school teams at Seward,
Cordova, Juneau, Sitka, Ketchikan, Petersburg, and
Skagway by a combined score of 328–79.

Robert P. Isaac Collection, Rasmuson Library

OUTDOOR WINTER SPORTS, INCLUDING SKIING,
ice hockey, and sledding were always popular
activities on campus. The toboggan slide (opposite
page), erected in 1927 on the south side of the
campus, was 210 feet long and 50 feet high. The
starting platform at the upper end was 18 feet off the
ground. At the bottom of the slide a toboggan could
approach speeds of up to 40 miles per hour.

Charles E. Bunnell Collection, Rasmuson Library

THE MEN'S 1927–1928 BASKETBALL *team won all seventeen games on a tour of southeastern Alaska. Holding the broom signifying their "clean sweep" was Captain Jack Boswell. The men's team was joined by the women's team plus a male quartet for this photograph taken in the Anchorage railway station on January 25, 1928.*

IN THE 1920S THE MAIN BUILDING HOUSED THE
entire college. On this postcard a student identified
some of the facilities including the gym, the
classrooms for calculus and the history of education,
the president's office, and the "domestic science"
room.

Charles E. Bunnell Collection, Rasmuson Library

(OPPOSITE) THE COLLEGE CURRICULUM FOCUSED ON
the applied practical benefits of higher education to
the people of Alaska, as demonstrated by this
advertisement from the late 1920s.

Rasmuson Library

The
Alaska Agricultural College
and School of Mines

OFFERS

Four-Year Courses

LEADING TO THE DEGREE OF

BACHELOR OF SCIENCE

IN

{
AGRICULTURE
BUSINESS ADMINISTRATION
CIVIL ENGINEERING
CHEMISTRY
EDUCATION
GEOLOGY AND MINING
GENERAL SCIENCE
HOME ECONOMICS
METALLURGY
MINING ENGINEERING
}

Short Courses for

THE HOUSEWIFE

THE FARMER

THE PROSPECTOR

THE MINER

BOARD AND ROOM AT COLLEGE DORMITORY

$55.00 PER MONTH

Tuition Free

WEAVING AND
*sewing in the home
economics lab.*

Charles E. Bunnell
Collection, Rasmuson
Library

HOME ECONOMICS TEAS PUT ON BY PROFESSOR
*Lola Cremeans (Tilly) counted among the social
highlights of the college's academic year. Seated at the
center table are Mrs. Kathryn Patty (left), wife of
Dean Ernest Patty, and Mrs. Minnie Gasser, wife of
agriculture professor George Gasser.*

Charles E. Bunnell Collection, Rasmuson Library

Lola Cremeans (Tilly)
Fairbanks 1929

LOLA CREMEANS (TILLY), HOME ECONOMICS
professor, dressed in winter finery, shortly after her
arrival in 1929.

Lola Tilly Collection, Rasmuson Library

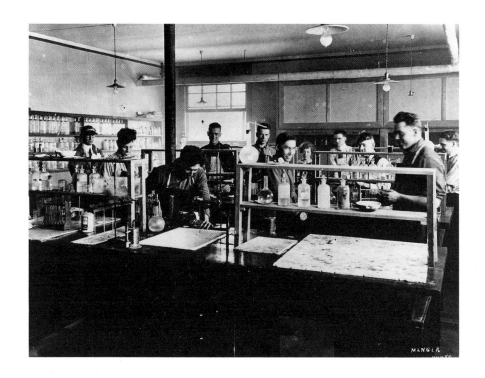

NEARLY THE ENTIRE *student body, gathered in the chemistry lab under the watchful gaze of Professor Herbert Bruce at the far left.*

PRESIDENT BUNNELL *took special pride that the college could boast of at least one graduate per year from its very beginning. The third graduating class with just one student was Jamie Cameron, the class of 1925. Cameron, the second woman to graduate from the college, received a B.S. in home economics. From left to right in the commencement "parade" are: Morton E. Stevens, president of the board of trustees; Dean Ernest Patty; Jamie Cameron; and commencement speaker Col. James Gordon Steese.*

PRESIDENT BUNNELL, *his daughter Jean, and the president's 1926 Buick. Bunnell could not drive, but according to his one-time chauffeur, Bill Cashen, the president had "an amazing collection of driving tips and suggestions at his command."*

Charles E. Bunnell Collection, Rasmuson Library

COLLEGE COEDS *from Fairbanks in 1929 on the steps of President Bunnell's house. The Main Building is in the background. Seated: Helene Durand, Genevieve Parker, Helen Franklin, and Helen MacDonald. Standing: Norma Clausen, Alaska Stewart, Janet Preston, and Maxine Raats.*

Charles E. Bunnell Collection, Rasmuson Library

(ABOVE) PRESIDENT BUNNELL, DRESSED IN HIS *academic robes, looks on as his old nemesis James Wickersham digs the first shovelful of dirt for the construction of the Eielson Memorial Building in 1934.*

Historical Photograph Collection, Rasmuson Library

(BELOW) ON MAY 20, 1935, BRUCE THOMAS *received the last of the ninety-three diplomas granted by the Alaska Agricultural College and School of Mines before it became the University of Alaska.*

Bruce Thomas

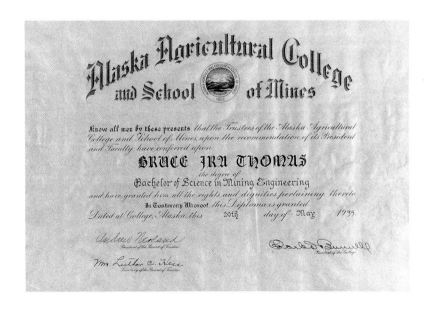

PRESIDENT BUNNELL POSES WITH SOME OF THE *proud alumni of the Alaska Agricultural College and School of Mines at the 1931 meeting of the alumni association. Top row: Ted Loftus '27, Charles O. Thompson '30, and Albert Visca '29. Center: Kenneth Sheggeby '31, George Lingo '27, Frank DeWree '28,* *Clifford Smith '27, W. W. Walton '31, William McCarty '27, and Fred Beeler '31. Bottom: President Bunnell, Florence Roth Thompson '27, Helen Franklin Heath '30, Dorothy Roth Loftus '27, and Jack Boswell '29.*

Alumni Services Collection, Rasmuson Library

A GROUP PORTRAIT OF NEARLY THE ENTIRE *faculty and student body in 1925–1926. (Some individuals appear on each of the facing pages, to prevent them from being obscured in the book binding.) The photo was taken in the college's first gymnasium, which was located on the top floor of the west wing of the Main Building. This copy of the class portrait belonged to chemistry professor G. Raymond Hood, (#19, standing about one-third of the way in from the right hand side). Hood, obviously a methodical person, went through the photograph and numbered the students he recognized, though he wrote on the back, "I don't know one-third the Frosh yet." In addition, he also noted which students he was then teaching, and which he had taught previously, as well as what he thought was their class year. "Two of my Chem. 111 students are not in the picture," he wrote. He also admitted that he could not tell the McCombe twins apart (#29 and #30). He said that one* was John and the other was Bob, but "God only knows which."

1. Charles E. Bunnell, president
2. Ernest Patty, dean
3. Lydia Jacobson, professor of home economics
4. Martha Park, instructor of home economics
5. Frances Carnall, secretary to the president
6. Grace Clark, librarian and instructor of physical education
7. Mrs. A. M. Truesdell
8. John Clark, chemistry major, '27
9. John Luss, '27
10. Donald Foster, chemistry major, '29
11. Charley Wheeler, '28
12. A. M. Truesdell, professor of math and civil engineering

13. Hanley Weiser, associate professor of metallurgy
14 & 15. Dorothy Roth, B.S. '27, and Arthur Loftus, her beau, '27
16. Florence Roth, B.S., '27
17. Clarence Isberg, chemistry major, '27
18. Leonidas Vernon, chemistry major, '28
19. Very Truly Yours. (G. Raymond Hood, professor of chemistry)
20. Earl Pilgrim, professor of mining
21. Lawrence McCarty, '27
22. Lynn Goyne
23. Robert Q. Brown, professor of physics
24. Ladessa Hall, professor of business administration
25. Leslie A. Marchand, professor of English and French
26. William Hering
27. Iris (Hinckley) Adler

28. Rev. Henry Chapman
29 & 30. The McCombe Twins. One is John. Other is Bob. God only knows which.
31. William McCarty, '27
32. Genevieve Parker, '28
33. Chester Tripp, '27
34. Jack Hosler, B.S., '27
35. Clarence Burglin, '27
36. Ray Hamilton, '27, instructor of military science
37. Helga Fohn-Hansen, '28
38. Albina Miller, '27
39. Clifford Smith, '27
40. Theodore Loftus, '27
41. Richard Schoeser, '28

STUDENTS OF THE ALASKA
Agricultural College and
School of Mines in 1929–1930.

Otto Geist Collection, Rasmuson Library

ONE OF THE SLOGANS FOR
the mining short course in the 1920s promised
prospectors "new vision in the hills."

Rasmuson Library

Short Course for Prospectors

𝕬laska 𝕬gricultural College and
School of 𝔐ines

"It will give you new vision in the hills"

Board and Room at College Dormitory $55 Per Month

GOLD MINING
A DEPRESSION PROOF BUSINESS

THE ALASKA COLLEGE
offers
THE MINING SHORT COURSE
For Prospectors and Small Mine Operators

This Year:-
Particular emphasis will be placed on gold prospecting and mining.

Training Will Be Given In:-
The tracing of "float"
Tracing of outcrops.
Study of gold mining districts in Alaska.
Fire Assaying for gold and silver.
Amalgamation of gold ores.
Cyanidation of gold ores.
Gravity concentration and flotation of base ores.
Mineralogy.
Shop work in repair and maintenance of gas engines.

There are no educational requirements.
The total cost of the course is about $25.00.
Room and board at the College Dormitory, $55.00 per month.

COURSE BEGINS NOVEMBER 28, 1931, AND
ENDS FEBRUARY 12, 1932

For Dormitory reservations make application promptly to
CHARLES E. BUNNELL, President
COLLEGE, ALASKA

DURING THE 1930S THE COLLEGE
attracted short course students with the
claim that gold mining was "a depression
proof business."

Rasmuson Library

A 1930 ADVERTISEMENT
for Alaska's "Virile, Young
Territorial College."

Rasmuson Library

The "Baldies" staged a memorable college
*stunt in 1929, when they decided to become human
billiard balls. Fred Beeler (front row on the far right
in a dark shirt) recalled that in 1929, he and several
other dorm residents, including "P. J." Doheny and
Buck Roberts, decided to form their own unique
billiard club. Each member got a "billiard ball" hair
cut, and had a red number painted on the back of
their heads. As a charter member, Fred Beeler was
No. 1. The club folded when their hair grew back.*

Charles E. Bunnell Collection, Rasmuson Library

TWENTY-THREE YEARS OLD, THREE YEARS YOUNG
An aerial view of the University of Alaska campus taken in 1938 by noted cartographer and photographer Bradford Washburn. Barely visible, halfway between the edge of the campus and the edge of the horizon near the center of the photograph, is the log home built by anthropologist

Froelich Rainey in 1937, on what was then called "Rainey Ridge." Now known as the Skarland Cabin, in honor of Ivar Skarland who lived in the cabin from the late 1940s until his death in 1965, the cabin is today behind the upper dorms built in the 1960s.

Bradford Washburn, Boston Museum of Science

90

THREE

Building a University 1935–1946

At midnight on June 30, 1935, bugler Albert Dickey of the college military unit stood in front of the Main Building and blew the mournful sound of Taps across the valley. The Alaska Agricultural College and School of Mines was no more. Glen Franklin, the president of the student association, then raised the flag for the first time over the campus of the University of Alaska.[1]

Ivar Skarland, a member of the college's final graduation class in 1935, wrote in an editorial in the *Farthest North Collegian*, "We are not writing an obituary over the Alaska Agricultural College and School of Mines; it is not dead; it continues to live as a part of the greater institution, the University of Alaska."[2]

As the *Collegian* had noted earlier that spring, "the new name will not only be easier to handle but also more appropriate for the expanding activities of the school." During its thirteen-year history, the Alaska Agricultural College had outgrown "the limited curricula of a professional, trade or technical school," and expanded into the "pure sciences, the liberal arts, literature and languages, the social sciences, and all other branches commonly associated with the wide interests and training of a university . . . ."[3]

As a small university—193 students in credit classes in 1935–1936—it continued to offer close personal contact between faculty and students, and at the same time provided a much greater range of courses. The new university offered full degree programs in ten different disciplines, including Arts and Letters, and provided courses for the first two years in fields such as prejournalism, prelaw, premedicine, forestry, aeronautical engineering and architectural engineering.[4]

The transformation from college to university brought great changes in the faculty, which now numbered nearly two dozen. After thirteen years with the college, Dean Ernest Patty—President Bunnell's right-hand man and the last of the six professors first hired by Bunnell in 1922—decided to return to mining and submitted his resignation. Patty said President Bunnell hated to see anyone leave the "college family," and was so bitter that not until three years later were they once again on speaking terms. Bunnell replaced Patty with four new deans, including Professor William Elmhirst Duckering as the new Dean of Faculty. Duckering, a professor of civil engineering and mathematics, had come to the college in 1932 at the age of fifty after a distinguished career in civil engineering.[5]

Dr. Murray W. Shields, professor of business administration, hired in 1934, had been the first and only faculty member with a Ph.D. on the staff of the Alaska Agricultural College and School of Mines. By contrast, among the faculty in the University of Alaska's first year were half a dozen professors with doctorates, including Shields, Alfred Bastress in chemistry, Ervin Bramhall in physics, James Hance in mining and geology, Froelich Rainey in anthropology, and Bruce White in education.[6]

President Bunnell thought the best symbol of the "coming of age of the University of Alaska" was its new fireproof library, opened in late December 1935. An appropriation of $35,000 by the territorial legislature enabled Bunnell to build the long-delayed second story library above the gymnasium. For the next quarter century, the students of the University of Alaska learned the power of concentration by studying on top of a basketball court and rifle range. John Mehler, the longtime head librarian after World War II, praised the day the rifle range moved to the Main Building, and congratulated the university engineer when he fixed the backboards so they would no longer vibrate and shake the floor.[7]

Though the location above the gym was hardly ideal, the library facilities were far superior to anything the college had previously known. Equipped with adjustable steel bookcases for the 12,000 volumes in the collection, the new library also provided students with a sixty-by-eighty-foot reading room, decorated with a large Sydney Laurence painting of Mount McKinley donated by Fairbanks businessman and university regent Austin E. "Cap" Lathrop.

"The (library's) central area is large enough to give the impression of spaciousness," the *Collegian* reported, "an impression which has been quite lacking heretofore, in University buildings. The interior of the library is beautifully lighted with twenty-four large electric lights, softened with large white globes."[8]

A corner of the new library was reserved for the 2,250 volumes from the personal library of the late Dr. Alfred H. Brooks, former head of the U.S. Geological Survey in Alaska. Some years earlier, Brooks' widow had chosen to donate his Alaskana collection to the Alaska College—over the claims of both Harvard and the University of Washington—with the stipulation that the books remain in storage until a fireproof, concrete library could be completed. The Brooks Collection, together with about 1,500 volumes that the U.S. Department of Agriculture sent the university in 1935 after closing the experiment station at Sitka, formed the nucleus of the library's growing collection of Alaskana.[9]

A year before the new university library opened, Judge James Wickersham promised Bunnell that the University of Alaska would inherit his personal library of about 10,000 volumes, a gift that would almost double the size of the university's holdings.[10] For years Wickersham had been building a huge personal library, with every intention of eventually leaving it to the university that he had helped to create. With the addition of the Wickersham Collection, the University of Alaska library would suddenly become the world's most comprehensive research library on Alaska.

In the 1930s, Bunnell and Wickersham seemed to have reconciled their differences, culminating with the honorary degree given to Wickersham in

1935. Yet the bitter feud erupted again in 1936. Wickersham had never given up his lifelong dream of writing a definitive history of Alaska, and he told Bunnell of his ambition in March 1935. According to Wickersham, Bunnell promised to help in any way he could. Wickersham noted in his diary that Bunnell said he "will try to get an appropriation from the Carnegie or Rockefeller Foundations to pay expenses" for Wickersham to write a history of Alaska.[11]

The following year the Rockefeller Foundation granted the University of Alaska $17,000 for the Alaska History Research Project, to catalog and translate the documents in Wickersham's library necessary for writing a history of Alaska. Unfortunately, Wickersham first learned of the Rockefeller grant when he read about it in the newspaper. Furthermore, Bunnell had hired Cecil Robe, who was then completing a Ph.D. at Yale but had been a history professor at Fairbanks since 1929, to direct the project; there were no plans to pay Wickersham for his time or for the use of his library. Upon hearing of this, the proud old judge decided he would never see his work of a lifetime given "to a group of strangers for two years to prepare what they think is a history, from which I am to be excluded." He charged that Robe and his associates were "to be paid big salaries," while *his* only compensation would be a copy of everything they translated and transcribed.[12]

If Wickersham had been physically up to the task of writing the history he dreamed about, then the translation project could have been of enormous value to him. Given his age and strength, however, the book was more daydream than reality, and failing to include him in the translation project was tanta-

mount to locking him out of his own library. Wickersham refused to let the university researchers use his library, and Robe and his three-member research staff went to the Library of Congress, the National Archives, and other repositories instead. When they finished work two years later, Robe and his team brought 5,807 typewritten pages of translated or transcribed documents back to Alaska.[13]

Judge Wickersham's fury was compounded by the fact that he truly needed the money that the history research project could have provided. By 1939 he was nearly blind and bankrupt; in failing health, he could no longer practice law, and his library was one of his few remaining assets. Even if he had still wanted to give his library to the university, he could no longer afford to do so. In the last months of his life, friends tried unsuccessfully to convince the legislature to appropriate funds to purchase his library, but not until almost two years after his death did lawmakers finally approve $20,000 to buy the Wickersham Collection for the Alaska Historical Library and Museum in Juneau.[14]

As the year 1939 progressed, the entries in the personal diary that Wickersham had kept faithfully for nearly forty years grew more illegible. "I am so blind I can hardly see," he wrote on May 12, 1939, a few months short of his eighty-second birthday, "and must quit my diary for the present . . . ." New glasses helped delay the inevitable, but on October 19, 1939, he made the last entry in the diary: "Cannot see—blind!"[15]

A week later the flag over the University of Alaska flew at half-mast in honor of the death of James Wickersham, the university's founding father. In the shadow of the flagpole was the concrete cornerstone that he had laid nearly twenty-five years earlier. "ALASKA'S WICK BURNS OUT," a headline in the *Juneau Empire* read, "BUT HIS LIGHT SHINES ON."[16]

One of the many lasting visions shared by both Wickersham and Bunnell was that Alaska's university should be a center of research about Alaska. No part of the institution fulfilled that goal better than the University of Alaska Museum. According to tradition, the university museum began in 1922 as a single display case in President Bunnell's office. By the mid-1930s the museum's collections contained more than 75,000 artifacts, including Eskimo baskets, ivory carvings, arrowheads, stuffed birds, human skulls, animal heads, an albino moose, whale bones and mammoth tusks. The man primarily responsible for assembling this conglomeration of treasures was a former truck driver and self-trained amateur archaeologist and paleontologist named Otto W. Geist.[17]

Born in Bavaria in 1888, the eleventh of fifteen children, Otto Geist inherited a love of history and natural history from his father. He was stubborn and fiercely independent. At the monastery where he was sent to school as a child, he was allegedly expelled for too often skipping classes in favor of wandering the fields to collect rocks, insects, and ancient Roman artifacts. Geist had the distinction of being a veteran of two armies that fought on opposite sides in the First World War. He served in the German army from 1908 to 1910, and after emigrating to America was called up for service by the U.S. Army in 1917. An expert mechanic and a skilled truck driver, Geist was once the personal mechanic

and chauffeur for Sterling Morton, the president of the Morton Salt Company. As a military driver, he chauffeured President Woodrow Wilson's daughter around France during the peace negotiations after the Armistice. Geist's small business as a general hauling contractor in Kansas City failed in the 1920s and he came to Alaska in 1923. After drifting from one odd job to another, including two summers as a riverboat engineer on the Koyukuk River—during which time he met Olaus and Margaret Murie—and a stint washing dishes at the Model Cafe in Fairbanks, Geist enrolled in the fall of 1925 in a mining short course at the college.

At age thirty-seven, Geist met Bunnell. The encounter led him to embark on a new quest that became his lifelong obsession: the collecting of artifacts and fossils relating to the history and natural history of Alaska. Neither Bunnell nor Geist had any formal training in archaeology or natural history, but both men were fascinated by the handful of museum specimens possessed by the college, and recognized the value of the archaeological, ethnological, botanical, and paleontological treasures in Alaska. Geist and Bunnell also realized that the answers to basic questions about the prehistory of the western world might be found in Alaska. In the 1920s, almost no systematic archeological work had been done in the territory, but scientists had long reasoned that the first inhabitants of North and South America had probably migrated to the western hemisphere through Alaska.

Lying in the Bering Sea about forty miles off the coast of Siberia, St. Lawrence Island appeared likely to have been in the prehistoric migration route between the continents. The first Bunnell-Geist

Archaeological Expedition to St. Lawrence Island in 1927 was originally funded with a personal $1,000 grant from President Bunnell (later reimbursed by the college).[18] During the course of about half a dozen years which Geist devoted to the archaeology of St. Lawrence Island, he amassed a huge collection of artifacts that formed the nucleus of the University of Alaska Museum.[19]

In his effort to build a museum, despite having no budget, no building and no curator, Bunnell found Geist to be the perfect collaborator: an independent bachelor without a family to support, willing to travel the territory in search of artifacts for the sheer joy of the task itself. Few scholars associated with the University of Alaska were ever more dedicated than Otto Geist; during the many years he spent collecting for the museum, Geist seldom received a regular salary.

Geist became noted as an archaeologist on St. Lawrence Island and as a fossil hunter in the gold fields of the Fairbanks mining district. Over the years, miners washing away the thick loess deposits in the area uncovered remains of virtual herds of prehistoric animals. In a cooperative agreement among the American Museum of Natural History in New York City, the University of Alaska Museum, and the Fairbanks Exploration Company—the dredging firm in the Fairbanks district—Geist recovered about four to five tons of bones a year, totaling approximately seven or eight thousand specimens. At the American Museum's Frick Laboratory in New York, he often spent the winters classifying what he had found.[20]

As Bunnell once reported to the legislature, "The value of the service rendered to the College and to science by Mr. Otto Wm. Geist can not be calculated in dollars and cents . . . ."[21] In fact, a 1941 inventory listing the university's assets stated that the irreplaceable archaeological artifacts and paleontological specimens Geist collected were probably worth at least $400,000—approximately twenty percent of the total book value of all of the university's other assets, and more than the total combined cost of the campus power plant plus all of the permanent buildings on campus.[22]

Critics rightfully complain that Geist's approach to collecting was not scientific by modern standards. Today, an archaeologist or paleontologist excavates a site with the patience and finesse of a fine artist, removing soil centimeter by centimeter, using a teaspoon and a toothbrush, in order to record accurately the context in which the artifacts or fossils are found. To a modern scientist, the context of a find is what makes the discovery scientifically important. Geist, however, was more interested in how much he could find rather than where he found it. Singlehandedly, Geist dug up more Pleistocene fossils in the north than anyone in America before or since. During his first dozen years of fossil hunting, Geist estimated that he collected about 50,000 "usable" fossils, not including truckloads of fossil scraps, which he used to line the driveway to his house in Lemeta, off College Road.[23]

A 1929 headline in the *Farthest North Collegian* succinctly described Geist's approach to collecting: "GEIST RETURNS WITH TONS OF SPECIMENS." In fact, his haul from that particular expedition to St. Lawrence Island consisted of "about ten tons of material or about thirty thousand individual specimens."[24] No one person could hope to catalog such a mountain of material scientifically; however, it was Geist's belief that his first duty was to collect and preserve whatever he could find, and leave the slow work of cataloging to future scholars. Even now, some thirty years after his death in 1963, boxes of material Geist collected still sit unopened and unidentified in the modern university museum officially named for Otto W. Geist.

Geist's expeditions to St. Lawrence Island marked the beginning of the university's involvement in Alaskan archaeology, a field in which it has continued to excel for the past sixty-five years. Except during World War II, the University of Alaska has sponsored archaeological field expeditions exploring the north almost every year since 1927.[25] As part of the change from college to university, Bunnell established on paper a half-dozen new departments that grew out of the museum, including anthropology, archaeology, ethnology, natural history, paleontology, and the Department of the Museum.[26] Among those at UA who distinguished themselves in northern anthropology or archaeology over the years were Froelich Rainey (hired in 1935 as the first professor in the newly created Department of Anthropology), and Ivar Skarland, J. Louis Giddings and Wendell Oswalt (all students who later became teachers).

Archaeologists who trained at the University of Alaska enjoyed the advantage of having an archaeological site at their doorstep. The university campus sits on top of a world-famous archaeological discovery made by local students in 1933, when they were digging a post hole for the freshman bonfire. The "Campus Site," located about one hundred yards southeast of the Main Building on the bluff of College Hill, contained microblade cores virtually identical to specimens found a few years earlier in the Gobi Desert. The startling similarity between the artifacts from interior Alaska and those from central Asia was the first solid archaeological evidence that the original inhabitants of America had indeed come from Eurasia, indicating that the Bering Land Bridge migration was more than just a theory.[27]

Archaeology was just one facet of the university's scientific exploration of the north that would blossom in the 1930s and in the years to come. Control of the Agricultural Experiment Station was officially transferred to the college in 1931. In 1932, one of the station's long-lived experiments came to an end with the slaughtering of the only known "galoyaks" on earth, animals that were a cross between a Tibetan yak and a Scottish cow. Students of the Alaska College long remembered the effort by Dr. C. C. Georgeson to crossbreed yaks, hardy animals native to the high plains of Tibet that could easily withstand the rugged winters of interior Alaska, with Galloway cows from southwestern Scotland, beef cattle which are also known to produce rich milk. Unfortunately, the male hybrid offspring all proved to be sterile, and the experiment had to be curtailed. In 1932, the scientists released the six remaining full-blooded yaks into the wilds of the Tanana Valley, while the hybrid "galoyaks" were slaughtered and served up to the students in the college dining room. Galoyak meat proved to be as hard to chew as it was to pronounce. Students who lived on galoyak stew, galoyak burgers, and galoyak surprise, found it tough, tasteless, and after a full year of it on the menu, unforgettable.[28]

Far more successful than the doomed campaign to breed galoyaks was the 1930 attempt to bring back muskoxen in Alaska. Muskoxen, huge northern mammals that can weigh up to half a ton when full grown, survived the last ice age, but were hunted to extinction in Alaska in the nineteenth century. These shaggy "arctic buffalo" were easy prey for hunters; when threatened, muskoxen often form a menacing defensive circle, a stance effective against attacks by wild predators but useless against hunters who can proceed to slaughter them easily one by one. Wildlife officials, prodded by Fairbanks resident Irving Reed of the Alaska Game Commission, secured a $40,000 congressional appropriation in 1930 for the Bureau of Biological Survey to capture and purchase a small herd of calves and yearlings from surviving muskox herds in Greenland in order to reintroduce the species to Alaska. They selected the experiment station on the campus of the Alaska College for raising the young muskoxen.[29]

In 1926, the Biological Survey had established a cooperative research station at the college, to undertake experiments on forage management and Alaskan livestock, such as crossbreeding caribou and reindeer to produce "carideer."[30] At the time, the station consisted of a corral located near where the Duckering Building now stands. By the late

Students in the Mining Short Course in 1936–1937.

Charles E. Bunnell Collection, Rasmuson Library

1920s, however, the facilities of the Biological Survey Station included a barn, granary, feed lot, five handling corrals, and miles of fenced pasture "on and adjoining the campus." In 1930 the Biological Survey shipped thirty-four young muskoxen 14,000 miles from Greenland to the college campus in Fairbanks, where the scientists hoped to begin the return of an entire species to Alaska.[31]

Among the many benefits from having a herd of these rare animals on campus was the opportunity to experiment with their wool, one of the world's finest natural fibers. Arctic explorer and promoter Vilhjalmur Stefansson once described the muskox as "a cow with a coat of wool," and in fact its Latin name *Ovibos* literally means "sheep-cow."[32] Lydia Fohn-Hansen, former professor of home economics who became assistant director of the newly established Cooperative Extension Service in 1930, began using muskox wool or *qiviut* in knitting and weaving courses. Getting an adequate supply of the wool required ingenuity. Shearing the muskoxen was impractical because of the animals' temperament and because the finer wool was hidden under a thick layer of coarse guard hairs. But the animals shed an average of about two and a half pounds of their finer fleece in the spring. Stuck to the bushes which the animals had brushed against in the pasture, the wool could be picked like cotton and made into scarves, gloves and mittens.[33]

For six years, scientists and students at the Alaska College watched the muskoxen grow to maturity, as the animals roamed 7,500 acres of pasture on and behind the campus stretching back into the Goldstream Valley. After the first muskox calves were born in 1934, the now full-grown herd was ready to be released from captivity. In 1935 and 1936, the animals were shipped to Nunivak Island, a national wildlife refuge in the Bering Sea free of predators, where it was hoped the muskoxen would prosper and multiply.[34]

The return of the muskox has been spectacularly successful. In 1975, four decades after muskoxen were first turned loose on Nunivak, the number of animals had grown so large that sport hunting had to be inaugurated to control the population, despite the fact that many animals had been culled from the Nunivak herd over the years so that wild muskox populations could be planted in other parts of Alaska.[35] In the 1980s, the total population of muskoxen in Alaska was estimated to be more than thirteen hundred, all descended from the original herd of thirty-four animals captured in Greenland and raised at the college in Fairbanks.

Today, the university's Large Animal Research Station (popularly known as the "Muskox Farm") is located on some of the same pastureland north of the campus on which the original herd once roamed. Dozens of muskoxen, caribou, and reindeer are maintained at LARS for nutritional and behavioral studies, physiological monitoring, and educational purposes, attracting more than 100,000 visitors each year.[36]

Another field of research in which the University of Alaska would become world famous also began in the 1930s: the investigation of the aurora borealis. With a $10,000 grant from the Rockefeller Foundation, physics professor Veryl Fuller set up the college's first aurora observation station in 1930. With specially designed

cameras, primitive when compared with the sophisticated tools of today's scientists, Fuller made thousands of photographs and measurements of the aurora over the next five years. His career was tragically short; while working in the garden of his home on campus in May 1935, Professor Fuller died of a heart attack at the age of thirty-nine.[37]

Dr. Ervin Bramhall, Fuller's replacement in the physics department and the man who continued his studies of the northern lights, received his Ph.D. from Cambridge University in 1931. Like many of the researchers attracted to the University of Alaska over the years, Bramhall was a scientist with a love of exploration and adventure. He first came to Alaska in 1932 with the Cosmic-Ray Expedition on Mount McKinley. The following year he was a key member of the scientific team on Richard Byrd's second expedition to Antarctica, for which he received a congressional medal. Bramhall took charge of assembling and publishing the data that Fuller left behind, and coauthored a 1937 book entitled *Auroral Research at the University of Alaska 1930–1934*. In his conclusion, he acknowledged that the University of Alaska's geographical location "makes it an ideal site for research on geophysical phenomena," and predicted that inevitably "a permanent observatory must sooner or later be established in its vicinity." His prediction was borne out with the opening of the Geophysical Institute on the University of Alaska campus a dozen years later.[38]

The 1930s were the last great boom years of placer gold mining in Alaska, and were also the heyday of the university's School of Mines.[39] Alaska's thriving gold mining industry, revolutionized in the 1920s with the introduction of large-scale dredging operations at Nome and Fairbanks, and boosted in the 1930s by the federal government's seventy percent increase in the price of gold, created a steady demand for mining engineers. The School of Mines in those years became the most professional and

99

well-equipped department on the campus; facilities included a complete mine shop, a stamp mill, metallurgical laboratories and an assay office, which the university operated in cooperation with the Bureau of Mines as a service to the miners of interior Alaska.

From the opening of the college until the U.S. entry into World War II almost twenty years later, twice as many students were enrolled in the mining school as in any other department, and nearly one-third of the total 271 graduates from 1922 to 1942 earned their degrees from the School of Mines.[40] Upperclassmen among the mining students were virtually guaranteed summer jobs with the Fairbanks Exploration Company. In fact, until the early 1930s, "one summer of practical mining experience" was a prerequisite for graduation, and the majority of graduates went directly to work in the mining industry when they finished school.[41]

Instructors used the Fairbanks mining district, one of the richest placer gold fields in America, as a "natural laboratory" for the School of Mines. Within a radius of twenty miles of the campus every mining method from hard-rock to hydraulic mining could be found, and students saw them all first hand. Furthermore the school operated its own "practice mine" directly underneath the university campus itself, where students handled the "actual drilling, blasting, timbering and mucking."[42] By the mid-1930s, student miners had dynamited a tunnel about six and a half feet high and five hundred feet long into the hard rock of College Hill, to a point near the southwest corner of the Main Building about seventy-five feet below the surface. In the 1940s, water was tapped in the mine tunnel and piped to the surface, and the tunnel became the main source for the campus water supply for many years. The tunnel entrance on the south side of College Hill was permanently covered up during road construction in the 1980s, sealing off the abandoned mining shaft that runs through the heart of the university campus.[43]

The College bus overtakes the Toonerville Trolley

Paul Greimann, a Fairbanks mechanic and garage owner, began driving a bus between Fairbanks and the Alaska College in 1931. The bus pictured here was placed in service in the mid-1930s. "The new College bus," the 1935 yearbook stated, "has all the style and comfort of the best in the States."

At first Bunnell had tried to talk Greimann out of starting his bus line, because the president feared—correctly as it turned out—that the competition from Greimann's bus would put the Alaska Railroad gas car out of business. If the bus service later failed, the college would be left without any reliable transportation. "If I had any idea I might fail," Greimann told Bunnell, "I wouldn't do it." Often Greimann and his drivers had to maintain College Road themselves, plowing snow in the winter and filling potholes in the summer. In wet weather Greimann sometimes carried female passengers across the bogs on the road, while the men on board helped push the bus out of the mud.

In 1953, after twenty-two years driving the road between Fairbanks and College, Greimann sold the bus business to another operator. Greimann claimed that during his two decades on the Fairbanks-College run, on only one occasion—a forty-eight-hour period during the 1937 spring breakup—did his bus fail to make it through.

Above ground, the university campus was rapidly outgrowing its old buildings. By 1936, the small campus power plant constructed eleven years earlier was on the verge of collapse, and housing facilities were inadequate for both faculty and students.[44] Bunnell predicted that the student population could easily double within two years, but only if more accommodations were available. To meet the crisis, the 1937 legislature appropriated funds for both a new power plant and a new dormitory for women: a reinforced concrete structure with room for eighty-four students, named for Harriet Hess, the woman whose handkerchief had marked the site of the cornerstone in 1915, and whose thirty-four-year tenure (from 1917 to 1951) as a college trustee and university regent would be the longest in the history of the institution.[45]

The first women students moved into Harriet Hess Hall at the start of the 1938 fall semester. All dorm rooms on campus rented for ten dollars per month, but since it was the first concrete dormitory on campus, Hess Hall held the most comfortable student accommodations available at the time. "The unique construction of the walls make this unquestionably the warmest building on campus," the *Collegian* noted. "With the hanging of curtains and the laying of carpets a homelike atmosphere is permeating the rooms and before long the routine matters of study and discipline will assume their natural precedence."[46]

Despite the addition of Hess Hall, the campus remained desperately short of housing. Enrollment in the fall of 1940 topped three hundred full-time students for the first time in the history of the university. In October that year, the *Collegian* noted that the dorms were "filled as full as some Midwest silos, and there are still students waiting to find spare corners to sleep in . . . ." Nevertheless Bunnell claimed as many as five hundred students could have been admitted if dormitory space had been

available.[47] To raise extra revenue, the university in 1940 charged its first tuition: twenty dollars per semester to nonresidents of the Territory of Alaska. Residents would not pay tuition at the University of Alaska until more than thirty years later, but all students paid a "community fee" of fifteen dollars each semester, which covered the "privileges of the gymnasium, library, laboratories and facilities . . . ."[48]

To visitors, the university's lack of funding was obvious. The grounds had the utilitarian look and feel of a construction camp rather than a college campus. Most of the buildings were wooden and supposedly temporary, and few architectural flourishes were bestowed on the permanent concrete structures. Bunnell claimed the nondescript look of the university buildings was visible proof of his thrift. Keeping construction and maintenance costs as low as possible in the subarctic environment left "only a

restricted opportunity for esthetic treatment." Furthermore, in the president's eyes "a certain austerity and Spartan simplicity of design" was required of construction in the north.[49] Some thought the campus more shabby than spartan. Alaska Governor Ernest Gruening said in the 1940s that Bunnell had always been forced to stretch every dollar "as far as it was humanly possible," and as a result the buildings on the university campus were "plain and simple almost to the point of ugliness."[50]

Like the typical Alaskan homesteader who keeps building new additions to the old cabin year after year, Bunnell almost had to build the university one room at a time. No structure demonstrated Bunnell's piecemeal, scratch and save approach to construction better than Unit 5, a portion of which still stands today as the north end of the first floor of the Eielson Building.

A midsummer night's strange, fatal air mishap

On July 12, 1944, at about 8:30 in the evening, a student pilot from Anchorage crashed a small blue and yellow plane into what was then the northwest corner of the Eielson Building. The picture at left was taken shortly after the crash that evening and shows the wreckage of the plane against the building. (Incidentally, the other building in the picture on the left is Unit 5, built in 1935 with scraps left over from the construction of the library, and whose first floor became the north end of the Eielson Building after it expanded in the 1940s.) Damage to university property amounted to marks on the side of the Eielson Building and the destruction of several antennae used in ionospheric studies; the plane, save for its tail section, was completely demolished.

The mysterious crash spawned one of the University of Alaska's genuine legends. The pilot, whose name was never publicly released, was said to be a soldier who had flown up from Anchorage that day. He was reportedly swooping down over the campus buzzing the buildings when he struck an antenna near the volleyball court adjacent to the Eielson Building and crashed into the wall. According to one story the pilot's former girlfriend, who had split up with him earlier in the year, worked in the Eielson Building. This led some to claim that perhaps the crash was not an accident, but the suicide of a spurned lover, or even more farfetched, an attempt to murder her. For years the mark on the side of the building from the crash was still visible, and with the few facts they knew, people told and retold the story the way they thought it happened.

Unit 5, built with odds and ends left over from the construction of the library in 1935, was apparently given its utterly colorless name because it was supposed to have been one of five permanent concrete buildings surrounding the library-gymnasium in the "campus quadrangle." According to the blueprints, this quadrangle was supposed to form the nucleus of the permanent campus, but half of the buildings designed for it were never constructed.

The first story of Unit 5 was similar in design to the original Eielson Building seventy-two feet to the south. The campus plan in the 1930s and 1940s envisioned Unit 5 and the Eielson Building at the northwest and southwest corners of the quadrangle respectively, and two twin buildings (neither of which were ever built) at the northeast and southeast corners. At the center of the quadrangle were to be the library-gymnasium (now Signers' Hall) and a four-story administration building (which also never made it off the drawing board). From this structure, designed to have sat at right angles in front of the library, administrators would have enjoyed "a panoramic view of the Alaska Range from Mt. McKinley in the west to Mt. Hess and beyond, in the east."[51]

Unit 5 was not a particularly distinguished addition to the quadrangle. When built in 1935, the concrete lower level of Unit 5 housed the campus post office, the barber shop, trunk storage, and laundry, while a temporary wood-frame second story and attic provided badly needed dormitory space for twenty-five men. At the time, Bunnell did not have the funds to build the second story of concrete. This temporary upper story served as a residence—and later as an office—for thirty-five years. In 1950 it was removed from the first story, and shifted forty feet to the west, where it continued to be used until it was demolished in early 1970 to make way for the construction of the Gruening Building. Meanwhile the original first floor of Unit 5 was incorporated into the expansion of the Eielson Building in the 1940s, and became the north end of the ground floor.[52]

To meet what he called the "essential needs" of the university, Bunnell submitted plans and cost estimates to the legislature in 1940 for an ambitious program of construction, including $80,000 for a building for the School of Mines, $125,000 for a men's dormitory, $80,000 for the completion of the Eielson Building and Unit 5, and $25,000 for an infirmary. Despite Bunnell's high hopes, in the spring of 1941 the legislature refused virtually all of the requests for new construction; the plans would have to be shelved until the next biennium, when Bunnell vowed he would try again.[53] But it would be far longer than Bunnell could have ever imagined, because late that year the Japanese attacked Pearl Harbor, and the grand designs of the University of Alaska, like those of the entire nation, would be radically and irrevocably altered.

The shadow of the Second World War, the bloodiest conflict in human history, darkened the globe from the Atlantic to the Pacific, from Europe to Asia. The astonishing advances in aviation in the 1920s and 1930s suddenly made the remote Alaskan wilderness a strategic stronghold in the fight against the Axis powers. From the air, the North Pole was no longer the end of the earth, but its center, and the shortest distance from Seattle to Tokyo was not through Pearl Harbor in Hawaii, but through Dutch Harbor in the Aleutian Chain. Fairbanks, which had been an isolated backwater in

the First World War, now stood on the front line of American defenses.

Ladd Field, an air base adjacent to Fairbanks, anchored the northern end of the Inland or Northwest Staging Route, a chain of airfields between Canada and Alaska which had been developed before the war to create a reliable air supply route to the north. In fact, the U.S. Army built the Alaska Highway in 1942 primarily to connect this chain of airfields. Between 1942 and 1945, the U.S. flew nearly 8,000 Lend-Lease fighters, bombers, and cargo planes along this route to Fairbanks, where Russian pilots took the controls and continued onwards to the Soviet Union. These aircraft helped the Soviets withstand the full force of the German Army until the Allied invasion at Normandy in 1944.

As air power rewrote world geography, the University of Alaska found itself in the middle of a war zone. In the panic of December 1941, no one knew where the Japanese might strike next. Immediately after Pearl Harbor, the faculty took turns guarding the campus power plant, while students practiced blackouts. In case of an air raid, campus residents were told to assemble in either Hess Hall or the Eielson Building, and to be sure to have flashlights and warm clothing, since there was probably "more danger of freezing to death than being shot."[54]

On January 1, 1942, Bunnell promised that come what may, the university would stay open "for the duration." But four months later, the difficulty of keeping open the university doors was apparent. In the ten years preceding the outbreak of war, the university had hired numerous young faculty and established new academic programs in the arts and

IN AIR AGAINST NAZIS—Lt. Lothar Fieg, former UA student, flies his P-51, named "Denali," in the air war against Germany.

Lt. Fieg Damages Three Nazi Planes Deep In Germany

AN EIGHTH AAF FIGHTER STATION, England—1st Lt. Lothar Fieg, of Oneonta, N. Y., damaged three unidentified enemy aircraft

Leased Space Relinquished

Army Vacates All But Dormitory, Garage

Official notice of cancellation by

AIR COMBAT VETERAN
Lothar Fieg, a University of Alaska alumnus and a decorated World War II fighter pilot, sits in his P-51 Mustang Denali *in this photo clipping from the August 1, 1944* Farthest North Collegian.

social sciences. "The war has wiped out those gains," Bunnell admitted in May 1942. "The music department is a total casualty. Many courses in the arts that had been gradually added must now be dropped. And most of the young instructors who joined the teaching staff during the past few years will be missing at next September's faculty meeting."[55]

As faculty and students were drafted, enlisted, or called up in the reserves, the campus population dwindled. Only eight of the thirty-eight faculty members on the staff in 1941 were still at the university

two years later. Full-time enrollment, which had reached its prewar peak of 310 in 1940, fell to less than 70 from 1943 to 1945. In 1944, for the first time in the history of the school, as the college yearbook noted, "the student body was too small to permit the formation of a basketball team . . . ." The entire graduating classes of 1944 and 1945 comprised three students apiece.[56]

With the reductions in students and faculty came drastic cutbacks in course offerings. The entire School of Mines closed in 1943–1944. This was a logical move following the federal government's October 1942 declaration that gold mining was a "non-essential" industry, and its subsequent shut-down of most gold mines on American soil.[57]

The university itself was nearly closed. As early as September 1942, U.S. Army officials warned that because of a severe housing shortage at Ladd Field, the army might need to take over the entire campus; however, General Simon B. Buckner, head of the Alaska Defense Command, relayed word that the army "did not want to do that unless there was an emergency of such a nature that they had to."[58] Though the university was able to keep a minimum amount of space for its reduced activities, it eventually surrendered about two-thirds of the campus to the army for more than two years. Hess Hall became a military convalescent hospital.

The compressed university crowded into the Eielson Building, and did its best to aid in the war effort by instituting night classes for soldiers and offering programs that were of immediate need. In 1944, for instance, when hundreds of Soviet Lend-Lease pilots were passing through Fairbanks each month, Bunnell hired Mrs. Ada Urieli, a graduate of the University of St. Petersburg, to teach the university's first courses in the Russian language, as well as Russian history and geography.[59]

Students and faculty from the University of Alaska served in the armed forces around the globe. Lieutenant Lothar Fieg, a former student of mining engineering, named his P-51 Mustang fighter plane "Denali." By early 1945 when he was promoted to captain, Fieg had flown seventy-eight combat missions. "'Denali' has taken good care of me so far," he wrote in 1944, in a letter reprinted in the *Colle-*

gian. "I let her get ventilated with 20 m.m.'s once and last week I brought back a souvenir from France in my left wing."[60]

Other UA alumni were not so lucky. Among the eighteen who died in uniform during World War II was Lieutenant Ernie Reece, who had enrolled at the university in 1940 to study mining and to learn how to fly, but quit school in 1941 to enlist in the air corps. On a mission over the jungles of Brazil in April 1943, Reece lost the left engine on his B-26 Marauder bomber, a plane he had named "Denali's Cheechako." Unable to bring the ship in with a single engine, he ordered the crew to bail out at 1,500 feet, while he remained behind at the controls trying to stabilize the plane and ensure that his men could parachute safely to the ground. His body was later found in the wreckage.[61]

Lieutenant Francis Harper was one of the few students of the University of Alaska to be captured and imprisoned in a German POW camp. Born in Rampart in 1918, Harper was an Alaska Native whose uncle Walter Harper had been the first man on the summit of Denali in 1913. In 1935 his sister Flora Jane Harper had been the first Native graduate of the Alaska Agricultural College and School of Mines. Francis Harper had studied Business Administration at the university for a few years in the 1930s, and had resumed his education in 1941. After Pearl Harbor, he enlisted in the air corps and trained as a bombardier.

Harper's B-17 Flying Fortress was shot down over Bremen on October 8, 1943. Following his capture, officers from the Gestapo interrogated him at about two o'clock in the morning with a single bright light shining in his eyes. "It was just like the

LIEUT. FRANCIS S. HARPER, Alaska-born bombardier with the U. S
Air Force in Europe, now a prisoner of war in Germany, who was awarded the Air Medal.—(Story on Page One.)

This photo of Francis Harper, an Alaska Native and UA student, was featured in the Farthest North Collegian. *Harper's B-17 was shot down in October, 1943.*

told a newspaper reporter that what he wanted to do more than anything else was "to get away from people and go fishing and chop wood" so he could "get his mind back to normal."[62]

Like nearly one million other soldiers who took advantage of the G.I. Bill of Rights, Lieutenant Francis Harper and Captain Lothar Fieg returned to school after the war. By the fall of 1946, the first full year of peacetime, Harper, Fieg and 237 other veterans (including 17 women) accounted for about two-thirds of the record-breaking enrollment of 379 students who crowded the halls of the University of Alaska in 1946–1947.[63] President Bunnell and the rest of the faculty would quickly discover that the men and women who came back from the war were not the same youngsters who had marched away five years earlier.

The fact that there still was a University of Alaska for veterans to return to was largely due to the perseverance of Charles E. Bunnell, who had refused to let the war destroy the school. But the aging president soon faced a fiscal nightmare that would nearly force the University of Alaska to close forever.

movies," he said. Altogether Harper spent a year and a half in German prison camps, including months of confinement in a stalag the size of a few city blocks with 27,000 other men. Harper was eventually liberated in the spring of 1945 by a dozen U.S. tanks; one of the Americans he met happened to be Forbes Baker Jr. of Fairbanks.

When Francis Harper finally returned to Fairbanks on leave at the end of the war, he had lost forty pounds. Because he had been malnourished for so long, he was still on a soft diet in August 1945. He

Portfolio
1935–1946

ON MARCH 12, 1935, WITH THE KEY FIGURES *in the creation of the Alaska Agricultural College and School of Mines looking on, Governor John Troy signs the act changing its name to the University of Alaska. Standing from left to right: James Wickersham, Charles Bunnell, Senate President Luther Hess, Reps. Andrew Nerland and A. A. Shonbeck (both members of the Board of Regents), and Speaker of the House J. S. Hofman. Seated: Regent Grace Wickersham, Governor Troy, and Rep. George Lingo, who was both an alumnus and a regent.*

Charles E. Bunnell Collection, Rasmuson Library

A TERRITORIAL INSTITUTION

FARTHEST-NORTH COLLEGIAN

LOCATED 64° 51' 21" NORTH LATITUDE

MONTHLY PUBLICATION OF THE UNIVERSITY OF ALASKA

VOLUME XIII. COLLEGE, ALASKA, JULY 1, 1935. NUMBER TEN.

A. A. C. Now University of Alaska

GEIST PARTY IS READY FOR NINTH EXPEDITION TO ST. LAWRENCE IS.

Archaeological Research Will Be Continued By Graduates and Students Of College

WILL FLY TO NOME

Valuable Excavations Of Ancient Cultures Anticipated

The ninth season of archaeological investigation on St. Lawrence Island by the Alaska College will continue this year under the second half of the two-year program begun last year under a Public Works grant administered through the Bureau of Indian Affairs. The Interior Dept.-Alaska College Expedition, Mr. Otto Wm. Geist, archaeologist in charge, is expected to leave for Nome by plane early in July. From Nome the party will be brought to St. Lawrence Island by the Coast Guard cutter "Northland", although there is a possibility of continuing the trip by plane.

Mr. Geist advises that preparations for departure are practically completed and that he is only awaiting word from the cutter before leaving. Meanwhile, the expedition personnel is at the College cataloging specimens excavated at the ancient village site of Kukulik last year. Already some ten thousand specimens have been labeled and cataloged. Baggage and instruments have been sent by freight by the Yukon River route. A recent telegram from the Island states that supplies for the summer have already been landed.

Again the expedition is made up of Alaska College graduates and students. Members of the Geist party this year are: Mary Mikami, Accountant; Roland Snodgrass, Ivar Skarland, Percy Lucha, Field Assistants; Olavi Kukkola, surveyor. C. A. Bryant of Fairbanks will accompany the Expedition as field assistant and radio operator. By radio he will keep in touch with Nome. Time sheets, payrolls, and reports will keep the accountant busy; while it will be the duty of the field assistants to supervise the lowering of the mound, to keep daily notes regarding specimens, houses, and meat caches unearthed. The surveyor will furnish the charts and maps by which the specimens may be allocated as to position in the mound and strata at which uncovered.

Intensely interesting as was the work last season, the work this summer should prove even more so. Much time was spent last year in removing muck and overburden and in unearthing the recent culture strata. With this preliminary work done, excavating can now be carried down through the ancient cultures revealed in the test cut made through the mound by Mr. Geist under the Alaska College Expedition of 1931-32-33. As in previous years the skeletal material encountered as work progresses will be collected. The human skeletal remains will be sent to Dr. Ales Hrdlicka at the U. S. National Museum for research and the animal skeletal material will be sent

Anthropologist

Dr. F. G. Rainey

ANTHROPOLOGY IS NEW COURSE U. OF A. OFFERS

DR. F. G. RAINEY OF YALE APPOINTED TO TEACH COURSE AND DO RESEARCH FOR THE AMERICAN MUSEUM

A course in Anthropology has been added to the curriculum of the University of Alaska for the ensuing year and Dr. Froelich G. Rainey of the Peabody Museum of Natural History at Yale University has been appointed professor.

Dr. Rainey was graduated with a Ph. B. degree in English from the University of Chicago. He has taught in the secondary schools at Legaspi, Philippine Islands, and has attended the American School of Prehistoric Research in France and Spain. Since 1931 he has been working in the Peabody Museum at Yale and at present holds the position of Assistant Curator of Anthropology. From Yale University in 1933 he received his M.A. degree and this spring his Ph. D.

His most recent major research was a review of the archaeology for the West Indies and a series of excavations in Porto Rico. In the course of these investigations, he discovered a new prehistoric culture and has been able to determine the relations of this culture to others in the area. This, according to his colleagues, is one of the outstanding contributions for the year. The results of these investigations were presented to meet the requirements for his Ph. D. degree.

Dr. Rainey is continuing research at Porto Rico this summer and will proceed from there directly to the University.

The course in Anthropology will be a general one, perhaps through the Iron Age, and a general resume of modern Ethnology. Besides conducting this course Dr. Rainey will give a considerable part of his time to the interpretation of St. Lawrence Island finds and to assist in the publication of a scien-

PRESIDENT OF UNIVERSITY

Dr. Charles E. Bunnell

LAST RITES HELD FOR PROF. FULLER

Funeral services for the late Veryl R. Fuller, Professor of Physics at the Alaska College since 1926, who dropped dead of heart failure while working in the garden of his campus home May 30, were held Sunday morning, June 2, from St. Matthew's Episcopal Church in Fairbanks.

The rites were conducted by Rev. Michael J. Kippenbrock, vicar. A large number of automobiles formed in the funeral procession to the Fairbanks Cemetery where interment was made.

Pall-bearers were: O. W. Geist, E. N. Patty, Chas. Cann, R. L. Sheely, A. W. Bastress and L. J. Palmer.

Prof. Bastress Delivers Commencement Address Fairbanks High School

Alfred W. Bastress, Professor of Chemistry at the Alaska College delivered the address at the annual commencement of the Fairbanks High School, held in Fairbanks, June 4.

Prof. Bastress talked on the secondary education in the United States, inasmuch as this year marks the three hundredth anniversary of the establishment of secondary schools in this country, pointing out the obligations the graduates owe to themselves and to society.

Harvey Hautala, School of Mines senior, is employed by the F. E. Co. at Chatanika.

Extension Service Has Heavy Summer Schedule

The spring and summer months have been busy months for the Extension Service workers. Director of Extension Ross L. Sheely, Assistant Director for Home Economics Lydia Fohn-Hansen, Veterinarian Jule B. Loftus have all been moving rapidly to contact as many localities as possible in the short length of time.

On March 20, Mrs. Fohn-Hansen left Fairbanks for a field trip to Cordova, Valdez, Seward, Anchorage, and Matanuska. At each of these places instruction was given in cooking, knitting, sewing, glovemaking, and weaving. Mrs. Fohn-Hansen spent two weeks with the colonists at Matanuska before returning to her headquarters at College.

Mr. Sheely was detached from the Extension Service during April and May to survey and select farms for the new Matanuska settlers. After being at the office for one month he again returns to the Valley on July 4. Both Mrs. Fohn-Hansen and Mr. Sheely are allowing as much time as possible in the upward building of this project. They are both of the opinion that only through careful teaching and close observation can such a large group of people learn to adapt themselves to existing conditions.

the fur farmers and tested the livestock along the railroad belt. Mr. Loftus has willingly aided the settlers and farmers doing any veterinary work which was necessary. He left Fairbanks, June 26 to spend the remainder of the summer among the fur farmers in southeastern Alaska.

The Bureau of Indian Affairs of Alaska is holding a summer conference at Eklutna for teachers of the central district of Alaska. This school starts June 27 and lasts for a period of six weeks and the Extension Service of the College has been asked to give demonstrations. Mr. Sheely will handle the work in gardening, greenhouse construction and management, and tanning. Mrs. Fohn-Hansen will assist with classes in clothing, nutrition and health.

Mr. Sheely plans to close the summer with a field trip to southeastern Alaska. He will aid the coastal farmers who for many years have been asking that he visit that section of Alaska and assist them with their agricultural problems. Mrs. Fohn-Hansen plans to spend the month of August in the Cook Inlet district visiting at Seldovia, Homer, Kasilof, Kenai, and Ninilchic.

About the University, it's in the

ACT OF LAST LEGISLATURE ESTABLISHING UNIVERSITY OF ALASKA NOW IN EFFECT

President Of Regents

Andrew Nerland

TENTH ANNUAL TANANA VALLEY FAIR AUG. 29-31

CONTRIBUTIONS FOR VARIOUS EXHIBITS OF FARM PRODUCTS, COOKING AND HANDICRAFT APPRECIATED.

Brightly colored posters are making their appearance to announce the tenth fair of the Tanana Valley Fair Association, which is to be held August 29, 30 and 31, at Fairbanks.

The Association is busy lining up exhibits of all kinds—agricultural products, handicraft and needlework, specimens of culinary art and educational exhibits. The Association would appreciate any exhibits that anyone would care to send it.

The premium lists for the Fair are being prepared and will soon be available. They can be had by writing to G. W. Gasser, President of the Association, or to Mrs. Eva McGown, Secretary.

PRESIDENT BUNNELL HOST AT BANQUET

One long table with forty one places, the flickering glow of pink and yellow candles in silver holders and slender glass vases filled with wild yellow daisies, blue lupins and pink roses greeted guests on Thursday June 27 when Dr. Bunnell was host at a savory roast pig dinner for Campus residents at the College dining room. Of singular attraction were the clever napkins and place cards, the corner of each bearing the design of a pig.

Besides Campus employees who regularly board at the dining room the guests were: Mr. and Mrs. George L. Keys, Prof. and Mrs. Alfred Bastress, Prof. and Mrs. George Gasser, Mr. and Mrs. L. J. Palmer, Prof. and Mrs. Albert Wilkerson, Mr. Jack Warwick, Mr. and Mrs. Joseph Flakne and Otto Wm. Geist.

Barbara Woodward, who will be a senior in Business Administration next year, is employed this summer at the First National Bank

Board of Regents Holds Organization Meeting Elects Officers and Adapts By-Laws.

4 DEANS APPOINTED

All Property of Alaska College Transferred To University

In accordance with an Act passed March 8 by the Alaska Territorial Legislature, the University of Alaska today succeeded the Alaska Agricultural College and School of Mines.

Pursuant to the provisions of Chapter 49 of the 1935 Session Laws, the Board of Regents of the University met at 9 A. M. today in the Geology room in the west wing of the main building.

The meeting was called to order by Regent Nerland who was elected temporary chairman. Mrs. Luther C. Hess was elected temporary secretary. A roll call showed seven of the eight regents present: J. W. Gilson of Valdez, A. E. Lathrop of Cordova, A. A. Shonbeck of Anchorage, George A. Lingo of McKinley Park, and Andrew Nerland, Mrs. Luther C. Hess and John H. Kelly of Fairbanks. Mrs. James Wickersham of Juneau was unable to attend. A letter from Mrs. Wickersham to Dr. Bunnell was read:

"My Dear Dr. Bunnell:

"I have just returned from the hospital after a very severe illness and find myself very weak. I will be unable to be at the meeting of the Board of Trustees at your office on June 30, or at any date thereto. I greatly regret my inability to be present to assist you and the Board in the work of establishing the University, for it will be an historic occasion, and I have looked forward to the occasion with much pleasure and pride. However, the doctor's orders are complete rest for at least a month and I can do nothing but obey.

"Please give my kindest regards to the other members of the Board and convey to them my deep regret at not being able to be present with them at this interesting meeting.

Very truly yours,
Grace Wickersham"

Take Oaths of Office

The eight oaths of office in duplicate were presented, the originals ordered to be forwarded to the Governor of the Territory and the duplicates to be filed with the Secretary of the Board.

Resolving itself into a committee of the whole with Regent John Kelly acting as Chairman, By-laws were agreed upon and upon presentation to the Board of Regents were adopted.

The By-laws provide for a regular meeting of the Board on the first Monday of October each year and for the annual meeting of the Board on the first Monday of May of each year.

All officers of the Board including the members of the executive

(LEFT) THE FRONT PAGE OF THE *COLLEGIAN*
on July 1, 1935, announces the birth of the
University of Alaska.

Rasmuson Library

(ABOVE) JAMES WICKERSHAM IN HIS LIBRARY.
In 1936 the feud between Wickersham and Bunnell
erupted once again over a history of Alaska, which
Wickersham wished to write.

James Wickersham Collection, Alaska Historical Library

Alaska College

THE ALASKA AGRICULTURAL
*College and School of Mines, before
the construction of the new library
above the gymnasium in 1935. The
buildings in the foreground from left
to right are: the first story of the
Eielson Building covered by a
temporary roof, the gymnasium with
its temporary roof, and the Main
Building.*

Charles E. Bunnell Collection,
Rasmuson Library

113

NEW CONSTRUCTION PROJECTS ON CAMPUS IN 1935
*included two structures, parts of which are still in use
today. A second floor was built on top of the gym (the
dark concrete structure near the center of the photo)
and would serve as the university library for more
than a quarter of a century. Today the old library/
gymnasium is Signers' Hall, an administration
building. With scraps left over from the construction
of the library, Bunnell also built Unit 5 (just to the
right of the center in the foreground). Unit 5 featured
a permanent concrete first floor—which is now the
north end of the ground floor of the Eielson
Building—and a temporary wood-frame
structure on top that was removed in 1950.*

Charles E. Bunnell Collection, Rasmuson Library

114

THE UNIVERSITY OF ALASKA CAMPUS IN THE WINTER *of 1937–1938, after the start of construction of the university's first permanent concrete dormitory, Hess Hall (the three-story structure on the left). The small house in the foreground was President Bunnell's home. In back of the president's house are the hockey rink the students built in the fall of 1937 and the first three "permanent" concrete buildings at the core of the campus quadrangle. Beneath the smokestack of* the campus power plant is the two-story library and gymnasium (now Signers' Hall). On this side of the gym adjacent to the hockey rink is the Eielson Building, at that time still one story and home to the music department and the museum. Immediately left of Eielson is Unit 5, which housed the post office, barber shop, and dormitory space for men.

Charles E. Bunnell Collection, Rasmuson Library

115

(ABOVE) OTTO GEIST EXAMINES PART OF A SEASON'S *haul of specimens literally spilling from piles of cardboard boxes.*

Historical Photograph Collection, Rasmuson Library

(BELOW) THE *COLLEGIAN* ANNOUNCED IN 1929 THAT *Geist had returned with ten tons of specimens from St. Lawrence Island.*

Rasmuson Library

LOCATED 64° 51' 21"
NORTH LATITUDE

FARTHEST-NORTH
COLLEGIAN

A TERRITORIAL
INSTITUTION

VOLUME VIII   COLLEGE ALASKA, NOVEMBER 30, 1929.   NUMBER THREE

Geist Returns With Tons Of Specimens

Mines Graduate Soon to Transfer To Boston Office

Genevieve Parker Will Be Office Assistant To G. W. Metcalf, Former General Manager Alaskan Operations.

Mining engineering, as a profession, is generally considered closed to members of the fairer sex. In Genevieve Parker, however, the Alaska College has an exception.

She received a Bachelor's degree in General Science from the College during 1928 and when she suggested the plan of returning for an additional year of work toward a degree in Geology and Mining, the Mines School faculty agreed, not without some misgivings. They recalled, however,

GENEVIEVE ALICE PARKER

Landscaping As Short Course
Next Semester

Reasons Given For Zeppelin Polar Flights

Meteorological Control Of Arctics By Means Of Wireless Stations Is Aim Of Expedition.

Why are the Graf Zeppelin Polar flights being made? That question is often asked since Fairbanks has been chosen as the Alaska landing field for the Graf Zeppelin.

The answer is.

To gain permanent control of the Arctics. Preparatory work in this direction includes: airship expeditions to pave the way toward an unbroken control of the Arctics, construction and testing of light wireless stations adapted to transportation by air and to arctic conditions, and closer cooperation of the existing subarctic and arctic

George B. Wesch Elected Position New Treasurer

Unanimously Elected By Board Of Trustees To Fill Vacancy Caused By Resignation Of George Hutchinson.

At an adjourned meeting of the Board of Trustees held on the 12th of November Geo. B. Wesch was unanimously elected to fill the vacancy caused by the resignation of Geo. Hutchinson, Treasurer of the Board. Matters of importance requiring the presence of the Treasurer at Fairbanks came to the attention of Mr. Hutchinson, and he promptly wired his resignation from San Diego where he and Mrs. Hutchinson are spending the winter.

The following resolution was

SPENT THREE YEARS ON ARCTIC ISLAND IN QUEST OF 'BURIED TREASURE'

As Member of Eskimo Family, Ate Their Food, Adopted Into the Tribe, Given Name "Aghvook," Witnessed Tribal Ceremonies.

By DEAN ERNEST N. PATTY

A voluntary exile on a lonely arctic island for three solid years where he lived with an eskimo family—eating their food which consisted mainly of seal, walrus, whale, fish, and in the summer wild birds—adopted into their tribe and given the Eskimo name of "Aghvook," meaning "bow-headed whale" —accompanying the Eskimos out onto the ice floes in search of game —as a member of their tribe, a

cultural material extends to additional depths.

Some extent of the collections can be surmised when it is told that Mr. Geist shipped to the College about ten tons of material or about thirty thousand individual specimens. This includes not only early cultural material but also a complete collection of the present-day paraphernalia of the primitive Eskimos who now inhabit the Island, and colored drawings of their

(ABOVE) THE UNIVERSITY OF *Alaska Museum, crowded for years into a corner of the Eielson Building, could show only a fraction of the thousands of specimens Geist collected every year. One of the museum's most famous exhibits was the albino moose standing at the back of the room.*

Otto Geist Collection, Rasmuson Library

GEIST LINED THE DRIVEWAY *to his home off College Road with scraps of ice age fossils and 10,000-year-old broken bones.*

Otto Geist Collection, Rasmuson Library

(RIGHT) IVAR SKARLAND, A 1935
graduate of the Alaska College who
later became a distinguished
anthropology professor at the
University of Alaska, examines a
skull on the 1935 expedition to
St. Lawrence Island.

Charles Keim

(BELOW) MEMBERS OF THE 1934
expedition to St. Lawrence Island,
jointly sponsored by the U. S.
Department of the Interior and the
Alaska College upon their return to
Fairbanks in October 1934. Standing
from left to right: Carl Franklin,
Wilbert Lane, Harry Brandt, Ivar
Skarland, and Roland Snodgrass.
Front row: Percy Lucha, Mary
Mikami, and Otto W. Geist.

Charles Keim

118

(LEFT) MEMBERS OF THE 1935
*St. Lawrence archaeological
expedition unload supplies.*

Charles Keim

(BELOW) THE "CAMPUS SITE," AN
*archaeological site located on the bluff of
College Hill overlooking the Tanana Valley,
provided the first hard evidence about the
migration of human beings over the Bering
Land Bridge. Among those who excavated the
site in 1935 were two University of Alaska
students, and two teenage assistants from the
American Museum of National History in New
York. Standing here from left to right (holding
paleontological specimens from the Fairbanks
mining district): Archibald B. Roosevelt Jr., a
grandson of Theodore Roosevelt; University of
Alaska students Albert H. Dickey and John
Dorsh; and Roosevelt's friend Walter Sullivan,
who years later went on to become the senior
science editor of the* New York Times.

Photo by J. Louis Giddings,
from Charles M. Mobley's *The Campus Site*

(Right) Agriculture *professor George W. Gasser (on left) directed the experiment station at the college from 1921 to 1945. He developed wheat and barley varieties, suitable for Alaska, which were named in his honor.*

Agricultural Experiment Station
Collection, Rasmuson Library

(Below) Joe Flakne, who *graduated from the Alaska College in 1934 with a degree in business administration and agriculture and served as the superintendent of the University of Alaska farm from 1934–1937, stands in the university's vegetable patch.*

LarVerne Keys Collection,
Rasmuson Library

University of Alaska Experimental Farm

THE UNIVERSITY OF ALASKA EXPERIMENTAL FARM *in the early 1940s. During World War II, the experimental farm had nearly 300 acres under cultivation in the effort to maximize food production, including 57 acres of potatoes, 26 acres of wheat, and 10 acres of vegetables.*

University Relations Collection, Rasmuson Library

PAUL GREIMANN'S
*bus on College
Road below
College Hill.*

Rogers Collections,
Rasmuson Library

(ABOVE) STUDENT HOUSING IN
the 1930s. A student "yurt" in
"Yertchville" on the college flats.

Rogers Collections, Rasmuson Library

(BELOW) DON MARKL, A MINING
engineering student originally from
Minnesota, does chores at his home
in "Yertchville" in 1938.

Rogers Collections, Rasmuson Library

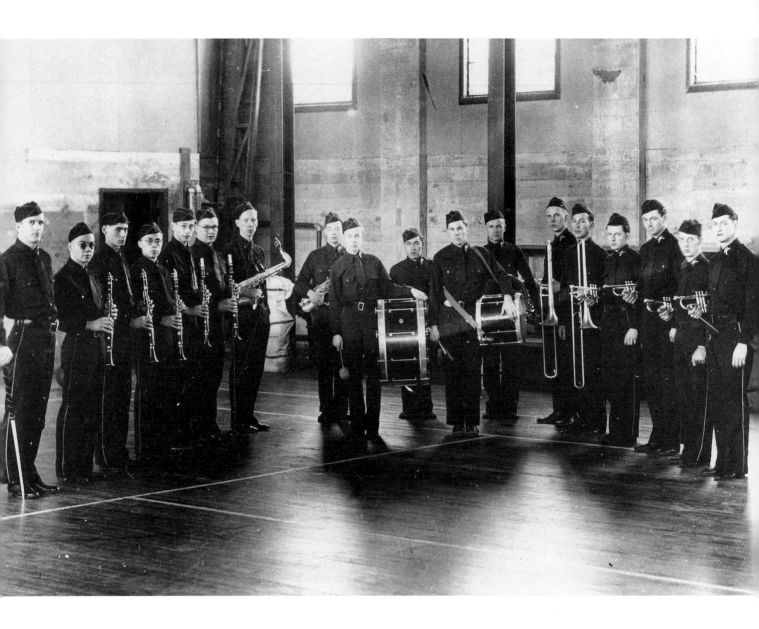

THE COLLEGE MILITARY BAND, FIRST ORGANIZED IN
*1933–1934, was a campus tradition for many years.
Shown here are the band members of 1935, with band
leader Glen Franklin on the far right. The musicians
are wearing the "snappy blue uniforms" that replaced
the khaki of previous years. From left to right: William
Cashen, Herb McClarty, George Henton, Leo Saarela,
Carl Parker, Clarence Carlson, Wendell Erickson, Bud
Browne, Earl Fosse, Andrew Peterson, Dean Stanley,
Reino Huttula, Eugene Uotila, Carl Weller, Johnny
Castle, Robert Hoppe, Albert Dickey, and Glen Franklin.*

(TOP) THE SCIENCE CLUB WAS ORGANIZED IN THE *fall of 1934 by students and faculty from chemistry, home economics, agriculture, and general science. From left to right back row: instructor Roland Snodgrass, Leo Saarela, Elinor Hukee, professor of agriculture George Gasser, Jack Adams, and George Henton. Front row: Albert Dorsh, Katherine Peterson, Gertrude Schlotfeldt, Winifred MacDonald, Cora Henton, Virginia Brown, Flora Jane Harper, and Howard Estelle.*

Rasmuson Library

(BOTTOM) THE COLLEGE YEARBOOK, *DENALI*, WAS *first published in 1934 and continued publication— more or less every year—until 1970. This picture shows the 1935 staff of the* Denali, *with editor Ivar Skarland seated at the right-hand table. Standing from left to right: Hilja Reinikka, Helen Linck, William Cashen, Helen McCrary, faculty advisor Leslie A. Marchand, Percy Lucha, Albert Dickey, and Bliss Harper. Seated: Glen Franklin, Vieno Wahto, and Ivar Skarland.*

Rasmuson Library

THE 1936–1937 BASKETBALL TEAM WAS NOT THE *powerhouse of other years. The team won five games and lost four, and was the first university team to lose to the Fairbanks High School in eight years. Standing from left to right: Al Malden, Stanley Hill, John O'Shea, Jack Wilbur, Milan Raykovich, Donald George, Harry Lundell, and Roy Moyer. Kneeling: Richard Mahan, Coach James Ryan, Manager Earl Beistline, and Ted Kukkola.*

Robert P. Isaac Collection, Rasmuson Library

THE UNIVERSITY OF ALASKA "POLAR BEARS" PULLED off a "seemingly impossible" upset in hockey, when they defeated the visiting team from Dawson by a score of 6–5 during the 1936 Winter Carnival in Fairbanks. The previous year Dawson had defeated the Polar Bears 11–0. The Collegian *described the victory as "more than an athletic contest," and said it not only "stunned Dawson supporters, but amazed students and friends of the University."*

The authors of this "miracle on ice" standing from left to right: Harry Mikami, George Karabelnikoff, Arnold Hoehner, coach (and chemistry professor) Dr. Alfred Bastress, Leonard Thompson, Glenn Bowen, Louie Smith, and Gordon Picotte. Kneeling: Pat O'Neill, Glen Franklin, Erwin Clahassey, and Manager Earl Beistline.

A. W. Bastress Collection, Rasmuson Library

ON THE BASKETBALL *court in the gym—now the lobby of Signers' Hall—a member of the freshman team (in white) puts up a shot against the varsity (in dark).*

Reuel Griffin Collection, Rasmuson Library

MEMBERS OF THE *university's 1936 boxing team—some of whom could barely keep from smiling or glancing at the camera—pose an "action shot" for Fairbanks photographer Reuel Griffin.*

Reuel Griffin Collection, Rasmuson Library

GEORGE KARABELNIKOFF, ONE OF *the pivot men on the university's 1936 tumbling team, supports his four partners: Hilja Reinikka, Hannah Yasuda, Juanita Cooper, and Elsa Lundell.*

Reuel Griffin Collection, Rasmuson Library

THE STAR OF THE COLLEGE *Tumbling Team in 1933 was Sidney Henrikson from Seward, second from the right in the back row. He was one of approximately eighteen University of Alaska alumni who died in uniform during World War II. Sgt. Henrikson was killed in the invasion of Luzon in January 1945. He served with the Army Engineers.*

From left to right in the back row: Coach James Ryan, Beatrice Harkness, Tom Givan, Frank Pettygrove, Sidney Henrikson, and Mildred Harkness. Sitting: Alice Mikami, Hilja Reinikka, Audrey Steel, and Mary Mikami.

Frank Pettygrove Collection, Rasmuson Library

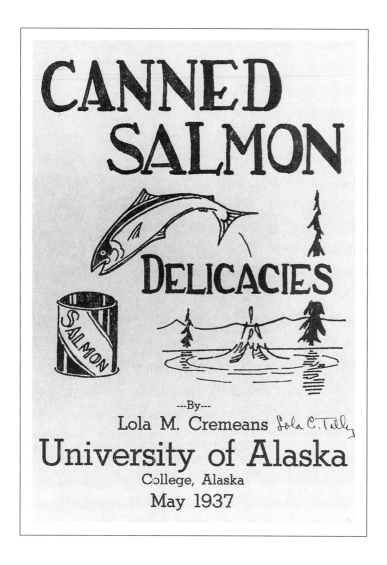

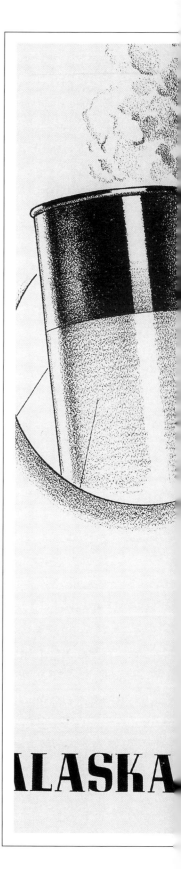

(ABOVE) ONE OF THE EARLY PUBLICATIONS OF THE
*University of Alaska was a 1937 collection of canned salmon
recipes by home economics professor Lola (Cremeans) Tilly.*

Lola Tilly Collection, Rasmuson Library

(RIGHT) AN ADVERTISEMENT IN THE 1941
Denali *on the eve of World War II.*

Rasmuson Library

(FAR RIGHT) A 1938 ADVERTISEMENT URGING STUDENTS TO
*reserve their rooms early if they wished to live on campus. Despite
the opening of Hess Hall, the "new dormitory for women," the
shortage of student housing would plague the campus for decades.*

Rasmuson Library

(LEFT) PRESIDENT BUNNELL, *shown here in the 1940s holding a head of cauliflower, always prided himself on the university's gardens, which helped lower food costs in the dining hall. The Eielson Building is in the background.*

Charles E. Bunnell Collection, Rasmuson Library

(RIGHT) PRESIDENT BUNNELL *tries unsuccessfully to encourage his baby moose to look at the camera.*

Charles E. Bunnell Collection, Rasmuson Library

(BELOW) BUNNELL IN THE 1940S *on the flats below College Hill.*

Agricultural Experiment Station Collection, Rasmuson Library

PRESIDENT BUNNELL ENJOYS A COKE. Charles E. Bunnell Collection, Rasmuson Library

ANNOUNCEMENT

Harriet Hess Hall, occupied by units of the U. S. Armed Forces for the past two years, is now being renovated, redecorated, and restored for dormitory use. The building will be available for women students upon the opening of the fall term, September 17, 1945.

Hess Hall has
- *Rooms for 80 Students*
  - *Spacious Lounge*
    - *Recreation Room*
      - *Laundry Rooms*
        - *Infirmary*
          - *Registered Nurse As Hostess*

Women students who expect to enroll next semester should make reservations early!

Rates for Board and Room on the campus are:

Single Rooms . . . . . $15.00 per month
Double Rooms . . . . . $10 per month each student
Board at University Club $40 per month

Beginning September 17, 1945, non-resident tuition will be $40 per semester. To be a resident one must have resided in the Territory one year prior to enrollment.

For further information or for room reservations write the Registrar

University of Alaska
College, Alaska

WITH THE END OF THE MILITARY "OCCUPATION" *of the campus in early 1945, the university could reopen its best dormitory, Hess Hall, for student use.*

Rasmuson Library

135

BUNNELL'S BUILDING FALLS, THE BUNNELL BUILDING RISES
*"Old Main"—the first building on campus, dating from 1918,
and the center of the university for almost forty years—is
demolished in the spring of 1960 after the completion of the
Bunnell Building, visible in the background.*

University Relations Collection, Rasmuson Library

136

FOUR

From Vulture Flats to University Park 1946–1959

Hundreds of veterans entered the University of Alaska following World War II, eager to start anew on the last frontier. Many found their postwar paradise in a place called Vulture Flats. By 1945, Jack Shanly's old homestead below College Hill was the site of a "new city . . . in the making," nicknamed Vulture Flats by students since it was a cold and hungry place to live. Charles Bunnell had purchased and subdivided Shanly's homestead in the late 1930s, and after World War II homes began to spring up along the avenues Bunnell had named for Mts. Deborah, Hess and Hayes in the Alaska Range, and the streets he had named in honor of the college's first three graduates, Shanly, Thomas, and Cameron.[1]

One of the proud citizens of Vulture Flats from 1947–1949 was Jay Hammond, a former fighter pilot with the U.S. Marines in the South Pacific, who, like other veterans at the overcrowded University of Alaska in those years, had to build his own house on the flats if he was going to have a place to live. Hammond graduated with a B.S. in general science in 1949. Twenty-five years later, he was the first University of Alaska graduate to become governor of the State of Alaska, and he whimsically recalled that he left the university after graduation because the

name Vulture Flats was abandoned in favor of the "singularly unimaginative" name of College. "I far preferred living in Vulture Flats rather than College," Hammond said, "and forthwith sold my property and departed . . . ."[2]

Despite Hammond's opinion of the virtues of Vulture Flats, Charles Bunnell cared for neither the name nor the other changes that occurred when ex-soldiers, sailors, and marines started to enroll at the university in such great numbers after 1946. Fearful that freeloaders would take advantage of the GI bill, Bunnell warned veterans in advance that anyone who considered the University of Alaska "a glorified loafing place" would be returning home on the next train headed south. "If you don't work and don't get down to business," he wrote in an article for *Army Times*, "you just have to find a haven elsewhere."[3]

Discipline at the university had always been rather strict, especially for women residents of the dormitories. In 1930, for instance, the catalog spelled out eighteen different restrictions for women and only nine for men. In the women's dormitory the lights were "flashed" at 10:45 and turned off at 11:00 P.M. Women were not permitted to hold "dancing parties" within two weeks of final examinations. They needed permission to ride in a car or to go to town more than twice a week. The men were prohibited from playing phonographs or "the making of disturbing noises" after the start of the 7:30 P.M. study period.[4]

By the late 1940s, the list of rules had shortened—though in 1946 female students could still only go to town twice a week, and any woman who left the dormitory between 6:00 P.M. and the 10:00 P.M. curfew, even to go to the library, had to sign out. "All students are expected to be punctual in attendance and to conduct themselves as ladies and gentlemen," the catalog stated. Any student could be expelled who failed "to make proper use of the opportunities which are offered by the University," grounds so broad that if Bunnell had wished he probably could have expelled the entire student body.[5]

Postwar students were not as content as their predecessors had been to heed the commands of the administration. Henry Kaiser, Jr., who enrolled in the fall of 1949, said the veterans attending the university in that era "were not the 9 out of 10 people you meet on the street, they were mostly number 10." These stubborn individualists had chosen the University of Alaska, Kaiser thought, because "they needed a place where formality was at minimum and individuality at maximum." He remembered seeing butchered moose and caribou carcasses hanging in dorm windows, and recalled a student truck driver who spent the winter months overhauling engines in his dorm room.[6]

Students activists in 1946 took the first steps to organize and officially incorporate the Associated Students of the University of Alaska, forming the first independent student government. The ASUA also began publication in October 1946—starting with a typewriter and a mimeograph machine—of the *Polar Star*, the first campus newspaper completely under student control, which would irritate university administrators for the next thirty-five years.[7] The establishment of the *Polar Star* marked the birth of a free and independent voice for UA students, and the start of a long-standing newspaper war between students and administration, a development that would have been unthinkable in the first twenty-five years of Bunnell's presidency. Under Bunnell, the *Farthest North Collegian* remained the official voice of the university, with President Bunnell reserving complete editorial control, although in 1938 as an "experiment," he agreed to initiate a *Collegian* Student Section and give students "carte blanche within reasonable limits" to publish what they wished.[8]

In selecting George Washington "Tex" Polk, a senior majoring in arts and letters, to be the first editor of the student section, Bunnell helped to launch the career of one of the most respected and courageous journalists of modern times.[9] George Polk's graduation from the University of Alaska in 1938 sent him from the *Farthest North Collegian* to a variety of news organizations around the world, including the *Shanghai Evening Post*. As a *New York Herald Tribune* correspondent in Paris and Washington, D.C., he covered the White House and the State Department. In 1945, Polk became a radio correspondent for CBS News under the tutelage of pioneer broadcaster Edward R. Murrow. After two years as chief CBS correspondent in the Middle East, he went to Greece in the spring of 1948.

On May 16, 1948, Polk's body was found floating in Salonika Bay, with his hands and feet tied and a

bullet in the back of his head. Both the right wing Greek government and the U.S. government tried to blame his murder on the communists, and the international scandal of this political murder has still never been completely resolved. In a nationwide broadcast on CBS news, Edward R. Murrow said his murdered young friend and colleague was "one of the ablest, most conscientious and courageous reporters" he had ever known. Later in 1948, the Journalism Department at Long Island University initiated the George Polk Award, one of the most prestigious honors in American journalism, given annually to newspapers and reporters who best exemplify "the ideals for which George Polk died."[10]

On December 7, 1946, the University of Alaska Alumni Association hosted a banquet at the Fairbanks Golf and Country Club to celebrate Charles Bunnell's twenty-fifth anniversary at the University of Alaska. About 150 friends, faculty and alumni gathered to pay tribute to the man who had started with no faculty, no students, and one empty building a quarter of a century earlier. The university now boasted 379 full-time students, the largest student body in its history up to that time. Throughout the evening, guests spoke about Bunnell's accomplishments, and read telegrams of praise from alumni and dignitaries across the country.[11]

Bunnell confidently predicted that in the next quarter century, America's only northern university would become "one of the most outstanding universities in the United States, if not the world." Within twelve months, however, he shocked Alaskans by announcing that the University of Alaska was on the verge of bankruptcy, and might be forced to shut down permanently before the end of the 1947–1948 school year.[12]

The 1947 financial emergency that nearly closed the university was part of a general collapse of the territorial government's rickety fiscal structure. By the late 1940s, Alaska simply did not collect enough taxes to support the services residents had come to expect. New Deal journalist and reformer Ernest Gruening—the first commencement speaker at the newly created University of Alaska in 1936—became the governor of Alaska in 1939, and President Bunnell was one of the first to alert him to the inequities of the territorial tax code. Under existing tax laws, absentee owners of the salmon canneries and gold mines paid relatively modest taxes compared with the huge profits they earned in Alaska. After meeting with the university president in December 1939, Gruening wrote in his diary that Bunnell felt the "one essential, indispensable thing that needs to be done is a general tax program. Everything, he considers, is secondary to that; I agree with him."[13] Throughout the 1940s Gruening would urge the legislature to enact a comprehensive tax program

composed of a personal and corporate income tax, a property tax, and a graduated business license tax, but lobbyists representing the two biggest industries in Alaska, salmon canning and gold mining, stymied his efforts for almost a decade.

Governor Gruening could genuinely appreciate Bunnell's efforts to keep the fledgling university alive in the absence of adequate funds. Gruening, an unusually versatile man, enjoyed life as both a scholar and a man of action. He had earned an M.D. at Harvard (though he never practiced medicine) and for four years edited *The Nation*, the leading liberal journal in the United States. Dr. Gruening wrote one influential book on public power and another on the Mexican revolution. During the Franklin D. Roosevelt administration he had been the senior official in the Division of Territories and Island Possessions (with responsibility for Alaska, Hawaii, Puerto Rico, and the Virgin Islands) before Roosevelt appointed him Governor of Alaska in 1939.[14]

In Gruening's eyes, the University of Alaska may have been a humble place, but he liked to quote Daniel Webster's famous line about Dartmouth: "It is a small college but there are those who love it."[15] In the memoirs he published many years later, Gruening would charge that due to legislative neglect "the university was a shabby, rundown, inadequate plant staffed by a wretchedly underpaid faculty."[16] Gruening once said that whenever legislators saw Bunnell prowling the halls of the capitol, pleading for more funds for the university, lawmakers greeted the president as if he were a cross between "a nuisance and a criminal."[17] The governor claimed, however, that the 1947 legislature hit "a new low in the disgraceful way it treated President Bunnell." Legislators "heckled and sneered" at Bunnell's proposed budget, which included $350,000 for construction that had been delayed since before the start of the war, and ultimately granted only about half of the $1.3 million he requested.[18]

President Bunnell was accustomed to getting less than he needed. The real problem was that this time the legislature had appropriated about $10 million to run the territorial government, against an estimated income of slightly more than $6.25 million; in other words, the legislature had written itself a rubber check for approximately $3.75 million. The check bounced in the fall of 1947, when a freeze on territorial appropriations left the university with virtually nothing in the bank. On November 1, 1947, the university's total available cash balance was exactly $1,104.09. For all practical purposes, the University of Alaska was bankrupt.[19]

The president feared that the university would be forced to close at the end of the first semester on January 15, 1948, and that it would take an act of Congress to reopen it. "The University would continue if it could do so by labor alone," the *Collegian* noted in December. "But food costs money. Books cost money. Electricity costs money. Coal costs money. And the University has no money."[20]

Bunnell had often been forced to pay for small expenditures out of his own pocket, but now, to meet his December payroll, the president gave the university a $20,000 advance from his personal funds. By asking students to pay their fees in advance, and receiving back payments from the territory, he managed to stay open for the 1948 spring semester. But

that still left the university with no funds for 1948–1949, the second year of the biennium.

Community business leaders rallied in support of the university. Fairbanks millionaire Austin E. "Cap" Lathrop, Alaska's richest resident, whose holdings included a chain of movie theatres, two radio stations, two banks, the *Fairbanks Daily News-Miner*, and the Healy River Coal Corporation, was vice president of the board of regents. A member of the board since 1932, Lathrop had never finished the ninth grade, but he prided himself on keeping the university to a practical course. Lathrop led the effort to solicit a total of $200,000 in interest-free loans to enable the university to remain open in 1948–1949. He personally pledged $25,000, as did Alaska Airlines, Standard Oil, the Fairbanks Exploration Co. and the Alaska Steamship Co. Andrew Nerland, the president of the board of regents, promised $10,000, and so did other Fairbanks business leaders such as Luther Hess, Martin Pinska, E. H. Stroecker, John Wachowitz and Mrs. James Barrack. Emma McKinnon of Juneau also gave $10,000, while President Bunnell gave the final $5,000 to bring the total sum to $200,000.[21]

Using a dozen personal loans to finance the operations of the university bordered on impropriety, as an audit by the accounting firm of Arthur Andersen and Co. would later note.[22] Nevertheless, the emergency loans saved the university until the 1948 election, when angry Alaskan voters cleaned out both the House and the Senate in Juneau, electing twenty-five freshman representatives and senators to the forty-member legislature. (Among the new representatives from Fairbanks was Democrat Glen Franklin, a 1936 University of Alaska

The Ice Bowl

Football at the University of Alaska never rivaled basketball or hockey in popularity, but from 1949 to 1952, the UA Polar Bears hosted the most unusual New Year's college bowl game in the country: the "Ice Bowl." Unlike the Rose Bowl, the Ice Bowl always took place under less than ideal conditions. In January 1949, the first time the game was held, the UA Polar Bears and the Ladd Field Flyers shivered to a 0–0 tie at 25 degrees below zero. During the second Ice Bowl the following year—shown in this photograph of the game on January 2, 1950—ten inches of snow covered Griffin Park in downtown Fairbanks. The Polar Bear ball carrier (No. 35) plowing through the snow is being chased by five Ladd Field defenders with dark patches on their shoulders. Despite the deep snow, hundreds of spectators crowded the stadium, while others listened to KFAR Radio's live play-by-play broadcast by Jack Warshauer,

an instructor in business administration. Leading up to the 1950 game, university coach Jim Welsch noted that deception was the key to winter football in Fairbanks. "The old plays would bog down in the snow," Welsch claimed. The Polar Bears planned to use their special "Arctic V" formation on offense, while the Ladd Flyer's boasted of their "Atomic Attack."

Neither the "Arctic V" nor the "Atomic Attack" proved highly successful. The Polar Bears won the 1950 game 3–0, when, as the *News-Miner* reported, Leo Helsby "kicked himself right into Alaska grid immortality" with a 35-yard field goal. The fact that there was any score at all was a near miracle. According to one reporter, "more times than could be counted" the snow drifts on the field "made the location of the ball obscure." The last Ice Bowl was held in 1952.

graduate.) In a special emergency session called by Governor Gruening in January 1949, and in the regular session that followed, the reform-minded legislators rewrote Alaska's tax code, instituting the territory's first income tax, a one percent property tax, and other revenue reforms to provide adequate funds for essential services such as the university.[23] At the end of the session, the university's 1949–1951 territorial appropriation was about $2.15 million, its first multi-million dollar budget.

Ironically, during the fiscal nightmare of 1947–1948, President Bunnell witnessed the achievement of one of his oldest dreams. In the spring of 1948, the U.S. Congress appropriated $975,000 for construction of the Geophysical Institute at the University of Alaska.

The Geophysical Institute grew out of nearly twenty years of geophysical research conducted on the Fairbanks campus, beginning with Professor Veryl Fuller's systematic photographic examination of the aurora in 1930. The first director of the Geophysical Institute, Stuart L. Seaton, had previously run the Carnegie Institution's ionospheric observatory in the Eielson Building during World War II. Working closely with the military, the Carnegie Institution had established several of these observatories worldwide to study radio waves in the upper atmosphere. The observatory on the Fairbanks campus functioned throughout the war, supplying invaluable data on radio communications and air navigation to Allied armed forces in the Pacific theater.[24]

The Second World War proved that arctic geophysical research was a vital weapon of national security. In July 1946, President Harry S. Truman signed the law authorizing the Geophysical Institute at the University of Alaska, the first American scientific laboratory of its kind in the north.

In 1948 Congress approved nearly one million dollars for construction of the Geophysical Institute on the university campus. Plans called for the new research facility to be located on about ten acres in a "wooded area" to the west of Hess Hall, where there would be sufficient land to build six new homes for the institute staff (which are today the faculty houses along Copper Lane) and the research building itself (now known as the Chapman Building). Stuart L. Seaton and an architect collaborated on the design of the three-story structure. It would include a wide array of modern scientific equipment, such as seismic recorders "constructed in such a way that they will be independent of the building and will be anchored in bedrock," as well as a "penthouse laboratory" and a retractable "astronomical dome" on the roof, equipped with telescopes, auroral cameras, and other meteorological instruments.

The laying of the cornerstone for the Geophysical Institute on Friday July 1, 1949 was performed with full Masonic rites, much as James Wickersham's cornerstone ceremony had been almost thirty-four years earlier. Among the scientific symbols Bunnell sealed inside the concrete box were a harpoon head Otto Geist had found on St. Lawrence Island and a modern vacuum tube.[26]

A local weekly newspaper commented that the ceremonies that rainy day in July marked the transition of the university "from a pioneer to an atomic age status," because in addition to the Geophysical Institute, the university also had a new chief executive for the first time in its history.[27] About one hour

before the ceremony at the Geophysical Institute, 71-year-old Charles Bunnell, in obviously failing health and suffering from diabetes, officially retired as the president of the University of Alaska.

For twenty-eight years, no detail had been too small to merit the president's personal attention. But stress from the university's near-bankruptcy and other pressing problems—such as the 1947 temporary federal take-over of the university's Agricultural Experiment Stations because of allegations of Bunnell's misuse of federal research funds—had taken their toll on his health. After a serious flare-up of diabetes, Bunnell required round-the-clock nursing care. Friends could see that the aging president was working himself to death. Nevertheless, convinced that no one could truly replace him, Bunnell vowed to remain on hand "to be available for counsel to his successor."[28]

On the morning of July 1, 1949, shortly before the dedication of the Geophysical Institute, Bunnell reluctantly became "President Emeritus," handing the keys to the university to a young investment consultant from Boston whom the board of regents had chosen to lead the University of Alaska into the second half of the twentieth century.

Like James Wickersham and Charles Bunnell before him, Terris Moore felt the lure of Denali and the other high peaks of the Alaska Range visible from the University of Alaska campus. In fact, Moore's climb to the presidency of the University of Alaska began at 20,320 feet on the top of Denali seven years earlier.

The man who took on the unenviable task of succeeding Charles Bunnell had impressive credentials as a scholar, an investor, a mountaineer, and a pilot. Born near Philadelphia in 1908, Terris Moore had graduated from Williams College with a degree in geology, before earning an M.B.A. and a doctorate in commercial science at Harvard University.[29]

While still in college, he became an avid mountain climber. Moore accompanied noted scientist Allen Carpé on the first ascents of Mount Bona and Mount Fairweather in the St. Elias Range in 1930 and 1931. On the first of these expeditions Moore made note of a 15,030-foot peak south of Mount Bona. Years later, by then president of the University of Alaska, Moore would name it "University Peak," part of a twenty-mile range of mountains called the "University of Alaska Range."[30]

In 1932, Moore made a remarkable first ascent of 24,900-foot Mount Minya Konka in eastern Tibet, for a quarter of a century afterwards the highest peak climbed by any American mountaineer. With his lifelong friend Bradford Washburn, the noted photographer and cartographer, Moore made the first ascent of Mount Sanford in the Wrangell Mountains in 1938. During World War II, the U.S. Army used Moore's mountain expertise on an experimental cold weather expedition to Denali, designed to test some 150 items of clothing and equipment in low temperatures. During the course of the expedition, Moore and three companions, including team leader Capt. Robert Bates, Bradford Washburn, and engineer Einar Nilsson, became the third party in history to stand on the summit of Denali. Moore told his biographer, T. Neil Davis, that it was in the summer of 1942, following the Army test expedition on Mount McKinley, that he first thought he might like to be president of the University of Alaska someday.[31]

In 1949, Moore was one of several dozen serious applicants to replace Bunnell. Unlike any of the other candidates, however, he flew his own plane—a Taylorcraft on skis—all the way from the East Coast to Alaska and around the territory in the spring of 1949 to talk personally with individual regents. His obvious enthusiasm for Alaska, his youth—at age forty-one he was close to the same age Bunnell had been in 1921—his distinguished academic background, and his successful career as an investment consultant seemed to make him the ideal man to be the second president of the University of Alaska. As Moore would discover, however, the problem with trying to fill the presidential shoes of Charles E. Bunnell was that Bunnell was still wearing them.

When Terris Moore arrived on campus in June 1949 with his wife Katrina and their two children, he realized that despite Bunnell's age and his ill health, the former president had no plans to step aside quietly. Bunnell, who continued to receive a salary as "President Emeritus," still resided in the "President's House" where he had lived since 1922, while the Moore family camped out for weeks in the infirmary in Hess Hall until the small quarters under construction for them were finished. Bunnell only reluctantly agreed to vacate the president's office in the Eielson Building, and moved directly across the hall to the new office of the president emeritus. After Moore's arrival, the University of Alaska essentially had two presidents and the campus was not big enough for both of them.

The most serious confrontation between the president and the president emeritus concerned the Geophysical Institute. Bunnell felt that the

The campus of the future

Visions of the University of Alaska of the future changed dramatically between the 1930s and the 1950s. President Bunnell's first campus plan in 1936 projected a quadrangle of concrete buildings at the center of campus, consisting of the Eielson Building, the library/gymnasium, and several other structures that were never built. By the late 1940s the expanding plan included more concrete dormitories and other facilities, all aligned in a precise rectangular pattern facing north/south or east/west. Architect Prentiss

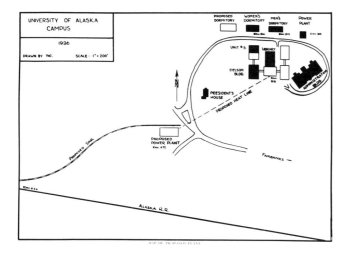

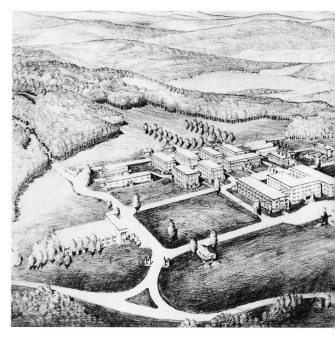

(Left to right)
The future as it looked in 1936, 1948, and 1951.

Rasmuson Library

establishment of the Geophysical Institute was the crowning achievement of his twenty-eight years as president, and he knew it would not have been possible without the help of his protégé, Stuart L. Seaton, the former head of the College Observatory and a 1942 graduate of the University. Seaton, like Otto Geist, was a largely self-trained scientist, and Bunnell had granted him an honorary doctor of science degree at the 1949 commencement. In one of his last official acts as president, Bunnell nominated Seaton as the first director of the Geophysical Institute.

Bunnell and Seaton envisioned the Geophysical Institute as an administratively and financially independent arm of the university, which would nevertheless serve as the core of the university's future graduate school. This confusing organizational structure caused immediate tension over numerous small issues, as well as the vital question of funding. The final rift came in the spring of 1950, when Seaton

French, hired by President Moore in 1950, thought the tidy, geometrical, New-England-college look which Bunnell had wanted was totally out of place on the rugged contours of College Hill. Instead the architect drew a more flexible plan, which he grafted on top of Bunnell's rigid quadrangle pattern. French recommended a new open "quadrangle," with academic buildings ringing the crest of College Hill to conform with the topography and take advantage of the view. Though greatly modified over the years, French's plan became the first draft of the blueprint of the modern University of Alaska Fairbanks campus.

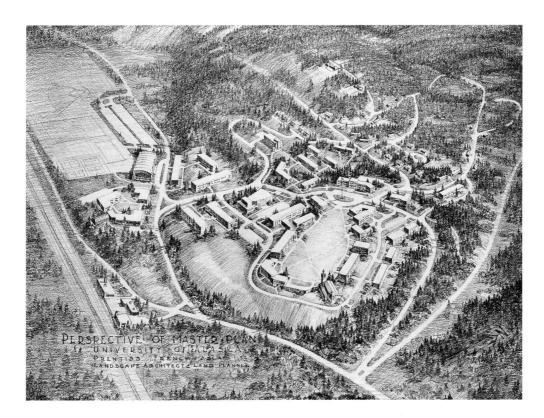

PERSPECTIVE OF MASTER PLAN
UNIVERSITY OF ALASKA
PRENTISS FRENCH A.S.L.A.
LANDSCAPE ARCHITECT & LAND PLANNER

and about two-thirds of the Geophysical Institute staff threatened to resign *en masse*, claiming that Moore was trying to take over the institute. The board of regents upheld Moore's position and fired Seaton and most of the institute staff.

For some time the Geophysical Institute, the finest research facility of its kind in Alaska, remained nearly deserted. Over the following years, however, Moore's administration assembled a first-rate research staff led by advisory scientific director Sydney Chapman and institute managing director Christian Elvey. These two distinguished scientists joined the elite names in the history of world science in 1970, when two craters near the north pole of the moon were named in their honor. On the university campus the first and second Geophysical Institute buildings were named the Chapman Building and the Elvey Building.

Under Chapman and Elvey, the Geophysical Institute became the core of the university's research and graduate programs. Its research projects, such as the study of polar radio propagation, neutron monitoring at the summit of Mt. Wrangell, mapping of ground conductivity throughout Alaska, and Syun-Ichi Akasofu's discovery of the magnetospheric substorm, were difficult for laymen to comprehend. The most dramatic demonstration of the value of the Geophysical Institute, however, came in October 1957, when the Soviet Union launched Sputnik, the first artificial satellite in our solar system. Observers at the Geophysical Institute, led by assistant director Gordon Little, successfully tracked the satellite's orbit and made the first confirmed visual sighting of Sputnik in the western hemisphere.[32]

Formal graduate study at the university began in September 1950 with the newly created Department of Wildlife Management. The University of Alaska granted its first graduate degrees in 1952, when Salvatore De Leonardis and John Hakala each earned a master's degree in wildlife management. In 1955, Masahisa Sugiura, studying with Sydney Chapman, earned the first Ph.D. at the University of Alaska for a dissertation in geophysics entitled "The Morphology of Magnetic Storms."[33]

Besides their differences over the Geophysical Institute, Moore and Bunnell held conflicting views over how to run the university. Bunnell saw changes Moore made as criticisms of himself and his administration. When Moore attempted to raise faculty standards by requiring advanced degrees for faculty promotion, Bunnell thought the newcomer from the Ivy League was looking down his nose at good scholars and teachers who had never enjoyed the luxury of formal graduate training. Moore wanted students to participate in the "self-government" of the university, as he believed it vital for "elders to listen more closely to the thoughts of the younger generation."[34] Bunnell had always prided himself on his ability to make tough decisions by himself no matter the consequences, and never wasted time consulting unnecessarily with students or other subordinates. He thought the dozens of committees Moore appointed, from the Committee on Keys and Locks to the Committees on Telephones or Office Arrangements, would produce nothing but paperwork and meaningless advice. To end the divisive competition for news and advertising between the *Farthest North Collegian* and the *Polar Star*, Moore suspended monthly publication in 1949 of Bunnell's cherished old *Collegian* to give "free rein" to the student newspaper.[35]

The first and second presidents agreed on the need for new dormitories and classroom buildings, but disagreed over where to put them. When Moore took office in 1949, he found a haphazard collection of wooden firetraps dating from the 1920s. The power plant and three concrete buildings constructed in the 1930s were still the only permanent structures on campus. An additional eyesore was the Veterans' Dormitory, a building constructed of two abandoned Army barracks from Seward which had been knocked down and shipped by train to Fairbanks, then reassembled on the campus.[36]

The still-uncompleted Eielson Memorial Building housed almost every office on campus, including the offices of the president and president emeritus, the book store, the student lounge, the post office, the university museum, the departments of physics, music and anthropology, and temporary housing quarters for junior faculty members. Before the Eielson Building's expansion in 1950–51 to its present size, President Moore said, "Something close to the extreme limit of compressibility in the amount of activity that could be carried on inside one building" seemed to have been reached.[37]

In 1950, President Moore hired Prentiss French, a San Francisco landscape architect and land planner, to draw up a new master plan for the university campus based on an enrollment of 1,500 students. French's plan—accepted by the board of regents in May 1951—recommended that the university abandon Bunnell's proposed "quadrangle," which the former president had envisioned for more than twenty years as the basic structure of the campus. The entire campus, except for the Main Building, the architect noted, had been planned on a rectangular north-south grid, with no regard for the contours of the hill. Existing structures stood like soldiers on parade, all aligned at right angles, ignoring the topography and the beauty of the natural setting. In French's opinion the long, narrow Eielson Building—shaped like a three-story freight train—was an architectural monstrosity, and duplicating it by completing the quadrangle would be a "serious mistake."[38]

The 1951 master plan grafted a new, more flexible layout on top of the geometrical grid of the Bunnell era. Instead of Bunnell's square quadrangle, the 1951 master plan called for new academic buildings to be constructed in a circular pattern around the edge of College Hill, leaving an open space in the middle—once the Main Building was torn down—as the heart of the campus. The architect further recommended the "simplest possible style of architecture," not only because of cost, but also because "the site is so magnificent as to make much elaboration of buildings seem superfluous, perhaps even ridiculous."[39] Though greatly modified over the years, the Moore administration's master plan was the first draft of the blueprint of the modern University of Alaska Fairbanks campus.

Two of the new structures on that blueprint were completed in the early 1950s, as substantial funds for new construction were available for the first time since the 1930s. The Alfred Brooks Memorial Mines Building, dedicated on July 22, 1952—the fiftieth anniversary of Felix Pedro's discovery of gold in the Fairbanks district—was the fulfillment of a thirty-year-old dream for the School of Mines. Equipped with ten classrooms and ten scientific laboratories, the Brooks Building was a state-of-the-art mining research facility. The second concrete dormitory on campus, named for Andrew Nerland, the president of the board of regents, opened in 1953 with accommodations for 102 men.[40]

Moore's drive to modernize the university campus, and in fact his very appointment as president, was rooted in the modernization of the board of regents which had begun in the late 1940s. For several years, Governor Gruening had believed that the university's governing board needed more "diversification." In 1947, six of the eight regents were over sixty-five, and four were over seventy.[41] Furthermore, five of the eight regents came from either Fairbanks or Nome, while the three members of the regents' executive committee, and the board's four officers—president, vice-president, treasurer and secretary—all lived in Fairbanks.[42] Improvements in aviation during the 1940s made it possible at last for regents from other communities to attend meetings in Fairbanks regularly, effectively ending the old Fairbanks monopoly of the board of regents. Gruening replaced half of the board between 1948 and 1950, and he drastically changed its composition by nominating four vigorous younger men from across the territory: William A. O'Neill and Leo Rhode in 1948 (both of whom were graduates of the university), Dr. C. Earl Albrecht in 1949, and Anchorage banker Elmer Rasmuson in 1950.

Born in Yakutat in 1909, Elmer Rasmuson was a 1930 honors graduate of Harvard University, who left a promising career with the accounting firm of Arthur Andersen & Co. to return to Alaska in 1943 to assist his father in managing the family-owned Bank of Alaska. When "Cap" Lathrop, the vice-president of the board of regents, died in July 1950 from falling beneath the wheels of a railroad car at his Healy River coal mine, Governor Gruening asked Rasmuson to replace him. During the nineteen years Rasmuson would serve as a regent, and especially after 1956 when he became president of the board, few men played a bigger role in charting the destiny of the University of Alaska. Rasmuson's tenure on the board spanned the administrations of three presidents—Moore, Patty, and Wood—during which enrollment increased from about 300 students to more than 3,000. Every year he pushed the administration to improve the university's long-range planning and budgeting; as president of the board he helped formulate an overall strategy, and

ably represented the university before the legislature in Juneau through the 1950s and 1960s. All three of the presidents with whom he worked would probably echo Ernest Patty's 1959 assessment of what Rasmuson's work behind the scenes meant to the University of Alaska.

"Perhaps we are flattering ourselves," President Patty wrote Rasmuson in June 1959, "but it always has seemed to me that you and I are the catalysts of the University. We are both impatient with mediocrity and drive ourselves and those about without any thought of personal popularity. When I say this I do not mean it as a slight against other members of the Board. Most of them have made valuable contributions, but in most instances they look to you for leadership."[43]

At his first regents' meeting in January 1951, Rasmuson introduced a resolution directing President Moore to study the feasibility of creating a "Junior College" in Alaska, and to find other methods "to take the university to the people in all corners of the Territory."[44] In many respects, the idea of the University of Alaska branching out from the Fairbanks campus was analogous to the development of a branch banking system, such as Rasmuson's pioneering National Bank of Alaska.

Residents of Southeastern Alaska had long clamored for a "Southern Branch" of the University of Alaska, but nothing ever came of the proposal, largely because each town wanted the new branch in their own community, or not at all. Few high school graduates from Juneau or Ketchikan even considered attending college in Fairbanks. Seattle was much closer and less expensive. For years, about the same number of Alaskans enrolled at the

University of Washington as at the University of Alaska.[45]

In October 1951, President Moore presented the regents with a detailed report on establishing community colleges in Alaska.[46] With a 1951 estimated population of 135,000, Alaska was approximately the same size as Albany, New York, but spread out over an area one-fifth the size of the continental United States. The western states had founded university branches, separate state universities, or teachers' colleges to satisfy regional higher education needs, but Moore believed that in Alaska these options would be ruinously expensive. Instead he proposed that the university work with local school boards throughout Alaska to establish true community colleges, by offering introductory courses at preexisting local facilities. Anchorage Community College, the first in the University of Alaska system, began classes at Anchorage High School in February 1954, while Ketchikan Community College opened in September 1954. Within ten years, four more community colleges had been established, in Juneau, Palmer, Sitka, and Kenai, making the Fairbanks campus the nucleus of an Alaska-wide system of higher education.

Though Terris Moore took the first steps to decentralize Alaskan higher education, he was no longer president by the time instruction began in Anchorage and Ketchikan. Moore left Alaska in October 1953, when Ernest Patty took over as the third president of the University of Alaska. In his farewell letter to the board of regents, Moore candidly admitted that during his four-year tenure, not everything had always gone smoothly. "At several times, of course, during these years we have had our difficulties and sharp differences of viewpoint," Moore wrote. "But for these I will think of that great line from Homer, 'Forsan ad haec olim, etiam meminesse iuvabit'—eventually even these will become pleasant to remember."[47]

The man who replaced Terris Moore as president was no newcomer to the University of Alaska. "Dean" Patty, fourteen years older than Moore, had been one of the original six instructors Bunnell hired in 1922 at the opening of the Alaska Agricultural College and School of Mines. As dean of the college and head of the School of Mines, Patty had been Bunnell's right-hand man for thirteen years—his assistant president. Patty was the senior member of the faculty when he left the college in 1935 to return to the mining business. For the next eighteen years he devoted himself to gold mining, running dredges in Alaska and the Yukon. He returned to campus in the spring of 1953 to receive an honorary doctorate and to give the commencement address.

At the time of Patty's speech, the regents were weeding through scores of applications to find a replacement for Moore. Patty was not among the candidates, but Bunnell strongly supported his old protégé. The regents found Patty's commencement address (entitled "Be Bold") so inspiring that they offered him the job. At first he refused. Not only did he lack an earned doctorate, but he was nearly sixty years old, and the president's salary would be about half of what he currently earned. But the decision was not a question of money. Elmer Rasmuson remembers telling Patty that if he turned down the job as president, he would regret it for the rest of his life. "I know," said Patty. He asked for a few months to think it over, and officially accepted the post in the fall of 1953.[48]

Ernest Patty was president of the University of Alaska from 1953 to 1960, and during those seven years the university underwent a remarkable transformation. Under Patty, the number of faculty increased by 190%, the number of students by 237%, and most impressive of all, the value of the physical plant increased by 650%.[49]

As a professional miner, Patty had spent most of his life moving dirt, and he did much the same as university president. Rebuilding the campus was the top priority of both President Patty and the regents. "For years the University went along without sufficient construction to give it a good physical plant," Patty wrote in 1955. "We want a University that Alaskans can be proud of. The alumni are ashamed of it and it causes many students to go elsewhere. Last September a group of students drove up from Anchorage intending to enroll. They spent a day here and then drove on to the States, frankly stating that the place looked 'too run down at the heels' for them."[50]

During Patty's tenure as president, construction never halted on campus; the construction budget, including large sums of federal funds from the Alaska Public Works program, averaged about one million dollars annually. Old alumni needed maps to learn their way around campus, as major new facilities were completed at the rate of at least one per year: in 1954 the new president's house—pictured on postcards as "one of the finest homes in Alaska, and probably the most photographed"; in 1955 Stuart Hall (apartments) and Constitution Hall

(Student Union Building); in 1956 McIntosh Hall (men's dormitory); in 1957 Wickersham Hall (women's dormitory); in 1958 Stevens Hall (men's dormitory); in 1959 Walsh Hall (married student housing); in 1960 the Bunnell Memorial Building (library, administration, classrooms).

With the new facilities constructed in the 1950s, the campus lost many of its old rough edges. Cement sidewalks were laid to connect all permanent buildings. Streets and large parking lots were paved; the installation of mercury vapor street lights meant students no longer needed flashlights to walk between buildings in the winter. When a physics professor complained that one of the new street lamps outside his front door ruined his view of the aurora, Patty told him to watch the northern lights from his back porch.[51]

By the end of the decade, the once shabby campus, which local Fairbanks residents had refused to show to visitors, was a prominent tourist attraction. In fact, a visiting journalist in 1959 wrote that in contrast to the run-down appearance of Fairbanks, where "at least every second place of business appears to depend on alcohol, either by the glass or by the bottle or both," the university campus was "truly beautiful, neatly landscaped in a mountain setting. The architectural motif is modern, and the bright pastel-colored buildings all look brand-new and extremely well kept. Alaskans are proud of the school, and they have good reason to be."[52]

Expansion of the University of Alaska made it possible for the campus to host Alaska's Constitutional Convention from November 1955 through February 1956. Hoping that a well-written consti-

tution would convince congress and the Eisenhower administration of Alaska's political maturity, and revive the stalled statehood movement, fifty-five delegates elected by the people of Alaska—including alumni like Jack Boswell and Jim Doogan, and Regent Mike Walsh—assembled in the just-completed Student Union Building in November 1955 to draft a state constitution.

Those accustomed to the interminable bickering of the legislature found the atmosphere of the academic setting to be a pleasant surprise. One week into the gathering, convention President William A. Egan told the *Fairbanks Daily News-Miner*, "It's wonderful and maybe a miracle to see how these fifty-five people have left politics out of this convention." According to Egan, when the legislature was in session in Juneau, Republicans and Democrats "wouldn't sit within half-a-mile of each other" in a restaurant. Here the forty-nine men and six women drafting the new constitution ate to-

gether in the new cafeteria on the second floor of the Student Union Building, rode the same bus to and from the campus every day, and forgot their differences. As the convention wore on, the work days for the delegates stretched to twelve and thirteen hours a day. Near the end of January 1956, Constitution Hall, as the Student Union Building came to be known, resembled a dormitory during final exams, with men and women buried in books and papers throughout the building.

In the seventy-five days delegates spent in Constitution Hall, they drafted a model document that became the legal foundation of the 49th state. "The good work of this convention," a memorial at the door of Constitution Hall states, "was rewarded with the granting of statehood on Jan. 3, 1959."[53]

University officials were especially pleased that the new constitution included a clause specifically designating the University of Alaska as "the state university." Furthermore, Patty claimed that the

The volcano that never was

The front page of the Polar Star on March 15, 1957, recounted the most outlandish college prank in the history of the University of Alaska, the "great volcano hoax" of March 13–14, 1957. The instigators were Peter Russell, a sophomore in geology, and associate professor of geology Harry Groom. The great hoax was inspired by a series of more than one hundred powerful earthquakes that struck Alaska and the Aleutian Islands in early March 1957, causing tidal waves that devastated parts of Hawaii and Japan, and awaking a volcano in the Aleutians that had been dormant for two hundred years. Russell and Groom had been scheduled to accompany a military research flight to investigate the volcanic eruptions in the Aleutians. Depressed and disappointed when their plans for the observation trip fell through, they went back to the snack bar at the Student Union Building. In a fit of black humor, they jokingly told

another student, Harvey Turner, that "the Brooks Range was bursting over with lava." Turner believed it all, until Russell and Groom confessed it was a gag, since of course there are no volcanoes in the Brooks

convention itself was one of best things that had ever happened to the university. "Practically every delegate told me how much they appreciated their stay here . . . . We have made lots of good friends and I think this convention was one of the finest pieces of public relations that was ever performed."[54]

Luckily the delegates did not have to write the Alaska Constitution in "Old Main," where strategically placed water buckets in the halls reminded everyone that the forty-year-old wooden structure was, according to President Patty, "the worst firetrap

in Alaska." Replacing Old Main with a new building was the capstone of Patty's career as president.

Old Main was the oldest building—and the oldest joke—at the University of Alaska; students claimed that the only thing holding up Old Main was the paint on the walls. Sitting through an English class in Room 221 in 1954, *Polar Star* columnist Al Baumeister bemoaned the fact that "this damned place didn't burn down." Nevertheless, he could not imagine the University of Alaska without Old Main, "for what would we do without the

Range. But it gave them the idea of pulling off a hoax. With the help of several co-conspirators they spread the wild story all over campus that a dozen volcanoes in the Brooks Range were simultaneously exploding—including a peak they invented named Stony Mountain. They further claimed that all men at the university had been asked to volunteer—and be paid fifty dollars a day—to paratroop into the region to investigate.

Panic and rumors spread that afternoon and early evening. The veterans and other older students in Main Dorm were skeptical, but the more gullible underclassmen swallowed the whole story, and jumped at the chance to earn fifty dollars a day exploring volcanoes. Many literally feared it was the end of the earth. One rumor had it that the Seward Peninsula was sinking at the rate of four inches an hour; around midnight someone set off a dozen sticks of dynamite on College Road, and some of the women in Hess Hall were convinced the campus itself had become a smouldering volcano sending "lava flowing through the streets." By five o'clock in the morning an estimated seventy-five to one hundred men with full winter gear, rifles and pack sacks had gathered at the supposed embarkation point in the hall of the Eielson Building to wait for trucks to ferry them to the airstrip. Two hours later, when no trucks or military commanders showed up, they finally realized it was all a hoax. In memory of the event the *Polar Star* published a song entitled "The Ballad of the Volcano That Never Was," which the paper claimed should be sung "to the mournful strumming of a sad guitar minus Elvis." The song said in part:

> *In the afternoon, Groom got the word.*
> *(Even though it seemed absurd.)*
> *That happening in the Brooks Range*
> *Was a phenomenon quite strange*
> *Where there was volcano none.*
> *Now there was an erupting one!*
> *Russell helped to spread the news*
> *And began to recruit the crews.*
> *Fifty dollars for a day*
> *That was to be the pay.*
> *For the help of college boys*
> *They made a hellova noise.*
> *To Brooks Range they would go*
> *To record the lava flow.*
> *Nerland Hall and McIntosh*
> *Went into hysterics; Oh my gosh!*
> *Strange it seems the men in Main*
> *All remained calm and sane.*

tantalizing aroma from the Wild-life Lab mixed to perfection with the rotten egg gas from the chem labs. And how I would miss the 25 watt light bulb hanging from the ceiling dangling in my face, the pitter-patter of little Elephant feet changing classes and the . . . Victorian privy downstairs with the slivered toilet seats."[55]

Despite its hazardous condition, Old Main was still the hub of the university in the late 1950s, where two-thirds of all classes were held. "Each year we keep pumping steam into it," Patty wrote in 1957, "and before winter is over it is heavily sheathed with icicles . . . . If it should burn down, we would have a holocaust on campus. The fire would sweep with it many other frame buildings, and severely damage adjacent permanent buildings . . . . We guard this old building night and day. So far, it has had a charmed life, despite the fact that it houses chemical and other laboratories which are severe risks."[56]

The threat that Old Main might ignite the entire campus led to the formation of the university's volunteer fire department in the 1950s under mining professor John Hoskins. Student firefighters could be called out of class at any time to man the jeep pumper (owned by the College community) or the university fire truck to respond to alarms from the campus or the surrounding area. In 1955, a small fire in Hess Hall started when a student "decided to heat a ping-pong ball to see if he could remove the dent." Fire Marshall Hoskins reminded everyone to sound the fire alarm, even for a burning ping-pong ball, because anyone could misjudge the danger of a fire, and furthermore "alarms keep the volunteer firemen in practice."[57]

The university finally tore down Old Main in 1960, shortly after completion of the Charles E. Bunnell Memorial Building. This four-story "multi-purpose building" on the south edge of College Hill showcased a "commanding view of the Alaska Range" and became the new campus hub. The east wing of the Bunnell Building housed the university administration and a large auditorium. The west wing was the new home of the university's 50,000-volume library; no longer would students in the library stacks listen to the sounds of basketball practice beneath them. Between the library wing and the administration wing were classrooms, laboratories, and several academic departments.[58]

As a working memorial to Charles Bunnell, the $2.9 million Bunnell Building was the perfect tribute to a "practical idealist" (as Dean Duckering once described the first president). By far the largest and most expensive structure on the campus up to that time, the Bunnell Building alone cost five times more than the three concrete buildings constructed in President Bunnell's 28-year reign. Speaking at the dedication of the Bunnell Building in the summer of 1960, the State of Alaska's first governor, William A. Egan, called the new facility the "prize jewel in the crown of buildings which in the last ten years have grown to adorn the crest of College Hill."[59]

Future UA students would only know Bunnell as the name of a building. The president emeritus had died four years earlier at the age of seventy-eight after a long illness. Even at the time of his death, a new generation of students, some of whom didn't even realize who he was, considered Bunnell "a name from the past; a figure clad in black who— up until a few months ago—could sometimes be seen making his way about the campus."[60]

But for old alumni and faculty, memories of Bunnell were everywhere. At Bunnell's funeral in the university gymnasium in November 1956, President Patty addressed his remarks directly to the Judge himself because he felt his spirit pervaded the entire campus. Without Charles Bunnell, Patty said, there would be no University of Alaska, "College Hill would be overgrown with brush and the chance traveller would come upon the shell of the Main Building—the windows broken and the winter wind whistling through." He recalled seeing President Bunnell before the opening of the college in September 1922, standing on top of the Main Building, pulling on a rope to help raise the flagpole. Some might remember Bunnell "working late at night in your office with coat off and sleeves rolled up," but Patty said, "I choose to remember you as a determined man of single purpose, pulling on a rope to elevate the University." Bunnell had requested in his will that he be buried somewhere on the campus, but he was laid to rest in the Birch

Hill cemetery outside Fairbanks, where, the *Alaska Alumnus* stated, "by light of sun or moon he can look down upon College Hill and the campus . . . ."[61]

As President Bunnell's second-in-command for thirteen years, Ernest Patty inherited his boss's concern for the practical value of higher education. Admittedly, Patty was not as interested in philosophy courses as he was in physics or physical education. Rudy Krejci, who founded the philosophy department in 1962 under William R. Wood—Patty's successor—said Patty once told him that the University of Alaska never had a philosophy department "and we'll never have it because we just don't need it."[62]

Like Bunnell, Patty was a stern disciplinarian, a traditional schoolmaster who took his role *in loco parentis* seriously. For instance, when the *Polar Star* ran several articles in the spring of 1954 that Patty thought were erroneous and generated bad publicity for the university, he called a special meeting of the students and faculty in the gymnasium and laid down the law. He would expel the writer of any article that harmed "the reputation of the University." To be on the safe side, he recommended that articles with "doubtful content" first be cleared with journalism instructor Charles Keim.[63]

Patty had spent most of his working life with mining crews. To him, running the university was not all that different from managing a mining camp, except that he felt the average miner was tidier than the average University of Alaska student. He crusaded against student beards, blue jeans, and bad manners, and considered offering a one-hour course to teach incoming students "how to make introductions, table etiquette, and general social behavior."

One idea he had was for the drama department to put on a skit in "etiquette instruction," which would be "a humorous play showing a man with his date making many of the social mistakes." In 1954, he recommended that "it would be nice to have the students dress for dinner once or twice a week this year. The boys could put on a white shirt, tie and coat, and the girls wear dresses."[64]

The effort to improve the "personal grooming" and "social amenities" of the student body was not received enthusiastically. "Mr. Patty, you don't seem to understand," he recalled one student protesting, "that many of us came to this university to escape the regimentation of civilization." Patty's response was, "Civilization has just caught up with you."[65]

In 1960, *Time* magazine published a notorious article about Patty's efforts to clean up the university and to reform its student body. Among other things *Time* claimed that when Patty first became president, the University of Alaska was "little more than a 'moose college' for young Alaskans who lacked the brains or money to attend colleges Outside," and that skeptics said it should be "converted into a penal or mental institution." According to *Time*, UA students who "used to brawl merrily in taverns" were now tamed by Patty's dress code and spent the winter watching *Maverick* on TV.[66]

Part of President Patty's effort to upgrade the image of the university was his attempt to do away with the place called College, Alaska. "The address 'College' was fine when this institution was a college," Patty explained in 1954. "Now we are grown up and it's time we changed the address."[67] Suggestions included changing the name of the College Post Office (which remained in the Eielson Building until it was moved off campus in 1961) to "University, Alaska" or "University Hill, Alaska," but the most popular proposal seemed to be "University Park, Alaska." The regents tentatively approved the new name, and indicated further that they would like to see College Road, the main highway to the university, renamed "University Boulevard."[68] In 1957, Patty told the Fairbanks Chamber of Commerce that he wanted to see "University Boulevard" from Fairbanks to University Park become a landscaped, four-lane-parkway with "no junk piles, no old mattresses, no eyesores." Fairbanksans needed to clean up the community and recognize the importance of the university to its long-range future, he thought, because although mining and military construction had long been the mainstay of the local economy, "the University of Alaska will be here . . . after the gold bearing gravel is worked out and the military bases are abandoned."[69]

But University of Alaska students preferred to live in low-rent College rather than high-tone University Park. "Dreams of Grandeur," claimed a *Polar Star* headline about Patty's proposal to change the name, while ASUA officially voted to oppose the idea. Student body president Stewart Butler complained to the board of regents in March 1957 that the university "has few enough traditions," and the name College called to mind the "proud heritage" of the University of Alaska's early history and its survival against the odds. Butler claimed that "the name 'College' is a name to be proud of, rather than ashamed of."

Despite Patty's wishes, University Park never became a reality—except for University Park Elementary School, which opened on the College flats in 1959. (The local school board chose the name University Park over both Bunnell Grade School and Vulture Flats Elementary.)[70] Perhaps one reason why students protested wiping out the name "College" was that they believed Patty was eliminating the most colorful traditions of the student body. Another of his edicts a few months previously banned one of the University of Alaska's oldest activities: beer drinking. His prohibition of alcohol on campus in 1956 unintentionally created the most famous underground tradition in university history, which for nearly forty years has commemorated Patty's administration: the Tradition Stone.

On November 30, 1956, the *Polar Star's* one-word-headline (in 96-point type) broke the news: PROHIBITION! The banning of alcohol, the newspaper explained, "struck without warning on the University of Alaska campus yesterday . . . ."

"The edict caused an immediate sensation among the students, and the campus was in an uproar last night as groups of students gathered to discuss the ban and ways in which it might be subverted." According to an editorial in the *Polar Star*, never known for understatement, news of the liquor ban caused such an explosion of anger that it was as if "an atom bomb had been dropped between the Eielson Building and Hess Hall."[71]

Patty decided to prohibit alcohol on campus after several drunken disturbances, including a brawl during the 1956 Starvation Gulch dance and celebration. He thought most students would welcome the move, and wrote Dean of Students William Cashen that the university would be better off

"It has been my experience that folks who have no vices have very few virtues."
—ABRAHAM LINCOLN

POLAR STAR

Associated Students of the University of Alaska, Inc.

Vol. XXII, No. 11   COLLEGE, ALASKA   Friday, November 30, 1956   By Subscription

PROHIBITION!

Annual Miners Ball Tomorrow Night

Queen of the Ball to Be Announced

Doffing their hard hats, mud encrusted pants and rowdy mannerisms, the Miners will sally forth in their best suits and ties and with their most gentlemanly behavior for their annual formal dance. Students, faculty, and even C.E.'s if they wear socks and ties, are most welcome to join the miners in the best formal dance of the year. The big social is planned for Saturday, December 1 at 9 p.m. in the Student Union

Dean Cashen's Memorandum, Based On Letter From President Patty, Establishes Prohibition On Campus

Dr. Patty Returns To Campus

President Ernest N. Patty returned

Open Letter To Dr. Patty Circulated

Prohibition—the cause of one of the wildest eras in the history of the United States—struck without warning on the University of Alaska campus yesterday.

The University administration, in a strongly worded directive, pro-

TRADITION'S OBITUARY . . .
The Polar Star's *headline announcing President Patty's decision to forbid alcohol on campus in November 1956.*

Rasmuson Library

159

. . . AND FUNERAL
Peter Schust unveils the Tradition Stone.

Alaska Airlines-Henry Kaiser Collection, Rasmuson Library

without the few troublemakers who would "resent these restrictions." Contrary to his expectations, 202 students—two-thirds of the students living on campus or about forty percent of the entire student body—signed an open letter protesting the ban. Students said they bitterly objected to the "dictatorial tone" of the pronouncement. "The edict rings of authoritarian discipline," wrote *Polar Star* news editor Ken Jensen, and was "contrary to the ideals of democratic people anywhere."[72]

Outraged by the attacks on himself and his administration, Patty not only refused to back down,

but forced the students to retract their accusations against the university. As Patty explained to the board of regents, dealing with students was sometimes "not very different from a family where at times the father and mother are at a loss to understand why their children do not show greater appreciation for the effort being made on their behalf."[73]

A few months later, on March 22, 1957, hundreds of students marched in a torchlight parade and assembled in front of Constitution Hall. They came to bury tradition symbolically by throwing empty beer bottles into a grave marked by a 400-

160

pound concrete headstone. On the top was a metal plaque with a welded inscription that read:

Here Lies
TRADITION
1957

Using their empty beer containers for candle holders, the marchers sang a few choice songs, including a parody to the tune of "The Old Rugged Cross," and then reenacted the scene from Shakespeare's *Julius Caesar*, where Mark Antony comes to bury his slain leader and pretends to praise the "honorable men" who murdered him. Led by master of ceremonies Peter Schust, students one by one recounted in solemn tones the traditions that President Patty had eliminated or watered down, like Engineer's Day, Starvation Gulch, etc., then dropped an empty beer bottle in the hole in the ground and said, "But Ernie is an honorable man."[74]

When the administration insisted that the Tradition Stone be removed and destroyed, it was instead stolen and ever since has remained a fugitive from justice, making only surprise appearances before the owners of the moment spirit it away again. Over the years the stone has been stolen, restolen, and stolen back again. There is no honor among the owners of the Tradition Stone. Legend claims it spent several winters on the bottom of the Chena River, and was at times shipped as far away as Texas, Brazil, and even Korea and Vietnam.

The travels of the Tradition Stone, even if only half of them are true, prove that whatever was buried in the cold grave in front of Constitution Hall in 1957 was not as dead as the students thought. On the contrary, Patty's successor, William R. Wood, like all American university presidents in the 1960s, found that many other cherished traditions truly were about to die.

Portfolio
1946–1959

THE UNIVERSITY CAMPUS IN 1949. UNDER
construction in the background left of center is the
first Geophysical Institute (now the Chapman
Building) and behind it are six houses for the institute
staff (now faculty housing on Copper Lane). On the
extreme left in the distance is the U.S. Coast and
Geodetic Survey's Magnetic Observatory located on a
40-acre tract of university land the Survey leased for
99 years. This observatory was the first of the
research facilities on what later became known as
"West Ridge."

Neil Davis Collection, Rasmuson Library

VICE PRESIDENT AND FORMER SECRETARY OF
*Agriculture Henry A. Wallace (third from left)
stopped to visit the university on May 21, 1944, while
en route to China on a secret trip. Wallace took a keen
interest in the scientific research at the university and
the experimental farm. From left to right: Gen. Dale
Gaffney, Charles Bunnell, Vice President Wallace,
and College Observatory director Stuart Seaton.*

Neil Davis Collection, Rasmuson Library

THE *COLLEGIAN* CLAIMED THAT ONE OF THE
*greatest moments in the history of the university
occurred at 10:00 A.M. on August 5, 1947, when the
motorcade of army chief of staff General Dwight D.
Eisenhower arrived on campus. In this photo,
President Bunnell (at left) shows a rather weary-
looking Gen. Eisenhower (standing next to him) some
of the university's scientific equipment.*

Charles E. Bunnell Collection, Rasmuson Library

(ABOVE) PRESIDENT BUNNELL PUTS THE
*"torch of knowledge" to the annual freshman
bonfire after World War II.*

(LEFT) PROFESSOR LOLA TILLY'S CAMP COOKERY COURSE
*taught many gold miners and University of Alaska students to
fend for themselves over a stove or a campfire. Professor Tilly,
like other female instructors, had been forced to resign when
she got married in 1937, due to President Bunnell's refusal in
the prewar years to employ married women. However, with the
labor shortages of World War II, the old prohibition
disappeared and she returned. Among those in this postwar
camp cookery class were Lothar Fieg on the left, Leo Mark
Anthony in the center, and Phil Hardy on the far right.*

Lola Tilly

THE EMERITUS DAY CEREMONIES ON JULY 1, 1949
*marked the official retirement of Charles Bunnell after
28 years as president. Early that morning, dozens of
alumni and other dignitaries, dressed in academic
robes, gathered with Bunnell around the Alaska
Agricultural College and School of Mines cornerstone
in front of the Main Building. Alumni wearing
academic gowns carried placards announcing the year
of their graduation.*

AT THE 1949 EMERITUS DAY CEREMONIES,
Bunnell and his replacement, Terris Moore, stand together near the right side of the cornerstone. Third from the left is Territorial Governor Ernest Gruening.

University Relations Collection, Rasmuson Library

(RIGHT) THE UNIVERSITY HAD FEW *Native students in its early years. In Bunnell's final year as president—1949— Arthur Nagozruk, Jr. became the first full-blooded Eskimo to graduate from the University of Alaska. Nagozruk posed with Bunnell at commencement, and the president used this picture for his Christmas card that year.*

Charles Bunnell Collection, Rasmuson Library

(BELOW) FRAIL-LOOKING, 71-YEAR-OLD *President Emeritus Charles Bunnell hands the key to the university to his 41-year-old successor, President Terris Moore on July 1, 1949. Sitting beneath the portrait of Bunnell painted by Eustace P. Ziegler is territorial governor Ernest Gruening.*

Neil Davis Collection, Rasmuson Library

(ABOVE) ARCHITECT'S SKETCH OF THE GEOPHYSICAL *Institute, a 1949 state-of-the-art scientific research facility, which included a radar lab, a solar telescope, an astronomical dome, an ionospheric lab, a spectroscopic lab, a seismological lab, and the institute library.*

Neil Davis Collection, Rasmuson Library

(BELOW) LAYING OF THE CORNERSTONE OF THE *Geophysical Institute on July 1, 1949 with full Masonic ceremonies. Institute director Stuart L. Seaton is at the microphone. Left to right: Frank Mapleton, Charles E. Bunnell, C. J. Woofter, Lou Joy, James Jorgensen, Les Nerland, and Seaton.*

University Relations Collection, Rasmuson Library

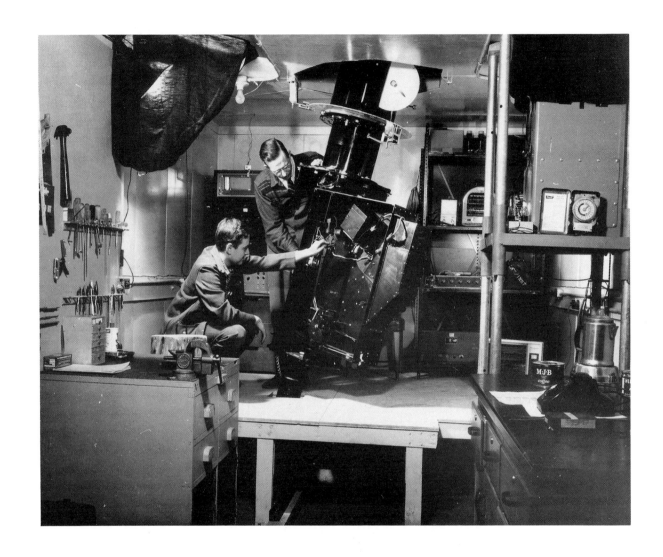

DR. KENNETH CLARK (UNIVERSITY OF *Washington) and Gerald Romick adjust the spectrometer in the old Geophysical Institute.*

University Relations Collection, Rasmuson Library

ERNIE STILTNER ON THE RIGHT, *Al George in the center, and John Henshaw lying on his back ostensibly scan the skies for Sputnik on top of the old Geophysical Institute. The Eielson Building is in the background.*

Geophysical Institute

(BELOW) RON DEWITT, CHUCK *Deehr, and Gene Wescott greet their fellow student, Syun Akasofu, upon his return to Fairbanks after a 1959 trip to Colorado with Sydney Chapman. Their greeting placards said, "Welcome Back" and "Kill the Dean of Students!"*

Geophysical Institute

173

PAUL GREIMANN'S BUS
*en route from Fairbanks
to the university.*

Paul Greimann Collection,
Rasmuson Library

(LEFT) PRESIDENT EMERITUS CHARLES *Bunnell in the early 1950s.*

Historical Photograph Collection, Rasmuson Library

(BELOW) THE DEDICATION OF THE ALFRED H. *Brooks Memorial Mines Building in July 1952 commemorated the 50th anniversary of Felix Pedro's discovery of gold in the Fairbanks mining district, and brought together the first three presidents of the University of Alaska for a rare photograph. Standing with a commemorative bust of Felix Pedro on the steps of the new building are from left to right: Patrick O'Neill representing the Pioneers of Alaska, dean of the School of Mines Earl Beistline, Regent William O'Neill, President Terris Moore, dean of the University Neal Hosley, Italian consul general Filippo Falconi, President Emeritus Charles Bunnell, president of the board of regents Andrew Nerland, and the first dean of the School of Mines, Ernest Patty.*

University Relations Collection, Rasmuson Library

(RIGHT) LEADING THE FAST BREAK, GUARD
Chuck Milles goes in for a lay-up in a 1957 game at
the university gym. The Polar Star claimed that the
new varsity uniforms, which the team began to wear
in 1954, were "really flashy and will remind fans of
the famed Harlem Globetrotter dress, or some similar
high-powered outfit."

University Relations Collection, Rasmuson Library

(BELOW) THE 1957–1958 BASKETBALL TEAM
hears a few instructions from Coach Dick Strait
during a time out in the university gym. From left to
right: Stan Gabriel (from behind), Coach Strait, Joe
Tremarello, and Bob Sliter. The bench warmers—
obviously not listening to the coach— are from left to
right: Gordon "Beans" Van Campan, Bob "Mouse"
Harris, and Ron Henckel.

University Relations Collection, Rasmuson Library

176

THE SPORT OF SPRINGTIME ON THE UNIVERSITY *of Alaska campus was mudball or "mud hockey" on the water-logged dirt inside the hockey rink. In the background is Vets Dorm.*

University Relations Collection, Rasmuson Library

A 1950s FORMAL DANCE IN THE UNIVERSITY GYM.

University Relations Collection, Rasmuson Library

PRESIDENT TERRIS MOORE AND THE BOARD OF *Regents present the university's 1953 budget request to members of the senate finance commxittee in Juneau. Seated around the table from left to right: President Moore, Senators John Butrovich, Howard Lyng, James Nolan, and John Gorsuch, Regent Elmer*

Rasmuson, and Don Irwin of the Palmer experiment station. Standing from left to right: Regents Walter Stuart, William O'Neill, Andrew Nerland, and Leo Rhode.

University Relations Collection, Rasmuson Library

ERNIE WOLFF, A 1941 GRADUATE OF THE UNIVERSITY *and former head of the College Observatory, taught mining and geology. A long-time resident on the College flats near "Wolff Run," he helped build the College Inn in 1945.*

University Relations Collection, Rasmuson Library

EXTRA!!

POLAR STAR

Associated Students of the University of Alaska, Inc.

PUBLISHED BY STUDENTS   FOR STUDENT INFORMATION

VOL. VIII, NO. 5   COLLEGE, ALASKA   FRIDAY, OCTOBER 24, 1952   Price 10 Cents

DR. MOORE RESIGNS

★ ★ ★ Had Previous Experience In Territory; Was In Finances

Dr. Moore came to the University in 1949, after having visited the Territory several times in the 1930s with mountain climbing expeditions.

For two years, 1937-39, he was instructor in finance and accounting in the college of business administration of the University of California at Los Angeles.

During the war, as consultant to the quartermaster general, he received a citation for outstanding contributions to the war effort after participating in a military expedition on Mt. McKinley in 1942.

Dr. Moore is a graduate of William College with the degree of Doctor of Commercial Science from Harvard University. In 1940 Dr. Moore was treasurer of Williams R. McAdams Inc., wholesale office supplies and printing business in Boston. Following that he served as financial and accounting advisor to the governors of Massachusetts and New Jersey.

From 1945 to 1948 Dr. Moore held the position of President of the Boston Museum of Science, and was treasurer of the Museum at the time he was named to head the University of Alaska.

He formally took over the University on July 1, 1949, at ceremonies honoring Dr. Bunnel's years of service.

Dr. Moore is a licensed pilot, and has become known throughout the Territory as the "Flying President."

Mrs. Moore is a graduate of Vassar. The Moores have two children, Katrina, a freshman here at the University, and Henry, in school in Fairbanks.

HOCKEY TEAM PRACTICE ON NOVEMBER 1ST

WILL END FOUR YEARS AS HEAD OF UNIVERSITY ON JULY 1ST, 1953

★ ★ ★ ★ ★ ★ NO SUCCESSOR NAMED TO FILL POST

★ ★ ★ ★ ★ ★ Board Confirms Action In Letter; Bestows Title of "Professor of the University"; Mentions Project

The resignation of Dr. Terris Moore, University president, was announced in a press release issued this morning by the Office of the President. The press release is printed below. THE POLAR STAR will print a more detailed story on the Regent's meeting in a later issue.

The first piece of business at the Board of Regents meeting at the University of Alaska today, was the presentation of the Biennial Report of the President, and presentation of the Budget Request of University Department Heads for the coming Biennial.

Copy of President Moore's letter of transmittal, and the Regents' letter of acceptance, made a part of the Regents' Minutes, are as follows:

October 15, 1952

"President, Secretary and Members of the Board of Regents University of Alaska College, Alaska

Dear Sirs and Madam:

"I have the honor to transmit herewith the outline of the Biennial Report of the President of the University of Alaska for the period July 1, 1950, to June 30, 1952, and the Budget Requests of University Department Heads for the 1953-55 Biennial. The usual subject matter required by Territorial Law is covered in the Biennial report.

"Additionally I feel that at the October 20, 1952 Regents meeting we should make definite and public the understanding reached at our May meeting, concerning effective continuity of administration after I have completed my best efforts in the work of the University President. As we know, it has proven impractical for me to take an adequate and normal vacation with my family, since the summer of 1950, despite your generous urging. With new phases of our long-range program still before us, I know the burden of being President will continue to be heavy, and I believe that by the summer of 1953 the University will best be served if at that time we are ready with a successor promptly to carry forward the work of this office. Also I believe that the opportunities in our proposed Mount Wrangell Inter-university Research Project are so promising that I can most usefully make my net contribution to the University by devoting full attention to it beginning in the early summer of 1953.

"Specifically, I urge that at this coming Regents meeting you announce there will be a vacancy in the Office of President effective say July 1, 1953. And that you promptly issue a call now for candidates in order to provide adequate time meanwhile to select the best possible individual for an effective overlap next year so the new Administration may continue to move the University forward without delay.

I continue to look forward to the work of the President of the University for the year remaining ahead of us, and to the satisfaction of serving under you as friends and fellow Alaskans.

Faithfully yours, Terris Moore, President."

October 23, 1952

"Dr. Terris Moore, President University of Alaska College, Alaska

Dear Mr. Moore,

"Your letter of transmittal of the Biennial Report which has outlined your future plans is hereby acknowledged. It is a decision which the Board of Regents after careful deliberation and discussion with you, reluctantly accepts.

"The Board of Regents recognizes the great contributions you have made during the years of your service as President of the University of Alaska. During your tenure of office, high quality standards have been maintained; the physical plant has been doubled; the overall student enrollment has been tripled by the addition of the military branches and summer school; a substantial increase has taken place in research activities so fundamental to an institution of higher learning and finally the introduction of modern methods of academic procedure and democracy have strengthened the administrative departments, during this time there has been a greater appreciation on the part of many more Alaskans of the significant value of its only institution of higher learning. We recognize the contribution of Mrs. Moore and your family in bringing a wholesome social atmosphere and enthusiasm to the campus, which has proven to be so worthwhile.

"We are fully aware that these accomplishments are an index of the heavy administrative load which you have carried and we accept the proposals you make regarding your future work for the University. The Mt. Wrangell Inter-university Reasearch Observatory, the project which you have outlined to us, we recognize, will help the University of Alaska greatly. By utilizing your ability we can actively participate in this important Arctic Research Project. With this in mind and as evidence of our appreciation of your services, we hereby bestow upon you the title of Professor of the University to be conveyed upon you at the time of the transfer of your present responsibility to that of your successor.

Under this plan you may carry out the responsibilities of the University of Alaska in the conduct of the Mt. Wrangell Inter-university Research Observatory.

"The very best wishes are extended to you and Mrs. Moore in this field of endeavor and with it goes our sincere satisfaction that you will continue to be associated with us in this new capacity.

Cordially yours, The Board of Regents, Andrew Nerland, President."

Reached for comment, President Moore said: "I believe that at this stage of the University's development, the work of the Presidency is something like a relay race. Four men running quarters can do a mile much faster than one man attempting the entire race alone.

"Also I would like to say I naturally appreciate the kind letter the Regents have written but wish to add that I claim no particular credit for the gains which have been made during my administration of the University. The credit goes to the generous citizens of Alaska who have made the funds available, to the hardworking faculty, scientists; and the assistants in administration and also, in no small measure, to many students in the University as well."

Starvation Gulch Dance In Eight Days

It's coming, there are only eight days left, are you ready for it? Well, what is it? You mean you don't know? You fool, it is the annual Starvation Gulch Dance. It is held every year at this time, one of the best dances of the semester, you better go get yourself a costume and make ready for the big event.

This dance, sponsored by the ASUA, is under the direction of Mr. Dean Hughes, President of the ASUA.

Remember the date now, November 1, the place, in the gym, and the event, THE STARVATION GLCH DANCE. Admission free to all ASUA members, $2.40 to all others, Non ASUA members will be required to have dates.

With the committees working full time you can be assured that we'll have full details in our GULCH-BIRTHDAY POLAR STAR out next week—watch for it.

(LEFT) THE FIRST "EXTRA" IN THE HISTORY OF THE
Polar Star *in October 1952 announced President
Terris Moore's departure. Moore actually continued
in office until formally replaced by Ernest Patty a
year later.*

Rasmuson Library

(ABOVE) MEMBERS OF THE BOARD OF REGENTS IN
1953, *when Ernest Patty replaced Terris Moore. Back
row from left to right: William O'Neill, Dr. C. Earl
Albrecht, former President Terris Moore, newly
installed President Ernest Patty, Elmer Rasmuson,
and Leo Rhode. Seated: Mike Walsh, Audrey Loftus,
Andrew Nerland, and Walter Stuart.*

University Relations Collection, Rasmuson Library

(LEFT, TOP) PRESIDENT PATTY (AT CENTER) AND *Les Nerland (right) congratulate Elmer Rasmuson on his elevation in May 1956 to the post of president of the Board of Regents, a position he would hold for 13 years.*

University Relations Collection, Rasmuson Library

(LEFT, BOTTOM) TO PROMOTE THE UNIVERSITY OF *Alaska, the university commissioned production in 1957 of a 27-minute color film called "Frontiers of Learning." President Patty is shown here during the shooting of the film with Joseph Raskie, the director of the film company. Inspired by "Frontiers of Learning," students at the university produced their own home-made "underground" film about love life on campus called "Frontiers of Yearning."*

University Relations Collection, Rasmuson Library

(BELOW) ROTC GRADUATES IN 1958 BEING *"pinned" are from left to right: Oscar Kawagley, Ira Blake McKinley, and Bernard "Happy" Holtrop. Standing in the rear is ROTC professor Col. K. C. Haycraft.*

ROTC Department

(ABOVE) STUDENT JOHN OWEN *studies in his dorm room.*

Alumni Services Collection, Rasmuson Library

(LEFT) DRUSKA CARR SCHAIBLE, DEAN OF *Women and the head of the university's Department of Biological Sciences, stands near her office in 1956. Schaible, a 1938 University of Alaska graduate, was the stepdaughter of Dean William E. Duckering and the sister-in-law of theatre professor Lee Salisbury. On November 23, 1957 she was killed in a $1 million fire that swept through the Lathrop Building in downtown Fairbanks. Schaible Auditorium in the Bunnell Building was later named in her memory.*

University Relations Collection, Rasmuson Library

(BELOW) AFTER HER DEATH IN THE 1957 *Lathrop Building fire, the university launched a memorial fund drive to create a scholarship in Druska Carr Schaible's memory. Her former students and colleagues are shown here in 1958 addressing envelopes for the drive in the typewriting laboratory. Seated from left to right: Joan Hume, Sandra Dalman, Joan Berry, and Irene Bechtol. Standing from left are: Virginia Walkley, Professor Minnie Wells, and Robert Kapelowitz.*

University Relations Collection, Rasmuson Library

THE 1956 GROUND-BREAKING CEREMONIES DURING *the construction of Wickersham Hall, with Vets Dorm to the right and the Geophysical Institute barely visible on the left. Among those at the ceremony were: chemistry professor Nalin Mukherjee (fourth from the left); Ivar Skarland (fifth from the left); university engineer Richard Russell and President Patty (holding the blueprints); Margarita Simpson (sitting on the* *bulldozer seat); history professor Donald Moberg (behind Simpson, in the distance with his head visible above the crowd); Helen Atkinson (holding the blue shovel with the Big Dipper painted on the end); Dean Neil Hosley (standing next to Atkinson); and Ann Tremarello (behind Hosley).*

University Relations Collection, Rasmuson Library

(LEFT) THE NEW STUDENT UNION BUILDING *(now called Constitution Hall) where fifty-five delegates wrote the constitution of the future State of Alaska in seventy-five days in 1955–1956.*

Alfred P. McNeill

(BELOW) CONSTITUTIONAL CONVENTION DELEGATES *at work in Constitution Hall, with William A. Egan presiding at the raised table in the front of the room. The massive tape machine in the far corner recorded all of their public deliberations.*

Ralph Rivers Collection, Rasmuson Library

(LEFT) DELEGATES TO THE CONSTITUTIONAL *Convention ate together in the university cafeteria. Former territorial governor Ernest Gruening, who gave the keynote address to the delegates on November 9, 1955, walks away with a full tray. Behind him is Laura Lofgren, a freshman student from Homer, and delegate Yule Kilcher. In the foreground on the extreme right, his face partially in the dark, is convention president William A. Egan.*

University Relations Collection, Rasmuson Library

ON FEBRUARY 5, 1956, CONSTITUTIONAL
Convention president William A. Egan signs his name
to the constitution of the future state of Alaska.
Though the delegates wrote the constitution in the
Student Union Building, they signed it in the
university gymnasium, the largest room on campus; in
memory of the occasion, the building is now called
Signers' Hall.

Ralph Rivers Collection, Rasmuson Library

THE QUEEN AND KING OF THE
*1956 Christmas Dance: Ann Maxwell
(Tremarello) and Joe Tremarello.*

University Relations Collection, Rasmuson Library

STUMPING FOR REPUBLICAN
*candidates in the soon to be born State
of Alaska, Vice President Richard M.
Nixon, his wife Patricia Nixon, and
their two children, Julie and Tricia,
visited the University of Alaska campus
in November 1958. The vice president
spoke to the students at an assembly in
the gymnasium describing the way to
win the Cold War. After his speech,
ASUA president James Boyd gave
Nixon two Alaskan dolls for Julie and
Tricia, and the Nixons examined
artifacts in the University Museum.*

University Relations Collection, Rasmuson Library

THE BURIAL OF BEER AND TRADITION ON MARCH 22, 1957. *Herman Nurnburger holds the flashlight for master of ceremonies Peter Schust. Onlookers include Mary Ann Kegler, Larry Irving, Ted Kegler, Norbert Skinner, and Margarita Simpson as the nun.*

THE CHORUS MEMBERS AT THE GRAVESIDE OF *tradition, using beer bottles for candle holders, included Anne Huber, Gladys Andrews, Hazel Owen, Madge McNavish, Dona McKechnie, and Anna May Grenac. The "funeral dirge" they sang was a student composition—to the tune of "Rock of Ages"—entitled "Traditions Farewell."*

> *Prohibition—Woe is me!*
> *Old tradition's gone you see.*
> *Engineers and Miners too*
> *Weep for their forbidden brew.*
> *Since the law has been laid down,*
> *Coke shall now our sorrows drown.*
> *We knew it was too good to last,*
> *When we had our busts and blasts.*

> *On our picnics, hayrides gay*
> *Now we'll bless the Good Old Days.*
> *Why did this happen to us?*
> *Nothing left to do but cuss.*
> *In the span of four short years*
> *Many things have brought us tears.*
> *When we used to brew our own,*
> *Old Main Dorm was just like home.*
> *Now this place has lost its jazz.*
> *Oh! It's just like Alcatraz.*
> *Sadie Hawkins was our dream*
> *When Olympia reigned supreme.*
> *Now together hear us wail;*
> *No more nights to spend in jail.*
> *From now on the Gulch is dry;*
> *Memories here beneath us lie.*

THE FULLY ARMED "DIS-HONOR GUARD" OF THE "Chena Ridge Militia," described by the Polar Star *as "an independent army of independent mercinary (sic) troops, (at present unemployed)," stands at attention at the 1957 tradition stone ceremony in front of Constitution Hall. Standing from left to right: piper Junius "Sparky" Jewett, Charles "Chaz" Lewis, Ben Zeller, Niilo Koponen, who later represented the university district in the state legislature for a decade,* and Larry Irving Jr. Kneeling: Mary Ann Kegler and Frank Stevens. Niilo Koponen said later that the "guard of dishonor" had been specially organized for the sad occasion. The vehicle in the background, Frank Stevens' U.S. Navy Pet Four Surplus Special, was decorated with the Chena Ridge Militia Emblem, "a ceramic container of homebrew overflowing," and their slogan: "In Hoc fer Plenti."

Alaska Airlines-Henry Kaiser Collection, Rasmuson Library

191

(LEFT) RON COSGRAVE, THE UNIVERSITY OF *Alaska's first chemical engineering graduate, performing a lab experiment in the 1950s. Cosgrave served as Charles Bunnell's personal attendant in the aging president's final years. In the 1970s, Cosgrave and another University of Alaska alumnus, Bruce Kennedy, assumed control of Alaska Airlines and transformed it into one of the most highly rated regional carriers in the industry.*

Alaska Airlines-Henry Kaiser Collection,
Rasmuson Library

(TOP RIGHT) AFTER BLASTING WITH *dynamite, student miners in 1957–1958 shovel out loose rock in the University of Alaska's practice mining tunnel underneath the campus. From the 1920s to the 1960s, mining students studied blasting, drilling, and underground mine surveying in the College Mine, and drove the six and a half foot high tunnel nearly the length of two football fields into College Hill. The blasting ceased in the early 1960s, as the university turned to the Bluebird Mine in Ester and later Tury Anderson's Silver Fox Mine for practical training. In the 1980s, road construction near the university power plant permanently sealed off the entrance to the abandoned mining shaft in College Hill.*

Rasmuson Library

(LOWER RIGHT) THE 1957 UNIVERSITY OF *Alaska Rifle Team. First row, left to right: Doug Barber, Joe Usibelli, Bill Ross, Wayne Hanson, Pete Weimer, and Marshall Ponko. Second row: Ron Rhodes, Tim Spencer, Fred Tampke, Don Able, Winfield Beach, Lonnie Heiner, and Roy Johnson.*

Rasmuson Library

(LEFT) CLAUS-M. NASKE WORKS ON *a term paper in his room in Harriet Hess Hall in 1959.*

Claus-M. Naske

193

THE LOUNGE IN WICKERSHAM HALL IN THE LATE 1950S.

Charles Keim

A FEW MEMBERS OF THE *University of Alaska's touring Choir of the North at the Fairbanks airport in the late 1950s. On the left is Glenn R. Bergh, music professor and director of the choir. Second from the right is Roxie Bergh, assistant director, and on the far right is Bill Boucher.*

University Relations Collection, Rasmuson Library

NOTED ALASKAN ARTIST AND UNIVERSITY ART
*professor, C. "Rusty" Heurlin, lectures
to a class in 1956.*

University Relations Collection, Rasmuson Library

A 1959 AERIAL VIEW OF THE RAPIDLY GROWING *campus, with the new $2.9 million Bunnell Building under construction in the foreground. During Ernest Patty's seven-year presidency, the physical plant of the university grew by 650%.*

Historical Photograph Collection, Rasmuson Library

DORMITORY SPACE TRIPLES IN THE 1960S
*Bartlett Hall, the third and final dormitory on
Rainey Ridge or upper campus, under construction
in October 1968. The central core housed all the
utilities, while preformed slabs were positioned
around the perimeter to form dormitory rooms.*

University Relations Collection, Rasmuson Library

The Boom Years 1959–1973

Across the nation in the late 1950s, university administrators viewed the approach of the 1960s with alarm. They had good reason to be fearful: millions of "Baby Boomers" were coming. "Here come the War Babies!" read the headline in a 1957 *Time Magazine* article, "U.S. Colleges Are Ill Prepared for Their Invasion." As the president of Haverford College confessed in the article, with so many more qualified students applying for admission every year, he sometimes doubted if he could have admitted himself.[1]

The rush of students who came of age beginning in the late 1950s descended on the University of Alaska as well. In 1957, the *Fairbanks Daily News-Miner* warned: "the University of Alaska is going to get part of this flood from the States. Students who cannot get into Stateside universities will turn to the Alaska university. In addition, Alaska is now experiencing a rapid population growth . . . . All of which means that our university is going to be 'caught in the deluge,' of the incoming tidal wave of university students."[2]

In 1959, due to the ever-increasing numbers of students enrolling at the University of Alaska, the regents established the first minimum standards for entrance to the university; henceforth Alaskan high school students had to carry a "C" average or better for admission, while non-Alaskan students would be required to take the standardized ACT test.[3]

The new stream of young students, together with Alaska's admission as the 49th state to the union in January 1959, indicated that enrollment at Fairbanks could double within three or four years. "So far as we know," President Patty reported to the people of Alaska in 1959, "no other university has ever doubled its enrollment in such a short period. We must plan now to house these students, to provide dining facilities and to provide faculty and classrooms" to avoid total chaos.[4]

Elmer Rasmuson, president of the board of regents, pushed his fellow regents and the administration hard to create a thorough but realistic long-range plan for the university so that the institution could begin to chart a course for the future instead of bouncing from one crisis to the next. "There is too much hand wringing and repetition of our obvious problems," Rasmuson told President Patty in 1958, "and too little specific and objective programming."[5]

To prepare for the coming surge in the size of the student body, the university administration and the board of regents used a $30,000 Ford Foundation grant in 1959 to begin developing a new master campus and development plan—including a three-dimensional model "intended as a guide for campus

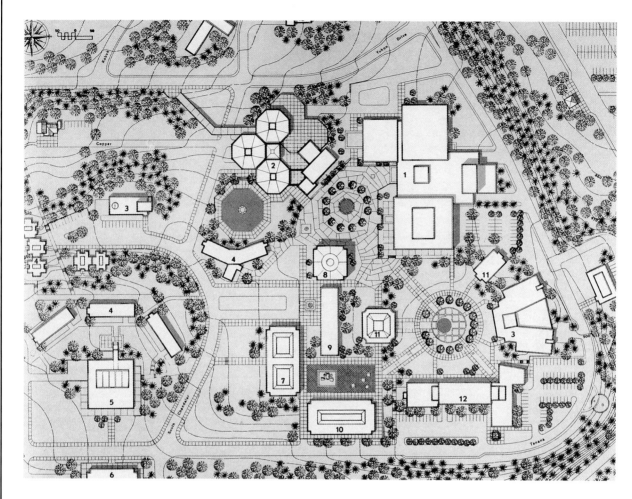

Rasmuson Library

building for the next 50 years." Several leading experts, including Dr. James MacConnell, Director of the School Planning Bureau of Stanford University, and noted San Francisco architects Lawrence Lackey, Donald Knoff, and Mario Ciampi, designed the plan over the course of a year, with input from university administrators, faculty and staff.[6]

As envisioned by the "Stanford Plan," the campus would eventually grow to as many as 5,000 students by 1975. (In fact, total enrollment at UAF would not top 5,000 until the restructuring of the university system in 1987.) The architects suggested that the Fairbanks campus—which was ten times larger in area than some schools with ten times as many students—could be developed with either a dispersed collection of smaller buildings or a concentrated grouping of larger structures "joined by underground passageways."

The regents unanimously preferred the dispersed or "open" campus plan with facilities spread out over

Campus planning in the 1960s

The "Stanford Plan" served as the basic blueprint for the planning of the UA campus. It was modified in the 1968 long-range development plan, which envisioned the campus core as a "closely knit pedestrian precinct" offering a "series of interesting spaces" and "stimulating environmental experiences." The 1968 plan is a close approximation of the campus as it exists today, though two of the proposed buildings (No. 6—a new museum and No. 7—a statewide administration building) were located on West Ridge, while two others were never constructed—a law-pharmacy-nursing school (10) and a general use facility on the site of the old gymnasium, now Signers' Hall (11).

The main open space, the circular Bunnell Memorial Plaza with a fountain at its center, was to be ringed by an "arbor of birch trees through which walks from many directions would penetrate, (and) would have as its focus the pool, sculpture, and the play of water." The sculpture was never built; wags dubbed the pool "Wood's Hole."

The structures on the plan included:

1. Library and Fine Arts Complex
2. Campus Activities Center (Wood Center)
3. Duckering Building and Chapman Building
4. Dormitories and "Modular Units"
5. Commons (Lola Tilly Dining Commons)
6. Museum
7. Administration, Statewide Services
8. High-rise general classrooms (Gruening Building)
9. Eielson Building
10. Law, Pharmacy and Nursing School
11. Brooks Building; and a new facility on the site of what is today Signer's Hall
12. Bunnell Building
13. Student Health Center

Campus planners recognized it as "manifestly impossible" to provide enough parking on the hilltop campus. One solution, first recommended in the early 1960s, called for the parking lot on the flats below the Library and Fine Arts Complex to be linked by "escalators or a moving sidewalk in a tunnel or covered passageway." Another suggestion was the eventual construction of a multilevel parking garage at the bottom of the bluff. Neither plan was ever enacted. The escalator proposal resurfaced thirty years later in 1992, but was quickly dropped due to strong public opposition over the estimated price tag of three million dollars.

a total area of at least 154 acres; this included 63.5 acres of residential space, 40 acres for recreation and athletics, 21 acres for a central academic core, and 20 acres of parking lots. The board reasoned that an open campus would retain more "vistas, light and air" than a collection of skyscrapers linked by underground tunnels.[7]

Under the open plan, the nucleus of the academic core was to be a park-like, "spacious landscaped 'green'" encircling Wickersham Hall, Constitution Hall, and the Eielson Building. On the three-dimensional model, these three buildings were virtually lost in a forest of birch trees. Surrounding the "green" was a "three-minute-academic circle" in which all classrooms would be within a three-minute walking distance of each other across a "pedestrian preserve." Automobile traffic would be routed to the periphery. Beyond the three-minute circle was a "six-minute circle," encompassing future residence halls, while research institutes "unrelated to

A Changing of the Guard
A 1960 banquet at the Travelers' Inn honoring retiring president Ernest Patty and welcoming his successor, William R. Wood. From left: Elmer E. Rasmuson, president of the board of regents; Neva Egan, wife of Governor William A. Egan; incoming president Wood; Ernest Patty at the podium.

Historical Photograph Collection, Rasmuson Library

undergraduate instruction" would be at a more distant location on the top of what became known as West Ridge. Though the Stanford Plan was to be modified and adjusted over the years (for instance the "green" at the center of campus never materialized), it nevertheless established the basic outlines of the overall campus as it exists today.

In addition to mapping the future layout of the university campus, the plan also recommended the reorganization of the university's administrative structure with the creation of six academic colleges and urged—as Charles Bunnell himself would have done—that the university build on its strength as an Arctic institution. "As the 'farthest north' University in the world," the plan stated, "the University of Alaska is uniquely located geographically for the pursuit of studies in Arctic and Sub-Arctic research . . . . Already there exists a scientific community at the University of Alaska that would do credit to a complex institution of many times the size of the present student population. The existence of an *extra-ordinary* scientific research activity can make a tremendous contribution to what otherwise might be an *ordinary* teaching situation."[8]

The task of helping to draft the Stanford Plan, and to make its recommendations become a reality, fell to William Ransom Wood, 53, the former academic vice president (and acting president) of the University of Nevada at Reno. Dr. Wood took over as the fourth president of the University of Alaska upon Ernest Patty's retirement in the summer of 1960.

William R. Wood attracted the attention of the regents for several reasons. An experienced administrator and teacher, with several edited books of readings to his credit, Wood had earned a Ph.D. in English literature at the University of Iowa in 1939; his dissertation was entitled "Pagan Mythology and the Christian Religion in the Poetry and Prose of John Keats." Following his service in the U.S. Naval Reserve in the South Pacific during World War II, he worked as a teacher, community college director and school superintendent in Illinois. He became an education specialist with the U.S. Office of Education before moving on to become dean of statewide development at the University of Nevada Reno in 1954.

The University of Nevada, a statewide institution in a large and sparsely populated region with a harsh climate, seemed to have many comparable problems to those facing the University of Alaska. "But what probably tipped the scales," Elmer Rasmuson later said of the decision to hire Wood, "was when we heard he had been crawling around the utilidors for first-hand investigation while on campus."[9]

Students and faculty quickly learned that Dr. Wood was irrepressible and nearly inexhaustible; he is still the only president in the history of the university to have done the Equinox Marathon—he walked it twice. The University of Alaska never had a more forceful cheerleader. While striding across campus or standing in line at the post office, he happily smiled and greeted everyone in sight. Wood liberally sprinkled his speeches and writings with rapid-fire ideas, italics, and exclamation points. Life at "65 North," as he liked to say, was a pioneering adventure, where so much had never been done before, and opportunities were lying dormant, waiting for

202

the right person to come along and take advantage of them. William Wood was a builder and a doer who relished the feeling of accomplishment that came from creating something new.

In Wood's inaugural address in October 1960, the new president listed a few of the opportunities that the University of Alaska had to offer. "Where but in Alaska could one find a single university with a fur farm, a musk-ox herd, a square mile of glacier, several tons of bones of prehistoric animals, an ice station on the Polar ice cap four hundred-odd miles North of land's end, a world-famous scientist with a special alarm system to awaken him whenever the aurora borealis flashes across our Northern skies, two satellite tracking stations, no social fraternities,

no sororities, and no losing football team for the Alumni to use as an excuse for firing the President."[10]

The presidency of the University of Alaska drove William R. Wood—like Charles Bunnell before him—to poetry. In a collection of Wood's poems published in 1983 entitled *Not From Stone* (i.e. from Wood) he confessed that he started scribbling verses as Christmas greetings soon after he became president. The poems had never been written with publication in mind. Some had been lost, and, Wood confessed, "It is probable that the present publication could have been improved by losing a few more permanently." A couplet from a composition called "To Be Or To Do" succinctly summarized his philosophy for a happy life:

To find yourself, the real you,
Just do and do and do

Another ditty he wrote reads in part:

Nothing clever.
Just Endeavor. [11]

Besides poetry, Wood also shared with Charles Bunnell a love of athletic competition that helped shape their philosophies of leadership. While Bunnell was a quarterback and a shortstop, the 6' 3" Wood was a former professional basketball player in the Midwestern leagues who once played nine seasons for barnstorming teams like the Michigan Meteors and the Springfield Kellys, while also buying and selling on the side for a sporting goods company. [12]

Whether on the basketball court or behind the president's desk, Wood believed that the needs of the team had to come above individual statistics or accomplishments. Without public-spirited citizens willing to sacrifice for the greater good of all, no institution could survive. "Somehow we have managed to weight the balance a bit too much in favor of the rights of the individual . . . ," Wood cautioned in his inaugural address. "At some point . . . the good of the *One* individual merges with or becomes subordinated to the good of the Many people." [13]

Of course, not all members of the university community would always share Wood's opinion of what constituted the general welfare. When President Bunnell was in office, few questioned the rights of a university president to exercise authority as he or she saw fit. By the 1960s that was no longer the case.

The GE College Bowl

In the early 1960s, nearly twenty million television viewers tuned in at 5:30 P.M. every Sunday night to watch the CBS General Electric College Bowl. Shown opposite "The Lone Ranger," GE's "half-hour intellectual basketball game" showcased teams of students from two colleges or universities each week, using the same hype and gimmicks of televised

SANDRA SCOTT   BILL STERN

F ALASKA

In early 1963, the GE College Bowl invited the University of Alaska to compete. Academic Vice President Howard Cutler recommended against going because he thought the university was "neither best known nor strongest in the areas from which the questions are drawn." Cutler stated that if the University of Alaska team did agree to field a team, it "should be developed with the same practice and rigor with which any football or basketball team is trained."

Despite Cutler's reservations, ASUA responded so positively that President Wood accepted the invitation. Arthur Wills of the English department agreed to coach the team. Out of a field of twenty-five applicants, Wills chose four finalists: Ben Harding, captain, whose strengths were history and geography; Jane Schaible, an expert on American and English literature; Sandra Scott (Stringer), whose specialties were the natural sciences, and biblical and children's stories; and Bill Stern, the team's foreign language specialist. "To provide the team with practice in hitting the buzzer quickly when they know the answer," the *News-Miner* reported, "the Electrical Engineering students constructed a simplified model of the buzzer system used on the show."

On Sunday, June 16, 1963, the University of Alaska made its first and only appearance on the GE College Bowl, against defending champion Temple University. The Alaskans won a practice round beforehand, but on the air, Temple dispatched the UA by a score of 280–85. An editorial in Fairbanks' *Jessen's Weekly* praised the UA team for their valiant effort, noting that Temple University's enrollment was thirty times larger than that of the University of Alaska. "Those Easterners can't be any smarter than our students," the editor explained, "but there is no overlooking the fact that they had a greater pool of more sophisticated people from whom to draw their contestants." A half-hour appearance on network television by four of the University of Alaska's top students was victory enough.

college athletics. Host Allen Ludden began the action with a "toss up" question; a referee's whistle signaled the half-time commercial break, and student audiences cheered correct responses. The program became a national phenomenon. *Reader's Digest* claimed in November 1960 that some College Bowl contestants "have become as well known and admired as any All-American fullback."

Wood served as University of Alaska president for thirteen of the most tumultuous years in recent American history. From the election of John F. Kennedy in 1960 to the Watergate crisis in 1973, college students and faculty across the nation—as well as Blacks, women, Native Americans, Hispanics, and gays and lesbians—struggled for greater individual rights, freedom of expression, and shared governing responsibility. Social upheaval and the "credibility gap," in a nation at war with itself over the undeclared war in Vietnam, eroded trust between young and old, polarizing American society in a way that had not occurred since the War Between The States. In such an environment, consensus proved to be impossible. Some students and faculty challenged the very notion of the university as a team, with everyone obliged to pull in the same direction, arguing instead that the institution must not only tolerate but encourage maximum freedom, even if it caused disharmony.

Debate at the University of Alaska over these and other issues—including the Vietnam War, sexual liberation, civil rights, drug use, and the protection of the environment—never generated the level of discord or violence that afflicted other universities. No riots took place on the campus of the University of Alaska. Nevertheless, bitter disagreements over the fundamental social questions of the day provided a stormy backdrop for Wood's tenure as president, a challenging era that marked the most rapid period of growth in the history of the University of Alaska. During this time it evolved into an enormously diverse and complex modern institution. Under President Wood, the little school on College Hill became a genuine university.

One of the first major changes Wood initiated—as recommended by the Stanford Study—was to divide the academic departments of the university into half a dozen colleges composed of disciplines and related professions. The six new colleges included:

Arts and Letters
Behavioral Sciences and Education
Biological Sciences and Renewable Resources
Business, Economics, and Government
Earth Sciences and Mineral Industry
Mathematics, Physical Sciences,
    and Engineering

The reorganization also created a Division of Statewide Services, run by Dean Arthur S. Buswell, to supervise continuing education programs and the growing network of community colleges.

Under the new organizational chart, mining shared the same college with geology, accounting with economics, and electrical engineering with mathematics. This unusual mixture of academic and technical fields was intended to provide students both a greater range of programs from which to choose as well as practical, professional training, generally only available at an institution many times the size of the University of Alaska. President Wood stated that this reorganization, giving the university a structure of colleges, was a historical landmark comparable to the admission of the first students in 1922. It signified the University of Alaska had truly come of age.[14]

The administrative structure of the university also grew more complex. Academic Vice President

George Adams (succeeded in 1963 by economist Howard Cutler) supervised the six colleges, while Vice President for Research and Advanced Study Christian Elvey (succeeded in 1964 by K. M. "Peter" Rae) took primary responsibility for the research and graduate programs.

Enrollment figures tell the story of the university's growth. In September 1960, the total graduate and undergraduate enrollment at the university in Fairbanks was 921 students; by 1970, enrollment had risen to 3,645, an increase of nearly 400%. Three times more students enrolled in the university during Wood's thirteen-year presidency than during the thirty-eight years before he took office. Wood signed nearly four times as many diplomas on the Fairbanks campus as had all three previous presidents put together. Upon his retirement, he pointed out to members of the alumni association that eighty percent of the alumni statewide had received their degrees since 1960.[15]

Paralleling the rapid rise in the numbers of students was the enormous expansion of the university's research mission. President Wood and the board of regents, headed by Elmer Rasmuson, envisioned the University of Alaska—through its research programs—as one of the driving forces in the actual creation of the State of Alaska itself. As the Stanford Plan stated, "Alaska cannot be a great State without an even greater State University, one that is expected to accomplish more than mere teaching."[16]

After almost a century of complete federal control of nearly every aspect of Alaskan life, statehood brought a new level of freedom from U.S. government bureaucrats who had once ruled Alaska. Policy makers and politicians in Juneau suddenly found themselves responsible for governing an area one-fifth the size of the contiguous United States. Resource development, conservation, selection of 103 million acres from the public domain to fulfill the statehood land entitlement, economic diversification, management of fish and game resources, the establishment of a new legal and judicial system, school and highway construction, and other issues were now to be tackled by state officials instead of settled from afar in Washington, D.C. At the same time, Alaska's precariously narrow economic base spelled an uncertain future. As economist George W. Rogers warned in 1962: "Statehood could be either a major contributing cause of Alaska's future economic growth or of its bankruptcy."[17]

President Wood and board president Rasmuson recognized the opportunity for the university to not only provide essential research needed to govern the new state, but also to establish scientific research itself as a basic industry for Alaska. With the United States and the Soviet Union locked in the multi-billion dollar Cold War, the strategic importance of arctic research grew steadily in the 1950s and 1960s. In 1954, the University of Alaska, under contract from the Office of Naval Research in Washington, D.C., took over operation of the Naval Arctic Research Laboratory at Point Barrow, America's flagship station for scientific research in the North. Under Director Max C. Brewer—who once appeared on the television program "What's My Line?"—the University of Alaska's management of NARL gave it a preeminent role among American universities in polar research. By 1966, the University of Alaska had almost as many arctic research projects underway at NARL in the social and biological sciences as the

The outcasts of Poker Flat

About thirty miles north of Fairbanks near Poker Creek lies Poker Flat Research Range, the world's largest land-based rocket range, and the only non-federal, university owned and operated range in existence. In the late 1960s, a team of scientists from the University of Alaska Geophysical Institute, inspired by the original "outcasts of Poker Flat" in Bret Harte's short story, struggled against all odds to build a $90,000 rocket launching pad from scratch on the outskirts of Chatanika.

In 1968–1969 the U.S. Department of Defense needed a site to launch a half-dozen barium-release rockets to simulate atomic bomb debris. Neil Davis of the Geophysical Institute, who had worked on auroral experiments at the sounding-rocket range in Fort Churchill, Manitoba, and had previously surveyed optimum rocket launch sites in Alaska for NASA, convinced the government to launch their simulated nuclear warheads north of Fairbanks.

The Poker Flat site was originally slated to be a "minimal launch facility" used only once; however, after the Defense Department's 1969 experiment, Neil Davis and others at the Geophysical Institute

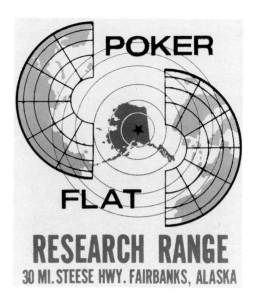

refused to let the site be abandoned. Over the years, new launching pads, support buildings, and related facilities were constructed. By 1991, Poker Flat had launched more than 1,500 meteorological rockets and 236 high-altitude sounding rocket experiments, with a record altitude of 870 miles. Possibilities for the future of Poker Flat include the launching of commercial satellites into polar orbits.

University of Washington and UCLA combined. Advance camps on floating ice islands in the middle of the Arctic Ocean, such as the famed T-3 ("Fletcher's Ice Island") and ARLIS I and ARLIS II (Arctic Research Laboratory Ice Station), enabled marine biologists, meteorologists, oceanographers, and ice physicists at NARL to explore the Arctic Basin.[18]

Wood believed the time was right for the University of Alaska to blossom as a major research

center, and the early 1960s saw the creation of an alphabet soup of research institutes dealing with Alaskan or arctic concerns. The Institute of Marine Science (IMS), headed by Dr. K. M. "Peter" Rae, began operations in 1961. With 6,640 miles of coastline—more than all of the contiguous states combined—and one of the world's largest and most profitable fishing industries, the State of Alaska desperately needed basic and applied research into the problems of the seas. To tackle Alaska's continuing

fiscal and economic problems, the legislature in 1961 authorized the founding of the Institute of Business, Economic and Government Research (today the Institute of Social and Economic Research or ISER)—sometimes called the "Institute for Everything," because its interdisciplinary programs could focus on almost any aspect of Alaskan life. The Institute of Arctic Biology (IAB), specializing in human and animal adaptation to arctic and subarctic conditions, and the Mineral Industry Research Laboratory (MIRL), dedicated to the development of the mining industry, were added in 1963. The Institute of Water Resources (IWR), an interdisciplinary program focusing on all aspects of hydrological studies, opened in 1965, and the Institute of Arctic Environmental Engineering, investigating problems of northern construction, became a full institute in 1969.

The University of Alaska's pioneering venture into big-budget science grew out of the Atomic

Energy Commission's ill-fated Project Chariot, one of the most controversial proposals in modern Alaskan history. Spearheaded by Edward Teller, the Hungarian-born physicist popularly known as the "father of the H-Bomb," Project Chariot originally called for the AEC to blast a harbor near Cape Thompson in northwest Alaska with half a dozen nuclear explosions equivalent to about forty percent of the total firepower expended during World War II. Teller, who received an honorary doctorate at the University of Alaska in 1959, praised Alaskans as "the most reasonable people" in the world for their willingness to experiment with the new technology.[19]

Not all were flattered by Teller's praise, or reassured by his claim that the explosions would not harm the people of the region or the environment. Biologists at the University of Alaska spurred the AEC to sponsor a full-scale scientific investigation of the plant and animal life of the region and study the possible impact the blast might have on the Eskimo population. Teams of University of Alaska scientists under AEC contracts helped compile a detailed assessment of the Cape Thompson region, a prototype of the modern environmental impact statement. Investigators like Don Foote, Les Viereck, Al Johnson, William Pruitt and others realized that radioactive fallout would be soaked up by the tundra's blanket of lichen; these rootless plants, the base of the arctic food chain for both caribou and the Inupiaq people, absorbed nutrients directly from the air and were therefore natural fallout collectors and concentrators.

The AEC shelved Project Chariot in 1962, but "fallout" of a different kind lived on following the aborted scheme. Two vocal critics of Chariot at the University of Alaska, Dr. William Pruitt and Dr.

Leslie Viereck, alleged that they lost their jobs and were blacklisted because they sounded the alarm about the environmental dangers of the proposed blast.[20] Federal indifference to the concerns of Inupiat inhabitants in Northwest Alaska, who were never consulted beforehand about whether they wanted a radioactive hole in the ground at the mouth of Ogotoruk Creek, prompted Alaska Natives to organize politically in order to protect their ancestral lands. Indignation over Chariot helped lead to the formation of the powerful Alaska Federation of Natives in 1966, which finally gave Native Alaskans a united political voice. Environmentalists were also inspired to band together by the threat of Chariot. Looking back on the last several decades, noted American conservationist Barry Commoner credited Project Chariot as the "ancestral birthplace of . . . a large segment of the environmental movement."[21]

In the fall of 1962, the same year that the AEC cancelled Project Chariot, the university's research mission received a boost: Alaskan voters approved $3.5 million in general obligation bonds to begin construction of a proposed "Arctic Research Center" on the ridge west of campus. The idea for this center was originally formulated in a draft proposal to President John F. Kennedy in 1961. Working with both the governor and the state's congressional delegation, the regents and the administration recommended that through cooperative programs with the federal government, the University of Alaska could serve as the focal point for American research in the North. In essence, they urged that the University of Alaska play the role in spearheading America's race to explore the Arctic that the National Aeronautics and Space Administration was playing in the race to the moon.

Separated from the main academic campus by the land which Charles Bunnell had leased to the U.S. Coast and Geodetic Survey in the 1940s, the cow pasture on West Ridge was to become the heart of the university's "Research and Advanced Study Area." On West Ridge the university could freely offer space to U.S. government agencies wishing to construct federally-funded arctic research facilities, thus creating—at minimal cost to the people of the State of Alaska—what regent Elmer Rasmuson styled as "the center of Arctic and sub-Arctic research for a free world."[22] The initial facilities in this arctic research park opened in 1965. They included the $2 million Alaska Water Laboratory of the Arctic Health Research Center, designed to research Alaska's water supply and water pollution problems, and the $2.9 million biological sciences facility (later named the Irving Building in honor of Dr. Laurence Irving, the eminent arctic biologist and founding director of both NARL and the Institute of Arctic Biology). The eight-story Elvey Building opened in 1970 to house the Geophysical Institute, and the distinctive William A. O'Neill Resources Building opened in 1973.

Board president Elmer Rasmuson helped rally an unprecedented level of public support for the university by convincing Alaskans across the state that teaching and research were sound investments for the future. The young state's fiscal outlook was precarious—predicted general revenues for 1965 amounted to only $54.5 million—but nevertheless, until the 1970s, voters approved every single

Castro Vote Rejected by City Council

FAIRBANKS
Daily News-Miner

"America's Farthest North Daily Newspaper" . . . Member of The Associated Press

LATE HOME EDITION

Vol. XL | 15c Per Copy | FAIRBANKS, ALASKA, FRIDAY, OCTOBER 19, 1962 | Twelve Pages | ☆ | 232

RESEARCH COMPLEX AT U OF A

Recount of Ballots Is Ordered Again by City

Ballot Termed 'Wasted' by 5 Seated Councilmen at Special Meeting Last Night; Alexander Still Leads by One

FIDEL CASTRO
Vote Rejected

The Fidel Castro write-in vote that threw the Seat D city councilman's race into a quandary has been rejected by the Fairbanks City Council on grounds that it was a "wasted ballot" Acting City Manager Robert Crow said today.

The action was taken by the five seated councilmen at a special meeting held last night.

In addition, the council ordered a recount of the ballots cast in Tuesday's run-off election between Stanley Sailors and Howard Alexander. The recount will be made tomorrow, with both candidates being invited to watch the ballot counting, Crow said.

As things now stand, Alexander, a Fairbanks car dealer, has 497 votes. Sailors, assistant school principal, has 496 votes. Castro had one vote, which if allowed would have thrown the council seat race into another run-off election.

If tomorrows' ballot count shows that the candidates have the same number of votes as the count now stands, and without the Castro vote, Alexander will have gained the seat by a simple majority of one.

However, there is a chance that the count may reveal new totals for both candidates, at which time the whole picture may change.

News-Miner Open House Scheduled

The second annual News-Miner open house will be held tonight and Saturday afternoon in conjunction with National Newspaper week.

For a first-hand inspection of the News-Miner and Commercial Printing Co. facilities the public has been invited by publisher C. W. Snedden to come to the offices between 7:30 p.m. and 10 p.m. today and from 2 p.m. to 5 p.m. tomorrow afternoon.

COMPLEX AREA—Conferring before a schematic drawing of a proposed scientific research complex for the University of Alaska campus are four principals of the planning group. From left to right they are E. K. Day; Lawrence Lackey, architect for the University; William O'Neill and Elmer Rasmuson, members of the Board of Regents. Day is a representative of the U. S. Department of Health to which the Regents yesterday granted space to construct a water pollution laboratory and other research facilities, the total cost of which will be about $14 million. —News-Miner Staff Photo

Go Ahead Given By Board of Regents

Regents Also Vote to Transfer 10 Acres to Health, Education, Welfare Department for Water Pollution Plant

The go ahead signal was given by the University's Board of Regents yesterday for the construction of the first installation in what ultimately will be a $43 million scientific research complex on the western end of the University hill.

The regents yesterday voted to transfer 10.4 acres of university owned land to the U.S. Department of Health, Education and Welfare for the construction of a water polution laboratory and other planned facilities to house a future Arctic Health Research center.

The water polution lab probably will be started in the spring of 1964, E.K. Day, a representative of the Bureau of State Services for the Public Health Department told the regents. Money for this installation has already been alloted by the Congress. Earlier construction is virtually impossible because the engineering and planning have had to wait until a definite site was agreed upon.

A Solution

The research complex conception was hit upon by the regents as a solution to many requests from federal government, other universities, and private institutions for facilities on or near the campus. Many of the requests either tie in with present university programs or future programs, primarily in the arctic research field. The research complex will offer room to these agencies, who will install their own facilities by and large, with no expense to the University of Alaska or the State of Alaska.

Besides the water pollution laboratory the U.S. Department of Health has definite plans for a $11.5 million Arctic Health Research Center. The total construction planned by this federal department will amount to about $14 million.

Other Facilities

Some other facilities expected to be included in the scientific complex are a biological science center and the U.S. Coast and Geodetic Survey which already has its seismograph and magnetic

(Continued on Page 7, Col. 4)

Kennedy To Send Word To Nikita

WASHINGTON, Oct. 19, (AP)—President Kennedy is reported to be sending word to Soviet Premier Khrushchev that he is willing to have an informal talk on the Berlin crisis and other world issues if Khrushchev decides to come to the United States in the next few weeks.

In a meeting with Khrushchev's Foreign Minister, Andrei A. Gromyko, at the White House, Kennedy, it was learned today, sought to avoid being either encouraging or discouraging on the prospective Khrushchev trip.

Neutral Response

His reaction to feelers about a meeting was described as a neutral response.

Gromyko spent two hours and 15 minutes in the White House conference with Kennedy, Secretary of State Dean Rusk and a number of advisers on both sides.

On leaving the White House, he said the exchange of views with the president on a number of topics, including Berlin, had been useful. Neither the president nor his press office had any comment.

Later, Gromyko and Rusk met at a working dinner at the State Department and continued the discussion for four hours and 15 minutes, until after midnight.

WEATHER

Cloudy with occasional light snow this afternoon, tonight and Saturday. Low tonight 25; high tomorrow 33; low last night 28; high yesterday 33. Temperature at 11 a.m. 30. Sunrise Saturday 6:59 a.m. and sunset 4:12 p.m.

Panamanian Ships Barred

PANAMA Oct. 19, (AP)—President Roberto F. Chiari forbade all ships flying Panama's flag from engaging in any kind of trade with Cuba.

Chiari's decree last night was a major boost to the U.S. campaign to clamp an economic blockade on Fidel Castro's regime. An estimated 8,000 ships fly the Panamanian flag, most of them foreign owned. Foreign owners register their craft in Panama to reap the benefits of lower taxes, lower wage rates and other advantages.

Ships violating the decree will lose their Panamanian registry automatically, Chiari said.

Third Straight Moonshot Fails; Electric Power Out

PASADENA, Calif., Oct. 19, (AP) — The United States' third straight attempt to scout the moon by television has failed—possibly because of damage to the Ranger 5 lunar rocket by radiation from recent high altitude nuclear blasts.

The 755-pound camera-toting spacecraft, launched yesterday from Cape Canaveral, Fla., ran out of electrical power eight hours and 44 minutes later.

Scientists said this meant it would be unable to correct its course and would miss the moon by 300 miles.

It also meant Ranger 5 would not be able to operate its television camera nor to land a quake-measuring device on the moon's surface.

Pasadena's Jet Propulsion Laboratory, which built Ranger 5 and is tracking it through space, said the spacecraft apparently failed to draw electrical power from its wing-like solar panels to operate its instruments.

Its only source of power then was a small reserve battery with a life of eight to nine hours. That battery went dead just as scientists were trying to command the spacecraft to fire a small rocket that would re-aim it at the moon.

Cause of the failure of the solar power system was not announced, but there was unofficial speculation by some space experts that the craft's delicate solar cells could have been damaged by radiation from recent high altitude nuclear blasts over the Pacific.

"It's too early to say what went wrong," a laboratory spokesman said. "We may never be sure. All we know at the moment is that the spacecraft failed to get power from its solar panels."

Radiation of the kind emitted in nuclear explosions sometimes is trapped in the dangerous belt of radiation surrounding the earth.

Ranger 5 had to go through this belt on its flight toward the moon.

This was the third straight failure in the hard-luck Ranger program to scout the moon electronically for upcoming manned moonships.

Army to Test Pershing Missile At Fort Wainwright This Winter

PERSHING MISSILE — This is the Pershing missile which will be tested at Fort Wainwright this winter. The missile, which is to replace the Redstone rocket will be tested for operation in arctic weather conditions.

The Army announced today that a new missile will soon arrive at Ft. Wainwright for testing under arctic conditions.

The missile, the mighty Pershing, is due to make its entrance in the Yukon area sometime next month, according to Lt. Col. Henry Septfonds, unit commander of the U.S. Army Ordnance Arctic Test activity at Wainwright.

An advance party of civilian and military personnel is scheduled to land here next week and begin segregating parts of the system as they arrive.

The missile itself, as well as all components, testing personnel and actual crew members attached to the Pershing, are slated to arrive by Nov. 25.

The Pershing is an inertially guided ballistic missile which is being developed to provide the Army in the field with a flexible weapon system combining nuclear firepower, high mobility and quick reaction.

Pershing is a battlefield weapon that can be transported on rugged terrain by four tracked vehicles only slightly larger than most of today's automobiles.

The firing unit carries its own launch pad and erector as well as communications and automatic equipment for guidance computation and last minute checking of critical system components.

The Pershing will be tested at three separate sites on Ft. Wainwright and a total of approximately 45 men will be involved in operating the Pershing and evaluating its performance under Arctic conditions.

The Pershing is a two-stage, solid propellant missile.

Czech Diplomat Kills Wife, Self

NEW YORK, Oct. 19, (AP)—A Czechoslovak diplomat, who killed his wife and led police in a wild two-state chase yesterday, died today of a bullet he fired into his brain after cracking up his big limousine.

The diplomat, Karel Zizka, about 40, died at St. Luke's Hospital at Fountain Hill, Pa., despite efforts by doctors to keep him alive.

Zizka stopped brea'thing around 7 a.m. Doctors immediately administered oxygen, began external massage of the chest around the heart and his breathing resumed. However, his heart stopped again a little after 10:20 and this time it could not be restarted.

Zizka was an attache of the Czech United Nations mission here.

He also had a shoulder wound inflicted by a Pennsylvania State Trooper.

The body of Zizka's brown-haired wife, Vera, 40, a bullet through her head, lay unnoticed in their apartment in the Czech mission on upper Madison Avenue for hours as Zizka, leaving behind a note telling of the murder and his suicide intent, began his frenzied 75-mile flight. He drove a black Cadillac, owned by the mission and bearing diplomatic license plates.

Roaring away from the mission building, Zizka's car was involved in two minor accidents near his home. He got out of them by claiming diplomatic immunity.

Zizka, 6-feet-2 and 240 pounds, then headed the car into New Jersey and stepped on the gas as he sped west on route 22. Three Jersey State Police cars were after Zizka at speeds up to 110 miles an hour when the limousine crossed the state line, where Pennsylvania highway patrolmen took up the chase.

Near Easton, Pa., Zizka's car roared off the road, down an embankment, and overturned.

Cpl. John Uditis, alerted by radio, found the limousine with Zizka lying beside it.

"The man was lying there on his stomach," Uditis said. "He had a cigarette in his left hand and his right hand was concealed from view under his body."

Advancing with gun drawn, Uditis ordered Zizka to bring his right hand into view. But, said the trooper, "he just kept on smoking and kept his eyes trained on me. Upon my second order to bring out his hand empty it came out with a revolver in it. He pointed it at me and I fired."

In the next instant another shot rang out. Zizka had put his revolver to his right temple.

Inside the car, police said they found two broken bottles of vodka.

In the Zizka apartment were broken bottles of wine, whisky and gin, and wild disorder. The official Czech statement said: "The flat was in a terrible state and demolished."

In Head

Mrs. Zizka, mother of two children still in Czechoslovakia was clad in a nightgown and lay on the bedroom floor. She apparently had been shot through the head while in bed, then rolled to the floor.

Miles Vejoda, mission counsel, told of breaking down the door to get into the third-

(Continued on Page 7, Col. 5)

Sourdough Jack Sez: **"Don't see why the University wants to build a research complex. When I went out there everything seemed complexin' enough already."**

University of Alaska bond issue by overwhelming margins. As a territory Alaska had not had the authority to bond itself, but after statehood, citizens willingly pledged their financial support for university expansion in one election after another. The first statewide bonding election in Alaskan history in 1960 included two million dollars for university utilities and construction of a new university gymnasium, the Patty Building. In 1962, the second bond election provided nearly six million dollars, most of which was used to launch the West Ridge research complex.[23]

As president of the National Bank of Alaska, Alaska's largest financial institution, Rasmuson proved especially influential in swaying Anchorage and Southeastern residents to support the university. At a meeting of the Anchorage Chamber of Commerce in October 1962, Rasmuson and Wood told business leaders in Alaska's largest city that the passage of the upcoming bond issue creating the arctic research center in Fairbanks could bring the state up to forty million dollars in federal grants within five years. "I am more excited about the economic potentialities of the Research Institute," Rasmuson told the chamber, "than any development since the discovery of oil on the Kenai and the construction of the pulp mills in Southeastern Alaska." He foresaw a "chain reaction" of research, teaching, and development in Alaska, similar to the way the space race was stimulating the growth of the "Golden Girdle" around Harvard and MIT, and what would become known as the "Silicon Valley" near Stanford. Federal support of arctic research and education was "the great economic breakthrough we have been searching for."[24]

During the 1960s nearly two dozen new graduate programs were added to the catalog in disciplines such as anthropology, history, English, creative writing, civil engineering, botany, zoology, biology, and business administration.[25] A Ph.D. in geology was offered in 1962, while the following year establishment of an interdisciplinary Ph.D. program enabled students to earn a doctoral degree in any field depending on the available "faculty and facilities." In 1965, the university awarded five doctorates, the greatest number in its history up to that time, including a degree in marine science to Vera Alexander (Dugdale), who became the university's first woman Ph.D. graduate.[26]

The regents and the Wood administration struggled to expand the university's physical plant to keep up with the expansion in teaching and research. University facilities erected throughout the state during Wood's thirteen-year presidency were worth ten times as much as all of the existing facilities constructed in the university's first forty years; the physical plant, valued at $10.5 million in 1960, was worth $102 million in 1972. Between 1960 and 1973, the square footage of buildings on the Fairbanks campus more than tripled from about 427,000 to 1.35 million square feet. Looking back over Wood's career in 1973, Harry Porter, Fairbanks businessman and former mayor, said President Wood's "vast accomplishments in glass and cement . . . will stand as their own testimony for years to come," while Congressman Don Young said Dr. Wood's name was "chiseled into stone on the campus he built."[27] On the day Wood arrived on campus in 1960, groundbreaking ceremonies were held for a new engineering building (later named in honor of former Dean

William E. Duckering). It was a sign of things to come. From that day on, new construction continued virtually without interruption during Wood's thirteen years as president. The News-Miner once said that Wood probably wore "working clothes under his cap and gown," as on average he completed more than two major building projects every year. "The smell of diesel and the roar of tractors," as the summer news bulletin stated in the summer of 1967, were familiar to anyone who ventured on campus during Wood's tenure. In fact, so much concrete was poured on College Hill in the 1960s that the Ideal Cement Co. of Denver, Colorado, featured an aerial photograph of the University of Alaska campus in Fairbanks as a national advertisement for the firm in *Barrons*, *Business Week*, *Fortune*, and *U.S. News and World Report*, under the heading: "Alaska: One of the growing markets building with Ideal."[28]

Construction of four new residence halls nearly tripled the number of dormitory beds in less than eight years. Lathrop Hall opened in 1962 and Skarland Hall in 1964. Moore Hall (1966) and Bartlett Hall (1970) held 322 students apiece; both were more than twice the size of Lathrop, which had previously been the largest dorm on campus. A dining commons capable of feeding 600 students at a time (now called the Lola Tilly Commons) was finished in 1963, while Hess Commons—for residents of Skarland, Moore, and Bartlett (the upper dorms)—opened in 1970.

An innovative and relatively inexpensive solution to the university's chronic married student housing shortage was the Modular Units. The "Mod Units" looked like a train wreck strewn along the steep hillside above Lathrop Hall. Resting on top of a maze of steel girders, which the News-Miner claimed resembled a "World War II tank trap," thirty-two prefabricated box car apartments were stacked on top of each other in a staggered fashion. This experimental modular housing, which attracted great interest from architectural firms and building contractors around the country, served for nearly two decades before the prefab units deteriorated so badly the fire marshal ordered them to be scrapped.[29]

By the early 1960s, the university also needed to replace the old gymnasium. Built in 1931, the first concrete building on campus was so small that even though the basketball court literally stretched from wall to wall, the court was less than regulation size. The narrow balcony held only about fifty spectators for sporting events. Audrey Loftus, executive secretary of the alumni association, called the university gym a laughingstock compared to the modern regulation-size gyms in any of Alaska's urban high schools.[30] Construction began on the new gymnasium in 1962 and was completed by the fall of 1963. With room in the new gym for 3,500 spectators for sporting events—seventy times the capacity of the old gym—as well as an Olympic-size swimming pool, three basketball courts, two handball courts, classrooms, a rifle range, ski room, and ROTC offices, the new Patty Building (named for former President Ernest Patty) "so completely dwarfs the present campus sports and recreation facilities," Larry Holmstrom wrote in the *Polar Star*, "that there is not much basis for comparison."[31]

Before the new shooting gallery in the Patty Gym opened, an old cafeteria served as the campus rifle range. But despite the makeshift facilities, University of Alaska riflemen and riflewomen were an intercollegiate target shooting dynasty in the 1960s. The newly established women's rifle team broke all national records and swept the national championship six times in seven years from 1962 to 1968. Sgt. Everad Horton, an ROTC instructor who coached the 1961–1962 team, claimed it was "the greatest women's rifle team ever seen in the United States." The men's varsity rifle team was always among the top teams in the country, turning out eleven All-Americans from 1961 to 1970; the men's team beat out the Air Force Academy for the national championship in 1964, and lost by a single point to West Point for the title in 1965.[32]

The new gymnasium enabled the university to begin competing for the first time on a sustained basis in intercollegiate basketball, the favorite sport of President Wood, who became a regular fixture in the bleachers for every home game. Though the UA Polar Bears had played their first intercollegiate basketball game in 1952, until the mid-1960s most of their competition still continued to be military and town teams; the Polar Bears' cumulative intercollegiate record for the 1950s was one win (a one-point victory against Eastern Washington State College in 1957) and nineteen losses.

The basketball team began to jet regularly to the states in the 1960s to play other college teams. After 1963, the Polar Bears—the University of Alaska nickname since the 1930s—became known almost exclusively as the "Nanooks" (after the Inupiaq word for polar bear) or the "Flying Nanooks," a name habitually ranked in national surveys among the top ten strangest nicknames in college athletics. (The Santa Cruz "Banana Slugs" currently hold the number one

ranking.) For years the symbol of the Flying Nanooks, the "flyingest squad in intercollegiate basketball," was a cartoon drawing of a basketball-dribbling polar bear, wearing blue shorts and riding on top of a Boeing 727. In 1972–1973 the Flying Nanooks reached one of the high points in UA athletic history when they went 20–9 and captured the NAIA district championship, defeating traditional powerhouse Central Washington State University.[33]

One of the most bizarre structures on campus solved the problem of an ice rink for hockey players and figure skaters. The "Beluga," an inflatable nylon dome, could be used for hockey in the winter and held three tennis courts in the summer. The seven-ton, white polyester Beluga—which some called the "Hindenburg"—came alive in February 1969 like a giant float in Macy's Thanksgiving Parade. It immediately became a Fairbanks landmark. A student-sponsored contest chose the name of the white whale for the cigar-shaped balloon because, as one student wrote, "the dome took on its own personality" and "the students felt that they just had to name it."[34]

Though the Beluga's total cost was a modest $60,000, a tenth of the price of a permanent facility, problems quickly surfaced which made it seem more like a white elephant than a whale. The uninsulated Beluga was not a great deal warmer than an outdoor rink, and high winds, heavy snowfall, and mechanical problems with the two large fans that kept it pressurized caused frequent Beluga blowouts. Vandals with knives posed a constant threat; one weekend, miscreants flattened the building by slicing forty-seven holes in it.[35] The Beluga deflated for the first time only about a month after installation, slowly collapsing while two maintenance men were walking around on top of it trying to clear off the snow. University engineer Ernest Kaiser explained that "the two men who were on top of the dome when it collapsed were not jumping up and down" intentionally. With the "balloon-like quality of the structure, it had the same effect as if they were walking on a trampoline," he said. "The men only seemed to be deliberately bouncing." The university then hit upon a novel and safer snow removal method: using a hovering helicopter as a huge snow blower to blast the snow off the top whenever it accumulated to a depth of three inches or more.[36]

Ultraviolet rays rotted out the first Beluga's nylon fabric, and it was replaced by a dacron polyester Beluga II in 1974. The following year construction workers moved the Beluga south a few hundred yards to make way for the construction of an all-weather ice arena which opened in the late 1970s, providing the university with its first truly comfortable indoor winter hockey rink and enabling the start-up of an intercollegiate hockey program. Subsequently, in 1984, the obsolete and decaying Beluga was dismantled and sold.

When President Wood took office in 1960, he found the university power plant to be nearly as antique as the old gym. The administration briefly considered a proposal from the Westinghouse Corporation to replace the 1930s heating plant with a nuclear reactor; however, the regents finally settled on a new $3.5 million coal-fired generating plant to be built near the mouth of the old practice mining tunnel next to the railroad tracks below College Hill. At forty degrees below zero, the new boilers would consume up to one hundred tons of coal every twenty-four hours, and by placing the plant adjacent to the railroad—where President Bunnell had long desired to locate it—the freight cars of coal could be dumped directly into the plant. The new steam power plant came on line in January 1964. The facility was subsequently named for Ben J. Atkinson, a 1947 graduate of the university and director of the Physical Plant and Campus Planning for nine years. Atkinson died of a heart attack at age 49 in 1966.[37]

Building the new power plant on the flats below College Hill removed the smokestacks once and for all from the center of campus, but the new location had a serious drawback which did not become apparent until August 1967. That summer the worst flood in the history of Fairbanks devastated the community. After two months of record-breaking rainfall, including about one inch of rain a day during the second week of August, the Chena River crested half a dozen feet above its banks on August 15, 1967, inundating the valley all the way to the foot of College Hill. The streets of Fairbanks were navigable only by riverboat. "Cruising through town was an experience I will never forget," Phil Deisher wrote in the *Polar Star*. "We went by the Music Mart and there were guitars floating in the windows."[38]

The university was not completely unprepared for disasters. In the wake of the 1962 Cuban Missile Crisis, the administration had officially designated fallout shelters in the lower levels of Duckering, Eielson, Lathrop Hall, the Patty Building and the Commons. "In addition," an article in the *Polar Star* had reassured students, "new utilidors will

216

provide extra shelter area in case of a nuclear attack."[39] On August 14, 1967, Al George, the university's civil defense director, estimated that the campus had about 300 beds available for refugees. But as the extent of the flood damage became apparent, President Wood announced that anyone who needed food or shelter could find it at the university. More than 7,000 men, women and children (and their pets) were evacuated to the high and dry university campus, including about 400 infants, as well as the residents of the Fairbanks Pioneers Home, who were housed on the seventh and eighth floors of Moore Hall. In less than a day the university campus grew to the size of Alaska's fourth-largest city, with evacuees camped anywhere

with room enough to throw a sleeping bag, in dormitories, hallways, laboratories, offices, classrooms, and closets. Even after the roads were cut off between the campus and the outside world, evacuees continued to arrive by helicopters, riverboats, and canoes. As one witness stated, the foot of the stairs going up College Hill "resembled a marina." One unfounded rumor was that the flood had displaced an army of rats in Fairbanks which were threatening to climb College Hill. After the flood waters had dissipated, however, signs of only two rats were found.

In the first two days, the commons served about 26,000 meals, including 14,000 frankfurters on August 16 alone. Supplies requisitioned on August 18 included among other items: 1,200 pounds of bone-less ham, 1,000 loaves of bread, 900 dozen eggs, 600 pounds of wieners, 100 pounds of bologna, and 50 cases of oranges. The parking lot south of the Bunnell Building was cleared for use as a helicopter pad where military relief flights and civilian officials regularly shuttled back and forth from other locations.[40]

Relief headquarters were set up in Hess Hall, with an infirmary in Wickersham Hall, a preschool nursery in Eielson, a Salvation Army food distribution center in the old Geophysical Institute, and movies all day long in Schaible Auditorium. Some 1967 refugees still cannot bear to watch "Cat Ballou" starring Jane Fonda, the only feature film available, which was shown repeatedly during flood week.

To keep the evacuees informed, the university began twice daily publication of *The High Water News*, a mimeographed news bulletin, which claimed that thousands of new "students" had enrolled in "a special non-credit short course in flood survival." As the flood waters subsided, later issues of the bulletin were called *The (Lower) High Water News*, and *The (Even Lower) High Water News*. In truth, the university actually did open a "Flood School," offering seminars for evacuees on topics such as caring for flood-soaked clothing; income tax preparation for casualty losses; and reconditioning of electric motors, generators, kitchen appliances, and automobiles.[41]

The safety of the 7,000 people who found shelter on the university campus depended on keeping the power plant below College Hill functioning, and it was directly in the path of the approaching flood waters. Early on August 15, a pair of bulldozers and a front-end loader started building a dike around the power plant, but the water was rising so fast that plant supervisor Gerald England realized the dike could not be completed in time. In response to a call for help broadcast over the radio and the campus public address system, hundreds of evacuees came streaming down over the crest of College Hill. "I've never seen anything like it," England said. "They started coming over that hill like caribou—men, women and children." Standing in water, mud, and sludge that was in places nearly waist high, the human chain of volunteers worked all day helping construct sandbag defenses around the power plant, and manning a "Frankenstein-like maze of pumps and hoses" trying to stem the flow of water through the flooded utilidor in the power plant basement. Though the waters came within an inch and a half of shutting down the power plant, the volunteers and physical plant workers, aided by a 12,000-gallon-a-minute U.S. Army pump, stemmed the flood and kept the fires blazing in the boilers throughout the crisis.[42]

Only a few days after the last of the evacuees left the campus in early September 1967, classes opened right on schedule. Flood losses in Fairbanks were estimated to be in the hundreds of millions, including the severely damaged St. Joseph's Hospital on the banks of the Chena River. Faced with the prospect of Fairbanks losing its only community hospital, President Wood helped lead the organization charged with building a new facility. A hospital-medical school complex at the university was one of the options briefly considered, but in 1972 the new state-of-the-art Fairbanks Memorial Hospital opened in south Fairbanks.

The heart of any academic institution is its library. By the mid-1960s the university library in the west end of the Bunnell Building, which had opened in 1959–1960, was already inadequate. By 1966, shelves were so crowded that the government documents collection had to be stored in a campus utilidor about a quarter-mile from the library. Estimates were that by the end of the decade, the old library would have about six times as many books as it had been designed to hold.

In a 1966 bond issue, voters approved $8.5 million to build a new combination library, humanities, and fine arts facility near the center of campus on the site of the old power plant. Completed in 1970 at a total cost of nearly eleven million dollars, this com-plex of four buildings—including the library, a music building, an art building, and a theatre building—totaled more than a quarter of a million square feet. The new five-floor library, seven times the size of the old library in Bunnell, could hold two acres of books. It was named in honor of Elmer E. Rasmuson, who had retired from the board of regents in 1969, and it evolved over the years into the premier library in the world on Alaska and the polar regions.

Unfortunately, there proved to be so many code violations throughout the library and Fine Arts Com-plex—such as a lack of drains in the roof, inadequate air circulation, and faulty acoustics—that the univer-sity had to sue the architect, who had taken off for Australia, for a million dollars. Despite its faults,

Conductor Gordon Wright of the Fairbanks Symphony Orchestra, with featured guest soloists for the "1812 Overture"—members of the 37th Field Artillery from Fort Wainwright with six 105-mm howitzers—at the 1974 inaugural performance of the Charles W. Davis Concert Hall. Wright conducted the orchestra from 1969 until his retirement in 1989.

Howard Ringley

however, the Humanities and Fine Arts Complex provided the first modern facilities for teaching music, art, theater, and broadcasting.[43]

Ever since the premiere performance of "His Majesty Bunker Bean" on March 14, 1925, student theater had been part of the ritual of college life in Fairbanks. In 1955 President Patty hired Lee H. Salisbury, a 28-year-old actor from New York with seven years experience on the stage, to teach theater and create a Drama Workshop. At the urging of his sister-in-law Druska Carr Schaible (professor of biological sciences and acting dean of women), Salisbury came to the university, thinking he might stay one year. In fact, he stayed thirty-three. At the start, he found drama facilities on campus to be rather limited. The only place for performances at that time was the old gym. "The sets had to come down every Friday night," he remembers, "to permit R.O.T.C. to do its drill every Saturday morning."[44]

Reportedly Schaible Auditorium (named in memory of Salisbury's sister-in-law) was originally to have been a fully equipped theater. However, the university had run out of money during the construction of the Bunnell Building and had been forced to delete the stage, leaving Salisbury to direct in a playhouse without a stage. Where the stage should have gone, workers installed a huge permanent blackboard, while the only storage space Salisbury could find for costumes and props was an empty elevator shaft in the still-unfinished Duckering Building. Actors had to erect a new stage platform for each show, and all the sets had to be U-shaped to fit around the blackboard. Nevertheless, the Drama Workshop staged its productions in Schaible Auditorium for a decade, beginning with "The Time of

Your Life" in 1961. The workshop truly came of age in 1969–1971 with the introduction of a theater major and completion of a new 481-seat theater in the Fine Arts Building, where the 1971 inaugural performance was "The Man of La Mancha." By the time of his retirement in 1988, Salisbury had established the "longest continuous tradition of theatre production" in the history of Alaska, directing on average two or more plays a year for more than thirty years.[45]

With President Wood, Charles Keim, and others, Salisbury also assisted with the creation of radio station KUAC-FM in 1962 and ultimately KUAC-TV Channel 9 in 1971. The university's radio station actually originated as KUOA, an unlicensed, student-owned and -operated carrier current station wired through the outlets in the dormitories. In 1955, KUOA began broadcasting with a fifty-dollar transmitter from room 115 of the Eielson Building. Due to transmission problems, the station spent far more time off than on the air. The signal was so weak that picking up KUOA in the dormitories was like trying to find an overseas broadcast on short wave. "No one listens to our station," the *Polar Star* complained in 1955. "No one could listen if he wanted to."[46]

In 1961, the students voted by the bare margin of 190–186 to sell KUOA to the university for $795. The 1961 sale cleared the way for the establishment of a new university-run KUOA-FM that would be the first educational broadcast station in Alaska and the first FM station in interior Alaska. The FCC denied those call letters, however, which had previously been assigned to a radio station at the University of Arkansas, and authorized the new station to

be called KUAC (the University of Alaska in College). Broadcasting from Constitution Hall with a used $1,500 transmitter, antenna, and board purchased from Edison Technical High School in Seattle, KUAC-FM signed on the air for the first time at 3:00 P.M. on October 1, 1962. After a few brief introductory remarks from President Wood, announcer Larry Holmstrom opened KUAC's inaugural broadcast with a recording of Beethoven's *Emperor Concerto*.[47]

To receive KUAC's signal, many Interior Alaska residents purchased FM radios for the first time, tuning in to symphony orchestras, Italian operas, foreign news, and educational programs from around the globe. When Congress established the National

Public Radio Network in 1970, KUAC-FM became the first member station in Alaska. Due to the strength of support KUAC enjoyed in the Fairbanks community, the network judged it to be one of the most effective local educational stations in the entire country. In April 1971, KUAC's studios moved from the third floor of Constitution Hall to the lower level of the newly completed Fine Arts Complex. Shortly before Christmas 1971, KUAC-TV commenced operations, bringing public television to Interior Alaska.[48]

Local art and music production also flourished in the new Fine Arts Complex, most notably the Fairbanks Symphony Orchestra. Founded by a small group of dedicated local musicians in 1958–1959, and initially managed by volunteer Chuck Rees—who said he liked music even though he only played the coffee pot—the Fairbanks Symphony Orchestra was a true child of the "town and gown" marriage between Fairbanks and its university. Throughout the 1960s, faculty from the music department took turns conducting until Gordon Wright arrived in 1969. During Wright's two decades as conductor, the small town symphony became an accomplished 80-piece orchestra, playing a full seven concerts a year. The Fairbanks Symphony found a permanent home in 1974 with the completion of the Charles W. Davis Concert Hall in the Fine Arts Complex. The inaugural concert, which could have literally brought the house down, was a stirring performance of Tchaikovsky's "1812 Overture," accompanied by a full battery of 105-mm howitzers from Fort Wainwright set off in the parking lot during the 1812's famed explosive conclusion. Wright, the master showman, invited the officer in charge of the cannons to take a bow in his army fatigues.

In 1970, Wright organized the first tour of the Arctic Chamber Orchestra. Accompanied by violinists Paul and Linda Rosenthal, the Chamber Orchestra brought "Bach, Britten, Boccherini, Boyce and Nielsen to Barrow, Kotzebue, Nome and Anchorage." The 1970 tour started an annual tradition, which over the years has seen the members of the Arctic Chamber Orchestra and their instruments log hundreds of thousands of miles by bus, boat, jet, bush plane and snowmachine, performing in more than sixty communities across Alaska, from Ambler, Aniak and Anaktuvuk, to Unalakleet, Valdez, and Venetie.[49]

Across campus new facilities and programs continued to be added as signs of the past disappeared. In 1970, the wrecking ball smashed Hess Hall, the first permanent concrete dormitory on campus. (Sorry to see the old building go, the UA Veterans Club talked of installing a gravestone "in a conspicuous place" that said "Rest In Peace—Hess Hall."[50]) Hess Hall was destroyed to make way for construction of an eight-story office and classroom building named for former Alaska Governor and U.S. Senator Ernest Gruening. When the fiery 85-year-old politician first saw the Gruening Building at the dedication ceremony in 1972, the long-time peace activist and opponent of the Vietnam War looked up at the massive fortress of reinforced concrete named in his honor and asked, "Don't they know I'm a dove?"[51]

Delays and design problems plagued the construction of the Gruening Building, which ran a year and a half behind schedule. Work had to be temporarily halted when someone discovered that the contractor had neglected to install steel ties on the outside of the seventh floor exterior columns. At first it appeared that all of the cement on the eighth floor would have to be torn up to correct the error. A consultant, however, advised the university that the ties were not essential to the building's structural integrity, but only to "help prevent cement from flaking off because of any seismic disturbances." The ties were not added. In fact, much of the exterior facing of the Gruening Building proved to be unsatisfactory. A substandard pour of concrete, faulty anchor pins, and other problems resulted in sheets of crumbling cement when the molds were pulled away. The architect's solution was to chip the facing to make it look intentionally uneven, and so for weeks before the building opened in 1973, students walked past crews of workmen with masons' hammers pounding away on the outside of the Gruening Building.[52]

But the biggest mistakes in the design of the Gruening Building were on the inside. The building was laid out with so-called "open offices" separated by low, movable partitions instead of the traditional closed offices with full-length walls and doors. When faculty revolted against the loss of privacy and confidentiality, the administration abandoned the open office concept and reluctantly installed walls and doors. "Apparently some of the teachers don't want to be accessible," planning director Donald Moyer angrily charged, "and want to be able to lock themselves behind a door."[53]

Moyer's comments drew a blistering reaction from numerous faculty, including Dr. William R. Hunt, the head of the history department. "In truth the concept of the Gruening Building is a stupid one that the faculty has been opposing since 1968," Hunt wrote. "Dr. Moyer inherited a foolish scheme and his best PR efforts to convince teachers that their needs compare with those of clerks in insurance offices have not prevailed."[54]

Another flaw in the Gruening Building was a peculiar approach towards the use of electricity. The Gruening Building was originally designed so that all the lights in the building would burn twenty-four hours a day; only one set of light switches were located on each floor. "We approached lighting from a different angle," Moyer explained. "Rather than turning on the lights that are needed, all the lights are turned on, and those which are not needed are turned off." The lights eventually went out in the Gruening Building after the 1973 oil embargo and the subsequent U.S. energy crisis (when even Christmas lights were temporarily banished from campus), which made it both uneconomical and embarrassing to light an empty building around the clock.[55]

Architecturally the most intriguing building constructed on campus was Wood Center, a $4.6 million student activities center that opened in January 1972. Wood Center was the house that ASUA built. Initially, it was to be totally paid for by the students themselves, who had grown tired of their old cramped recreational quarters in Constitution Hall, and had voted in the mid-1960s to increase their activity fees to contribute to a new student union building fund. ASUA lobbied the legislature for a special four million dollar low-interest construction loan to the university, which would be paid back from student fees over the next twenty-five years. (Actually, in 1980, state Rep. Brian Rogers of Fairbanks, a former UA student and former editor of the *Polar Star*, succeeded in passing a legislative appropriation to take over the remainder of the debt payments for Wood Center.)[56]

Wood Center's angular copper roof—early accounts claimed the copper would show an "aurora effect" when lights were shined on it"—rises towards the sky like a mountain of metal in the shape of Denali. The *Polar Star* once joked that the uniquely configured building was actually a "surplus USAF dirigible hangar." At one stage, plans called for the lower level of Wood Center to be connected to the other buildings on campus by an underground pedestrian tunnel (an idea which was subsequently dropped). Four times the size of the

old SUB, the new student union featured an eight-lane bowling alley, six pool tables, a darkroom, a multilevel lounge described as the "students' living room" (with a fireplace on one level and a color TV on another), a small "discotheque-pub" pending approval of a liquor license, a spacious indoor "mall" designed to combat cabin fever, a "sidewalk cafe" with an espresso machine, and an inspirational staircase to nowhere.[57]

The most controversial aspect of the new student center was probably its name. At the groundbreaking ceremony in May 1970, the board of regents had taken the unprecedented step of officially naming the new facility the William Ransom Wood Campus Center. Admittedly, as President Wood stated, it was "strictly against the rules" to name a new structure after a sitting president. Though flattered by the recognition, he said he wondered if someone was trying to tell him something![58]

Apparently dean of students Robert Hilliard had submitted a petition to the board of regents, signed by five students, four administrators, and two faculty members, recommending the center be named for President Wood. The *Fairbanks Daily*

Former ASUA president Phil Holland joined the Peace Corps and went to India after graduating with a degree in philosophy in 1969. When Holland died of meningitis in New Delhi in February 1971 at age twenty-five, some students wanted the new student union building to be named in his honor. Instead, after Wood Center opened, its Memorial Conference Room was dedicated in memory of all the university students who like Holland had died young.

Celia Hunter

News-Miner praised the name Wood Center, noting that perhaps the only more appropriate one might be "Woods (plural)" Center, since Dorothy Jane Wood played such an important role in the life of the campus. "It may be breaking precedent to name a building after a man still active in the University," the *News-Miner* stated, "but this is one student revolution with which we agree wholeheartedly."[59]

Some students were upset that the student body as a whole did not have a greater voice in choosing the name for a building that was being paid for by the students. In an open letter to President Wood published in the *Polar Star* in October 1970, managing editor Howard Ringley wrote that students certainly wished to see a building on campus named Wood "to preserve symbolically your efforts to provide facilities for the University." Furthermore, Ringley wrote, any name for the student center would be "better than condemning it to a lifetime of painfully sterile titles such as SUB and Commons." He merely questioned why students could not have had more say in naming their own building. A protestor in 1972 went so far as to hang up a sign over the entrance of Wood Center that read "Student Union Building," because he felt "that the building should have the word student on it."[60]

Some students suggested the new activities center be named in memory of former ASUA President Phil Holland, an adventurous and idealistic young Peace Corps volunteer who had died in India in February 1971. Holland was a thoughtful and skilled student politician who had successfully rallied both student and legislative support to finance the new student center. Some called him the best student body president the university had ever seen. After graduating in 1969 with a degree in philosophy, he went to India as an agricultural advisor for the Peace Corps. "Periodically (usually at the end of a particularly frustrating day)," Holland wrote from India in 1970, "I'm overwhelmed by the presumption of a U of A philosophy graduate in assuming he can show Indian farmers how to improve their farms . . . ." Holland expected to return to the States in the fall of 1971 to start law school; however, he died of meningitis in New Delhi on February 26, 1971. He was 25. Shocked at the news of Holland's death, his friend Normand Dupre wrote, "The world owed it to itself to keep Phil Holland alive. Perhaps it just didn't deserve it."[61]

Students were the catalyst in the naming of Skarland Hall, the first of the upper dorms on Rainey Ridge, located near the cabin that anthropologist Ivar Skarland had inherited from Froelich Rainey. On New Year's Day 1965, Skarland died of a heart attack right outside the door of his cabin on the ridge. He was sixty-five. Shortly afterwards, students petitioned the administration and the Board of Regents to name the new women's dormitory in his memory, making it the first dorm not to be named after a former regent. Skarland was one of the best-loved and most respected faculty members. Dean Charles Ray said he thought Skarland "taught more students during his tenure at the University than any other staff member past or present," and that his three-credit anthropology course on Alaska Natives should have been listed in the catalog as "Ivar Skarland 342."[62]

Taking off through the woods north of the Skarland Cabin and Skarland Hall was a network of about thirty miles of hiking and cross-country ski trails, which, by student request, were also named in memory of Ivar Skarland. A native of Norway and the skiing champion of the 1934 Winter Sports Carnival in Fairbanks, Skarland did as much as anyone to popularize Nordic skiing in Alaska. In 1934, Skarland and George Karabelnikoff had blazed a tricky four-mile ski trail around College Hill, "full of Hazards" for college competition. For years Skarland's cabin had been a favorite warm-up spot for tired skiers he welcomed in from the cold.[63]

In part to preserve the ski trails on campus, students Nat Goodhue and John Samuelson organized the first Equinox Marathon in September 1963, which over the past thirty years has grown into Fairbanks' fall sports classic. Goodhue, who competed in the U.S. Ski Association's 1963 national cross-country championships, feared that the campus "Bulldozer Revolution" in the 1960s would eventually destroy all the ski trails unless the university accepted them as a "permanent facility" for runners, dog sled racers, skiers, and hikers. Goodhue blazed one of the most grueling marathon routes imaginable from the Patty Building to the top of Ester Dome and back, the standard marathon distance of 26 miles, 385 yards, with a cumulative vertical climb of about 3,000 feet. "The hill climbing makes this marathon unique," Goodhue said. "That first Greek warrior did not have any hill climbing. There isn't any in the Olympic marathon and there isn't any in the Boston marathon . . . ." A total of 143 runners participated in the first Equinox Marathon on September 21, 1963. Appropriately enough, Nat Goodhue crossed the finish line first with a time of 3 hours, 54 minutes and 22 seconds.[64]

Naturally, skiers and hikers viewed the rapid expansion of campus buildings with alarm; others decried the university's incongruous collection of architectural styles and building types. Freshman Cynthia Lee complained in 1971 that the university's buildings looked like "big blocks of stone all stuck there haphazardly." According to Lee, there seemed to be "no harmony between the buildings and the land." Another student thought the university an "architectural disaster."[65]

Wildlife biologist David Klein wrote in a 1971 essay that Alaskans were "indeed fortunate that the founders of the Alaska Agricultural College and School of Mines chose a site with such high potential for growth into a beautiful and distinctive university campus." But Klein charged that potential for beauty was being eroded as the campus stands of birch and spruce were replaced by the "'pavement and concrete' look so common to recent urban development throughout the United States." Too many California planners hired by the university seemed unaware of the slow speed of tree growth in the boreal forest, while Alaskan bulldozer operators saw every standing tree as an unanswered challenge. The result was the deforestation of the campus, even though the architects continued to "spot new trees on their drawings of new campus buildings as if we were in a tropical rain forest."[66]

Another rather acerbic critic of the University of Alaska's architecture was writer Norman Mailer. He and Ralph Ellison, the author of *The Invisible Man*, appeared as guest lecturers in the Patty Gym in April 1965 for the university's annual Festival of Arts. Mailer told a crowd of about 1,600 people that Alaska was the only place he had ever visited in

WRITERS IN THE SKY
The Flying Poets, the avant garde poet-professors who ran the Alaska Creative Writers' Workshop until 1968, at the Fairbanks International Airport with their Piper Cherokee 180. Front, from left to right: Don Kaufmann, Ken Warfel (a student poet), Robert King, and Laurence Wyatt with the dark glasses and cigar. Ed Skellings stands in the cockpit.

Ed Skellings

America that he found to be truly extraordinary. "There's something about this country that has more to say about life, about the nearness of death, than any place I've ever been," he said. "And it has extraordinary powers and qualities. And also is an unbelievably vulgar and tasteless state."

According to Mailer, this vulgarity was not in the people themselves. "But it certainly exists in the buildings. For instance in this college . . . part of the sheer insanity of American architecture has already visited this joint." According to Mailer, the Patty Gym seemed to him to be a "very chaste version of op-art," reminding him more than anything else of an operating room for a whale.[67] Mailer claimed that he especially admired the "existential quality" of life

in Alaska, a theme which he developed in the first novel he wrote following his 1965 visit to Fairbanks, a strange book set in Alaska entitled *Why Are We in Vietnam?* Ostensibly, it is the story of two draft-age young men from Texas who go grizzly bear hunting in the Brooks Range. Though the only mention of Vietnam is on the last page of the book, Mailer's parable about Lyndon Johnson's war in Southeast Asia became one of the notorious books of the decade. A Mailer biographer described *Why Are We In Vietnam?* as "possibly the most obscene book of American fiction ever published."[68]

Mailer's trip to Fairbanks had been engineered by Dr. Ed Skellings of the English department, the poet who also created the legendary Alaskan literary phenomenon known as the "Flying Poets." Skellings had received his Ph.D. in 1962 from the University of Iowa, home of probably the most distinguished creative writing program in America. Hired in 1963, at age thirty-one, to promote creative writing at the University of Alaska, Skellings' freewheeling approach to life and literature was bound to shake things up. Together with Laurence Wyatt, a theatrical novelist and playwright who came to the UA in 1964 and was partial to thin cigars, dark glasses, and silk-lined capes (and who later changed his name to Wyatt Wyatt), as well as Donald Kaufmann and Robert King, fellow Iowa graduates who followed Skellings to Fairbanks in 1964 and 1965, he made the Alaska Writers' Workshop into one of the most stimulating and controversial programs on campus. Patterned after Paul Engle's program at the University of Iowa, the innovative Alaska workshop encouraged uncensored student self-expression in poetry and fiction, and generated enormous enthusiasm among the students. Famed Russian poet Yevgeny Yevtushenko paid the workshop a surprise visit in 1966. Other prominent writers who sat in over the years were Karl Shapiro and Joseph Langland.[69]

In the days of the Alaska Writers' Workshop, hundreds of people were known to gather and listen to readings. An overflow crowd jammed the aisles of Schaible Auditorium in April 1968 to hear Skellings and King present a "page-ripping, book-throwing, word-zapping" multi-media "happening." Poet Ken Warfel, also a member of the workshop, described the evening as "a riot of lights, words and emotions, stretching in all directions at once." Warfel wrote that the "poems flung from the stage challenged us.

They could be offending, they could be argued, but they could not be denied."[70]

After arriving in Alaska, Skellings, who once jumped out of airplanes for a living as a member of the Army's 82nd Airborne Division, took flying lessons from Don Jonz, a pilot and member of the workshop. (A decade later, in October 1972, Jonz disappeared on a flight somewhere between Anchorage and Juneau, carrying U.S. Representatives Nick Begich and Hale Boggs; no trace of the plane wreckage has ever been found.) Skellings earned both a multi-engine and an instrument rating, and discovered more than half a dozen of the students in the workshop were also flyers. It was then he conceived the idea of taking the workshop "on the road"—by air—to other Alaskan towns and villages, and the "Flying Poets" were born. Not all of the poets were expert flyers, but they all at least took lessons.

Like a high-wire circus act, the Flying Poets brought a sense of adventure to the study of literature and poetry. Across the state from 1965–1967 they performed on more than fifty occasions in front of at least five thousand Alaskan high school students. Though some of their university colleagues thought the Flying Poets were showboats, student reactions were overwhelmingly enthusiastic to the most flamboyant goodwill ambassadors the University of Alaska ever had. Following an appearance of the poets at Seward High School in 1966, one teacher wrote President Wood that their visit had been a tremendous success: "Since all too often many high school students dislike or claim to dislike poetry and anything which even faintly smacks of the poetic, we English teachers here were completely delighted . . . ."[71]

The Flying Poets' longest tour, a month-long aerial swing sponsored by Upward Bound, covered a dozen states between North Dakota and Texas in June and early July 1967. Skellings, Kaufmann, King, Wyatt, and graduate student Ken Warfel claimed they set out to "dispel the notion of the dull professor and the dry writer." As a press release announcing their trip stated, "Poets are usually thought of as men with their heads in the clouds, but five young writers from Alaska are bringing literature down to earth in a light plane."[72] To the dismay of many students, the Flying Poets were essentially dismissed at the end of the spring semester in 1968. Simply put, their Bohemian lifestyle and uninhibited approach towards creative writing did not fit in with the image that the administration wanted to portray of the University of Alaska. Certainly some faculty and students were pleased to see the four poets fly south—Skellings, Kaufmann, and Wyatt all went to Florida, where Skellings eventually became the state's poet laureate, while King went to teach in North Dakota—but many students were outraged at their departure and the collapse of the Writers' Workshop, one of the most popular programs the university would ever offer. Earlier in the year a student election had named Denny Mehner of the psychology department, Sarkis Atamian from sociology, and the four members of the Writers' Workshop (Skellings, King, Kaufmann and Wyatt) as the six most popular professors at the university. An editorial in the Polar Star complained, "Do the students have a voice in this university? Doesn't their opinion count for anything?"[73]

Another contentious case of a faculty dismissal involved economics professor Harold Dinkins, whom the regents fired "for the good of the university" in the spring of 1970, after Dinkins had publicly complained about Dean R. London Smith of the College of Business, Economics and Government.[74] But it was the firing of four professors in the spring of 1971—all of whom were members of the English department—that spurred the first large student demonstrations against university policies. A Polar Star survey in March 1971 reported that eighty-five percent of those questioned felt they had not been "properly informed" by the administration in the decision to terminate the four English professors, two of whom, Hilton Wolfe and Susan Kalen, contested their dismissals. A group calling itself the Students for Academic Freedom (SAF) mobilized to stage sit-ins, protests, and rallies in their support.[75]

An estimated crowd of six to eight hundred people attended an SAF rally in the commons on April 6, 1971. According to one enthusiastic participant the "Commons was transformed into a northern version of good old Sproul Hall (Berkeley 1964) and like wow man, an honest to goodness free speech movement ushered forth." The Polar Star alleged that false "rumors of impending violence," due primarily to poor communication, had spread in advance of the meeting. "This lack of communication was further compounded," the paper complained, "by the mobilization of the Alaska State Troopers, the Fairbanks City Police, and the stationing of guards in the financial and records offices of the Bunnell Building Tuesday evening, presumably at the request of the Administration." One stated SAF goal was to involve "students at all decision-making levels of the university." In late April SAF delivered a petition to President Wood signed by more than four hundred students, demanding positive action within forty-eight hours, threatening a public campaign to boycott the university. Wood ignored the deadline and refused to respond to what he called the "persistent pressure tactics pursued by a self-appointed group of students and non-students." He upheld the decision not to rehire Wolfe, and gave Kalen a terminal contract for 1971–1972.[76]

Frustrated with some of the students and faculty, at the 1971 commencement Wood told the graduating class that he could not consider them part of a "vintage year," a statement which infuriated many faculty and students. "When it was pointed out that students are not grapes," the *Polar Star* commented, "and probably learn as much during periods of strife and dissent, Wood said while this was true . . . students can study best in a quiet library so their academic life is better (with) peace and quiet on the campus."[77]

While some faculty saw the SAF protest as a promising sign of student activism, others viewed the political nature of the protest with alarm. A half-dozen tenured senior faculty, including Orlando Miller of history, Walter Benesch and Rudy Krejci of philosophy, Jack Distad of mathematics, William Mendenhall in civil engineering, and James Morrow of biology, signed a statement which publicly condemned both the SAF student activists and the junior faculty allied with them, charging that the insurgents' intention had been "to attack and disrupt the university because they regard it as the symbol and most vulnerable part of a society which they describe as wholly corrupt." The senior professors claimed that the rebels' ultimate goal appeared

to be "complete dominance over the university." The weapons with which they planned to take control, the statement announced, were student evaluations of professors, which officially began in 1970. Letting students become the arbiters of teaching excellence would water down academic standards, rewarding "those junior faculty members who win student approval by making fewest demands on them" and punishing "professors who cling to standards of academic excellence."[78]

The SAF protests in 1971 demonstrated that at the University of Alaska, as on nearly every other American college campus in the era, both students and faculty felt the need for a greater say in determining the destiny of the institution, though there was hardly unanimity in how to achieve it. Power sharing did not come easily. Faculty tenure, which the education community regards as essential to academic freedom, became an established policy only in 1966, though skeptics claimed that a "financial exigency" clause, which could be invoked when needed at the sole discretion of the administration to permit the layoff of tenured faculty, made tenure a hollow guarantee. In 1967, after an extended battle between the administration and the faculty, the regents approved creation of the University Assembly, composed of faculty, administrators, and students. Though the president maintained veto power over all assembly actions, the body gave faculty and students some rights and responsibilities of leadership.[79]

In 1964, the board of regents had effectively killed ASUA Inc. as it had existed since 1948, ruling that a corporation could no longer operate as the student government. This "stunning blow to the

The Khyber Inn

Beginning in the fall of 1968, University of Alaska students found occasional refuge from the toil of studying at the Khyber Inn, the world's farthest north college coffee house. Operated by students, the Khyber Inn opened in the back of the old SUB in November 1968, providing a candlelight atmosphere for music, dancing, poetry, and quiet conversation.

The name "Khyber Inn" came from one of the founders of the coffee house, Enayet Aziz, a student who grew up in the mountains between Pakistan and Afghanistan. Aziz explained that he and his wife were from two warring tribes in the area near Khyber Pass, which had recently settled a pointless long-running feud, but only after killing thousands of people. "The purpose for the Khyber Inn is to have a place to talk to each other and to exchange ideas," Aziz said. "The name Khyber will always remind us of what can happen when people don't communicate with each other."

The opening act for the first Khyber Inn was a student rock band named "The Styrofoam Mountain People," whose members included Doug Hering, Jim Bartlett, Carol Choat, Greg Nillson, and manager John Collette. The first performer at the Khyber Inn in the fall semester of 1969 was famed guitarist Carlos Montoya. In later years, ASUA-sponsored dances at which alcohol was served by special permit were known as Khyber Inns, until the opening of the Wood Center Pub in November 1975 ended the name and the tradition.

---

student body," as ASUA President Phil Holland later called it, was prompted in part by a student lawsuit from those who opposed paying the mandatory student government fee to a private corporation like ASUA in order to attend a public university. Opponents of ASUA argued that the nonprofit corporation was incompetently run, and since it had originated as a protest organization independent of university control, could therefore not work effectively with administrators. On the other hand, ASUA supporters were eager to protect the broad freedom and autonomy that the corporation enjoyed. Over the protests of some student leaders like Pat Rodey, who argued that the death of the corporation would be an admission "that we are unable to govern ourselves in the great democratic tradition," the ASUA corporation was dissolved and student government was reborn in 1965 as a constitutional association of students.[80]

Even after ASUA became an official part of the university hierarchy, it continued to be an unpredictable force in campus politics. In the spring of 1972 "Dick Hertz," a fictitious write-in protest candidate invented by four residents of McIntosh Hall, actually won election as ASUA president. Among ASUA's notable accomplishments were securing the four million dollar state loan for the university to build Wood Center, and successfully lobbying for amendments to state liquor laws, including a provision which lowered the drinking age in Alaska to nineteen, and others which enabled the university to receive a liquor license and open the Wood Center Pub in 1975. Student leaders such as University Assembly representative Phil Younker and ASUA president Chip Wagoner were instrumental in 1971–1973 in obtaining legislative approval for a permanent student seat on the board of regents, despite the opposition of President Wood who said it was a "sad mistake to let vested interests" be appointed to the board.[81]

The times encouraged the relaxation of many of the old restrictions on student life, most notably for women living on campus. When Moore Hall opened in 1966, it became the first so-called co-ed residence hall, with the third and fourth floors reserved for women. Also beginning in 1966, "key privileges" were extended to senior female students with a GPA above 2.5, enabling them for the first time to come and go as they pleased without a curfew, as was the case for male students. Not until the fall of 1971 were mandatory restricted hours abolished for all women living in the dormitories.[82]

As dormitory rules were relaxed, one resident advisor said the job of running a dorm changed from that of "prison warden" to guidance counselor.[83] Though the administration insisted in 1971 that it still had the authority to enter and search any dorm room at any time if necessary—a blanket policy which Fairbanks lawyer and ACLU activist (and future governor of Alaska) Steve Cowper said was probably a violation of the 4th Amendment—random inspections of student rooms had become a thing of the past. "We're not interested in a student's personal behavior in his own room," Harris Shelton, the head of student housing, said in 1971, "until it infringes on other persons' rights."[84] Prohibition officially ended on campus in 1972, when President Patty's 1956 ban on alcohol was lifted. For the first time in sixteen years, students of legal drinking age were permitted to consume alcohol in their own dorm rooms, though previously the ban had not discouraged thirsty students. As the *Polar Star* had admitted in 1970, "a thorough raid of every dormi-

tory on campus would produce enough alcohol to open a tavern."[85]

As on any college campus in the 1960s, a raid would have also turned up stashes of marijuana. "Bright students from Berkeley to Princeton smoke it as a normal part of the college experience," *Newsweek* reported in 1967, "to escape from the deadening routine of exams, to heighten esthetic experience, to learn more about themselves or, in some cases, simply to do it because square adult society says it is taboo." *Newsweek* quoted officials, admittedly "guessing in the dark," who claimed that perhaps twenty million Americans had smoked dope at least once. Many young people thought marijuana no more harmful than a martini, and claimed it was hypocritical for one to be illegal and not the other. Folksinger Judy Collins referred to a cultural war between the "marijuana generation" and the "alcohol generation."[86]

In early 1968, a dispute over the extent of marijuana use at the University of Alaska made headlines. An unlikely figure raised the issue, 23-year-old Republican State Representative John Sackett from Huslia, the youngest member of the state legislature and a senior at the university majoring in business accounting. Sackett had joined three other former UA students in the freshman legislative class of 1966: Willie Hensley from Kotzebue, an activist in the Native land claims movement; Mike Bradner from Fairbanks, a future Speaker of the House; and Terry Miller from North Pole, a future President of the State Senate and Lieutenant Governor.[87]

Sackett demanded in early February 1968 that the university crack down on students and faculty who either used or advocated the use of marijuana, and threatened the school with a legislative investigation if action was not taken. President Wood responded that though the university did not tolerate anyone using an illegal substance like marijuana, it would strongly "defend anyone's right to openly discuss any subject on this campus." Even economics professor Arlon Tussing, an admitted "oftentime critic" of the Wood administration, praised the president for his staunch defense of the necessity for free speech on such a controversial topic.[88]

Students arranged a marijuana open forum a few days later. The crowd—which a News-Miner reporter estimated to be about a thousand people—elbowed into the commons to hear an eight-member panel, including educators, law enforcement officers, and a physician, debate the pros and cons of smoking marijuana. No consensus emerged. Outspoken sociology professor Sarkis Atamian claimed that most pot users were urban "Negroes, Spanish-speaking Americans, and some Jewish people," groups whom the reporter said Atamian characterized as "apathetic, lethargic and suffused with a feeling of futility." On the other hand, English professor Ed Skellings said artists and writers believed that smoking dope led to "increased perception," and that some of the best student poetry he had seen had been written by students "when they were high."[89]

After months of bitter debate, the 1968 legislature amended Alaska's marijuana laws, passing what some considered at the time to be model legislation. Possession of small amounts became a misdemeanor instead of a felony, and judges were given leeway to require medical treatment in lieu of other punishment.[90] In 1975, the Alaska Surpreme Court ruled that under Alaska law the possession of small amounts of marijuana for personal consumption was legal, a ruling which stood until passage of a voter initiative in 1990 recriminalized its possession.

Some of the students who attended the university in the 1960s or early 1970s, like their predecessors in Vulture Flats or Yertchville twenty or thirty years earlier, lived in shacks or log cabins off campus seeking the low cost and relative freedom of life in the woods. Mike Keim, a student whom the Polar Star interviewed in October 1967, lived and studied in a BMW motorcycle crate. He used Coleman lanterns for heat. Keim said he enjoyed simplicity, and claimed that one of the advantages of his tiny home was that it floated during the 1967 flood.[91] W. Findlay Abbott proposed in 1971 that students and faculty consider living with him on a model 160-acre township he wanted to create about five miles from the university near the Goldstream Valley that would be called "Bearflanks," a name inspired by a Walt Disney comic book. He proposed selling or exchanging for labor five-acre parcels with small cabins, restoring the old Tanana Valley Railroad grade into a wagon road, and establishing a primitive gold mining operation. "I am in partnership with a geology student to do this," he wrote, "but would encourage anyone in the School of Mines to observe and take part as it will be conducted throughout in an educational manner, rather than in a wholesale, destructive, profit maximizing spirit."[92]

The free spirits who lived off campus spent many hours camped out in Wood Center or the 24-hour Reserve Room of the Rasmuson Library. In fact, in 1972, the Reserve Room became so crowded with "permanent residents" that the library ordered a mass eviction of its unwanted tenants. "The room was not designed as a dormitory," the *Polar Star* explained, "and the smell of cheese and crackers and hot chocolate combined with other scents of human habitation nauseated many." One man—who turned out not to be a student—literally set up housekeeping in a locked graduate carrel at the library. "Staff who investigated his carrel found a small apartment: five loaves of bread, cheese, honey, boots and shoes, and other clothing . . . and a sleeping bag."[93]

Underlying and exacerbating student discontent in the 1960s and early 1970s was the Vietnam War, the longest and most divisive conflict in American history since Lee had surrendered to Grant in 1865. Though the *Polar Star* asked all state legislative candidates in 1970,"What would you do if a student riot broke out on the UA campus?" no violent confrontations ever materialized in opposition to the war.[94] But fear that a demonstration could get out of hand persisted. Partially declassified records obtained by writer Dan O'Neill under the Freedom of Information Act reveal that the FBI kept tabs on antiwar demonstrators at the UA as early as 1965.[95] In reality, the only mass violence on campus usually occurred on Engineer's Day, the annual St. Patrick's Day celebration, during which mining and civil engineers might chain the doors of classroom buildings, steal all the desks, or set off enough dynamite to blow out a few windows. In contrast to the rowdies with slide rules, UA antiwar protestors were models of decorum. Following the Cambodian invasion and the killing of four students at Kent State University in early May 1970,

student protesters near the Memorial Plaza Fountain doused an effigy of President Nixon with gasoline and set it on fire. The *News-Miner* condemned the violence of symbolically torching Richard Nixon—even if the president's body was just an old suit of clothes stuffed with hay—as an unwarranted act of militancy. Yet compared to the days of rage that swept other universities after the Kent State killings, the UA response was mild indeed.[96]

After President Wood made one of several trips to South Vietnam as a government consultant on higher education, the ASUA Senate passed a resolution in 1971 by a 13–12 margin condemning "the University of Alaska for its silent support of the genocidal program of the United States government against the peoples of Indo-China." Larry Kerschner, a Vietnam veteran with a Purple Heart and cosponsor of the resolution, said he objected most strongly to indiscriminate B-52 bombing runs that killed and mutilated noncombatants. Kerschner claimed that "petrified Wood's" trip to Southeast Asia did nothing but support the dictatorial Thieu regime in Saigon.[97]

Alaska's largest antiwar demonstration occurred on October 15, 1969, the first "Moratorium Day," part of a nationwide protest called "the greatest organized expression of pacific sentiment in American history."[98] That day as many as 500 UA students, faculty, and local residents joined hundreds of thousands of other Americans across the country, calling for the immediate and unconditional withdrawal of U.S. troops from Vietnam. After the rally on the Memorial Plaza in front of the Bunnell Building, police estimated as many as 350 people slowly marched four miles from the campus to downtown Fairbanks along College Road. The Moratorium Day

RALLY FOR PEACE
Students opposed to the war in Vietnam gather
at the Bunnell Plaza fountain on October 15, 1969,
the first Moratorium Day, a nationwide protest
against the war.

Rasmuson Library

committee requested all faculty to cancel their classes Wednesday afternoon to let students participate. "If any professor is unable to cancel classes, we would urge him to devote his class periods to a discussion of our involvement in the Viet Nam War."[99] The orderly demonstration met a crowd of anti-protestors, protesting the protest, on the streets of downtown Fairbanks. One Fairbanks businessman claimed the marchers were "Communist led and inspired, friends of Ivan's. They make me sick." The *Fairbanks Daily News-Miner* condemned the moratorium as a "cowardly solution" to the crisis, sponsored by an "odd assortment of well-intentioned peace at any price advocates, political opportunists, students and some outright supporters of Hanoi . . . ."[100]

Vice President Spiro Agnew blasted the "effete corps of impudent snobs" who organized the moratorium.[101] UA faculty and student supporters of the war effort who agreed with Agnew staged an "Americans for America Day" two weeks later in Schaible Hall, charging antiwar protesters with tearing down the United States. Organizer Pat Bookey started the festivities by leading a recitation of the Pledge of Allegiance. "We must support our leaders," Bookey said, "if not we have nothing." Music professor Jean Paul Billaud charged the moratorium had been a cowardly "male prayer that the war end before he's called upon." Sociology professor Sarkis Atamian's cures for dissent were to "put a moratorium on all moratoriums, recognize the U.S. flag, raise hell and don't weaken, (and) initiate a fund in Congress for youths who want to leave the country." Atamian, a veteran of World War II, concluded by saying, "God Bless you Old Glory, if you need me again I don't want to go but I will!"[102]

ROTC units across the United States were lighting rods for opponents of the war, especially when the program was mandatory, as it was at the University of Alaska. Until 1967, all physically fit male students who were American citizens between the ages of fourteen and twenty-three without previous military experience were required to enlist in ROTC for two years. Until the late 1950s, military drill had been mandatory at every land grant college, but when numerous institutions dropped the requirement in the early 1960s, UA students resisted continuation of forced ROTC training.[103] "The educators fail to realize," student Robert Stafford wrote in the *Polar Star* in 1963, "that even though there would be a substantial decrease in the enrollment if it were on a voluntary basis, the calibre of persons who would be participating in this program would more than offset the decrease in number. Better to have a few who believe in the organization, than a large number who are either indifferent or vehemently opposed."[104]

In 1966, a freshman, claiming to be a conscientious objector, was forced out of school full time because he refused to sign an Army loyalty oath. As *Polar Star* editor Kent Sturgis wrote at the time, the issue to the majority of students appeared to be whether the institution was really a boot camp or a college: "Does the University of Alaska exist to produce officers for the U.S. Army or is its function one of educating free men to live in a free society?" In the spring of 1967, at the request of both ASUA and the advisory faculty council, the board of regents declared ROTC optional on a trial basis, a decision made permanent in 1972.[105]

As on most college campuses, student sentiment was largely antiwar. In an April 1968 straw poll, UA students voted overwhelmingly for Sen. Eugene McCarthy, the "peace candidate" whose challenge to Lyndon Johnson in the primaries helped topple the sitting president. Among UA students, McCarthy polled more than twice as many votes (309) as his nearest rival, Sen. Robert Kennedy (150), and more than triple the total of third place Richard Nixon (101). Among the others receiving votes were Lyndon Johnson (24), George Wallace (16), and Ronald Reagan (14).[106]

Another race with a direct bearing on the war was the 1968 re-election campaign of 81-year-old Sen. Ernest Gruening. Though one of the oldest members of the senate, Gruening became a hero to American youth in the 1960s for his opposition to the war in Vietnam. He had been the first U.S. Senator to go on record opposing the war. The dictatorship in South Vietnam was not worth "the life of one American boy," he said in 1964, at a time when only about 200 Americans had died in the conflict. "I consider every additional life that is sacrificed in this forlorn venture a tragedy." Eventually the total American death toll would reach more than 57,000.[107] Gruening and Sen. Wayne Morse of Oregon were the only two members of the U.S. Congress to vote against the infamous 1964 Tonkin Gulf Resolution, the decree based on a fabricated incident that essentially gave Lyndon Johnson a blank check to wage war in Southeast Asia. Since 1964, Gruening had traveled the country blasting LBJ's Vietnam policies, becoming a hero to student antiwar protestors, and earning the condemnation of his opponents.

Gruening's unexpected defeat in the 1968 Democratic primary by Mike Gravel, a hawkish 38-year-old real estate developer and former Speaker of the State House from Anchorage, inspired a grassroots write-in campaign to keep him in the Senate. Students and faculty from both the University of Alaska in Fairbanks and Alaska Methodist University in Anchorage spearheaded the write-in effort; co-directors in Fairbanks included political science professor Ed Webking, who used his home in faculty housing as campaign headquarters, and philosophy professor Walter Benesch.

A highlight of the Gruening campaign was the visit of comedian and supposed presidential candidate Pat Paulsen to the UA campus on the night before the election; a regular on the Smothers Brothers television show who staged his own satirical campaign for president to express concern about the war and other issues, Paulsen spoke to an estimated crowd of 4,000 people in the Patty Gym. He joked that Gravel's campaign promise to solve Alaska's problems was "only fair since he created most of them."[108]

Gruening privately admitted that he probably could not win, but professed to hope that at least the write-in would split the Democratic vote and throw the election to the Republican nominee, UA regent Elmer Rasmuson. Gruening had known Rasmuson for many years, having appointed him to the board of regents in 1950, and considered him far more honorable and trustworthy than Gravel. In the end, however, Rasmuson and Gruening came in second and third, splitting the anti-Gravel camp, and sending Gravel to the senate with only forty-five percent of the vote.[109]

When the campaign was over, Walter Benesch said that Ed Webking was left with a basement full of Gruening pamphlets and campaign biographies, "which, I understand, the Webkings ate with condensed milk and artificial sweeteners of various sorts."[110] Webking later wrote his Ph.D. dissertation on the Gruening campaign, and a corps of students learned the harsh realities of practical politics. They had allegedly been under FBI surveillance; a photograph of a Gruening rally was filed in city police records under "suspicious persons." Student volunteers were routinely called communists and traitors; some were physically assaulted. "The abuse was unwarranted and undeserved," Webking wrote, "especially for a group whose only unconventional belief was that one shouldn't trust anyone over 30—unless he's also over 80."[111]

Nearly as emotionally divisive as the Vietnam War was the emerging battle in the late 1960s and early 1970s over the environment. Students and faculty at the University of Alaska celebrated Earth Day in 1970, the first national examination of the human impact on the environment, with a three-day long environmental teach-in headlined by Secretary of Interior Walter J. Hickel. The former Alaska governor, who had resigned in 1968 to join the Nixon administration and had earned national praise for his exemplary environmental record as secretary, flew in from Washington to spend Earth Day at Fairbanks, where concern was focused on oil development in the Arctic and construction of the proposed Trans-Alaska Pipeline.[112]

In early 1968, the Atlantic-Richfield Company (now ARCO) and Humble Oil (now Exxon) discovered the largest oil field in North America; on Alaska's Arctic coast at Prudhoe Bay they hit an estimated 10 billion barrels of oil and 26 trillion cubic feet of natural gas. Life in Alaska would never be the same again. To bring the oil to market would require a nine-year environmental, legal and political battle, and completion of the most expensive private construction project in history—an $8 billion steel pipeline four feet in diameter spanning nearly 800 miles from Prudhoe Bay to Valdez, the ice-free harbor on Prince William Sound where the oil would be pumped into tankers.[113] Many environmentalists opposed all development on the North Slope, contending that the pipeline would despoil the last great expanse of wilderness in the United States. Transporting billions of barrels of oil across hundreds of miles of permafrost—permanently frozen ground—without damaging the fragile ecosystems of the north, and without harming the vast herds of caribou that roamed the arctic plains, posed engineering and environmental hazards for which no one had any ready solutions in 1969–1970. Furthermore, Alaska Natives relied on the land for their subsistence, and rejected any pipeline plans until their century-old land claims were settled.

In late September 1969, only weeks after the State of Alaska earned a record $900 million from North Slope oil lease sales, TAPS (the Trans-Alaska Pipeline System, later officially incorporated as the Alyeska Pipeline Service Co.) displayed sample forty-foot-long sections of the steel pipeline in various locations around Fairbanks, including one outside the University Museum. Within a day, someone had crudely painted the words "SELL OUT" on the side of the university's piece of pipe. "This is thought to be the work of conservationists," reported the *News-Miner*, "who are against the pipeline for

OPPONENTS BEGIN "PIPING UP"
Critics of the proposed Trans-Alaska Pipeline repeatedly voiced their objections on the forty-foot sample section of pipe displayed on campus in 1969.

Rasmuson Library

239

RESEARCHERS TRY "PIPING HOT"
The Trans-Alaska Pipeline's buried "hot pipe"
experiment on the West Ridge in the early 1970s was
designed to test the impact of the proposed oil
pipeline on permafrost.

Don Borchert

ecological and other reasons." Though the university quickly painted over the graffiti, during the following year the pipe became a favorite target of midnight spray-paint artists opposed to the pipeline. "Hickel plays T.A.P.S. for Alaska," read a typical phrase that appeared one morning on the pipe. Shocked by the vandalism, Fairbanks businessman Harry Porter said, "I would think that people at the university would not 'sell out' intellectually until they knew all aspects of this pipeline. Some very keen minds out there are addressing themselves to the problems of the pipeline."[114]

University researchers, in fact, performed innumerable research studies related to the pipeline in every discipline from archaeology to wildlife management. One unusual experiment at the Institute of

Arctic Biology on West Ridge involved burying a 600-foot long pipe of corrugated aluminum behind the Irving Building to determine the effect of a hot oil pipeline on permafrost.[115]

As everywhere in Alaska, proponents and opponents of the Trans-Alaska Pipeline on campus found little on which they could agree. Dr. Wood characterized those who opposed the pipeline as "anti-God, anti-Man and anti-mind."[116] In response, Greg Moore, a wildlife major, professed to find it baffling that anyone could argue "we require Prudhoe crude, not only to live, but to maintain integrity with this so-called God." Moore closed with a prayer of his own: "May the Valdez terminal be moved to your front door, Dr. Wood, and drown you in your 'progress.'"[117]

In 1973, the U.S. Congress authorized construction of the Trans-Alaska Pipeline. That same year William R. Wood retired as university president at age sixty-six. Wood's departure did not take him far from the president's house on campus; he and Dorothy Jane moved about five miles to downtown Fairbanks, as they had decided they wanted to stay in Alaska. Except for Charles Bunnell, Wood is the only ex-president of the University of Alaska to retire in Alaska. Without a regular job, Wood suddenly had the opportunity to "do and do and do," as he always wanted, for any cause he considered worthwhile; he took on the unofficial role of first citizen of Fairbanks, organizing community activities ranging from the creation of downtown Golden Heart Park, to cleaning the streets, helping the Boy Scouts, raising funds for charities, promoting economic development, and even serving a stint as city mayor. Though some would decry the changes the pipeline would bring to Fairbanks, Mayor Wood relished every minute of the oil boom adventure. Later he said the pipeline days were "a lovely time, packed with excitement. I wouldn't have missed them for the world."[118]

Dr. Wood was the last of the university's pioneer presidents, the final leader cast in the mold of a builder like President Bunnell. Wood left behind a statewide institution that had grown so rapidly in thirteen years that the campus would have hardly been recognized by the class of 1960. The first three presidents—Bunnell, Moore, and Patty—had laid the foundations of the University of Alaska, but it was William R. Wood who built the rest.

Portfolio
1959–1973

AMONG THE NEW CONSTRUCTION PROJECTS
underway or recently completed in this 1963 aerial
view are the power plant and warehouse, the
Duckering Building, the Bunnell Memorial Plaza and
Fountain, the Lola Tilly Commons, Lathrop Hall, the
Patty Building, the utilidor to West Ridge, Skarland
Hall, and dozens of new faculty houses.

Historical Photograph Collection, Rasmuson Library

(ABOVE) THE 1960 UNIVERSITY CATALOG FEATURED *this photograph of history professor Herman Slotnick identifying the 49th star belonging to the new state of Alaska.*

Rasmuson Library

(LEFT) ERNEST AND KAY PATTY LEAVE *Fairbanks after retirement in June 1960.*

Alumni Services

(RIGHT) A 1959 DIAGRAM OF THE *statewide mission for the "49th State University."*

Rasmuson Library

State University

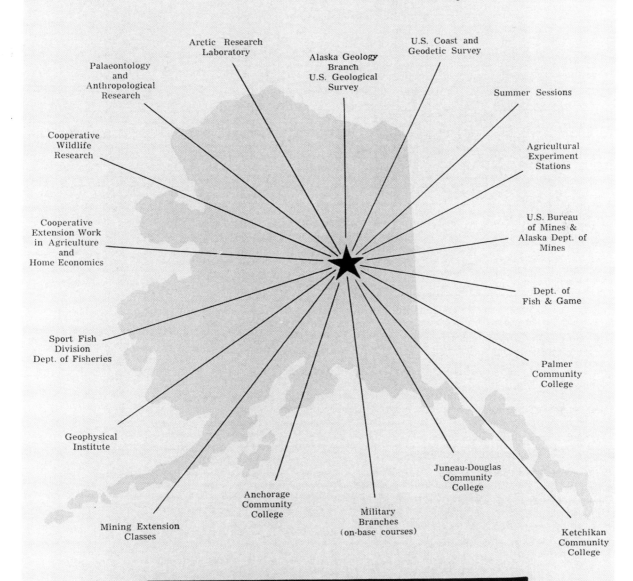

Arctic Research Laboratory

Alaska Geology Branch U.S. Geological Survey

U.S. Coast and Geodetic Survey

Palaeontology and Anthropological Research

Summer Sessions

Cooperative Wildlife Research

Agricultural Experiment Stations

Cooperative Extension Work in Agriculture and Home Economics

U.S. Bureau of Mines & Alaska Dept. of Mines

Dept. of Fish & Game

Sport Fish Division Dept. of Fisheries

Palmer Community College

Geophysical Institute

Juneau-Douglas Community College

Mining Extension Classes

Anchorage Community College

Military Branches (on-base courses)

Ketchikan Community College

The University of Alaska is a statewide organization for teaching, research, extension and public service. Some phase of University work—or the work of its cooperating agencies—affects the life, directly or indirectly, of practically every citizen of Alaska.

(ABOVE) ANTHROPOLOGIST IVAR SKARLAND
*(in academic robes) with three old friends and
distinguished scientists: left to right, biologist Adolph
Murie and his brother Olaus Murie, Skarland, and
Otto Geist.*

Alumni Services Collection, Rasmuson Library

NOTED CONSERVATIONIST MARGARET MURIE
*(the entire class of 1924) and her husband, biologist
Olaus Murie, the director of the Wilderness Society,
stand with the Rusty Heurlin portrait of themselves
hiking the Sheenjek River Valley in Northeast Alaska.
The Muries' expeditions to the Sheenjek were
instrumental in the campaign which eventually
created the Arctic National Wildlife Refuge in 1960.
The UA Alumni Association donated Heurlin's
painting to the university shortly before Olaus
Murie's death in 1963.*

Alumni Services Collection, Rasmuson Library

247

(ABOVE) THE CAMPUS "BULLDOZER REVOLUTION"
*commenced in 1960 with contractors scraping about
ten feet off the top of College Hill where Old Main
once stood, flattening the ground in front of the Mines
Building and the first floor of the new Duckering
Building. Both the Mines Building and the old gym
were now on the same grade, eliminating the flights of
stairs that previously made a walk across campus an
obstacle course and clearing the way for construction
of the Bunnell Memorial Plaza and Fountain. ". . . at
last, the campus buildings seem united," the* Alaska
Alumnus *noted in 1960, "and the university city
begins to emerge."*

George Soli Collection, Rasmuson Library

(ABOVE) ONE OF THE EARLY VERSIONS OF AN
architectural plan for the university's new gymnasium.

Farthest North Collegian

(BELOW) PROGRAM COVER FROM THE 1963
dedication of the Ernest N. Patty Building.

Rasmuson Library

Ernest N. Patty Building

For Health, Physical Education, Recreation and ROTC
University of Alaska, College, Alaska

THE "FLYING NANOOKS" IN 1967–1968, THE
*inaugural year for long-time head basketball coach Al
Svenningson. Front row, left to right: Milo Griffin,
Leo Kouremetis, Benny Ramos; second row: Steve
McSwain, Greg Mitchell, Randy Boyd, Pat Tielborg;
back row: Dan McHenry, Glen Boggess, Jackie Lewis,
Gary Schaefer, and Scott Loll.*

*It was only appropriate for 5' 11" Milo Griffin to hold
the ball. The team's top scorer averaged 26 points a
game, and by the end of his collegiate career in 1969,
Griffin held most of the university's all-time scoring
records.*

University Relations Collection, Rasmuson Library

THE 1969 REUNION PHOTO (SPLICED TOGETHER) *of the championship 1933–1934 Alaska Agricultural College and School of Mines basketball team. From left to right: John O'Shea, Bob Henning, George Karabelnikoff, Bill O'Neill, and Harry Lundell.*

Alumni Services Collection, Rasmuson Library

AFTER 1963, THE UA BASKETBALL "POLAR BEARS" *became known as the "Nanooks" (from the Inupiaq word for polar bear). The "Flying Nanooks" ranked among the strangest nicknames in college athletics. The dribbling polar bear atop a Boeing 727 served as the team symbol for many years.*

Rasmuson Library

HOCKEY PRACTICE IN THE BELUGA, THE INFLATABLE *structure that housed the campus ice rink after 1969.*

University Relations Collections, Rasmuson Library

(BELOW) THE START OF THE 1971 EQUINOX *Marathon. In September 1963, skier Nat Goodhue inaugurated the grueling 26-mile endurance race from the Patty Gym to the top of Ester Dome and back, in part to preserve the hiking and ski trails on university land. Over the years, the marathon has grown into a fall classic regularly attracting hundreds of hikers and runners.*

All-Alaska Weekly

JACK AND FRIEDA
*Townshend and their three
children—Brenda, Donna,
and Donald—ostensibly
train for the 1968 marathon
under the watchful eyes
of basketball coach Al
Svenningson (kneeling) and
race director Bill Smith.
Townshend, the chief of the
College Observatory,
became a dedicated runner
years later, and helped
spearhead the 1992 cam-
paign to mark the trail
permanently with
metal signs.*

University Relations Collection,
Rasmuson Library

TWO WEARY HIKERS
*approach the halfway point
at the top of Ester Dome on
the 1968 marathon:
President William R. Wood
and Dorothy Jane Wood.
The Woods completed the
race that year in just under
ten hours, finishing last
respectively in the men's
and women's hiking
divisions. It was Dr. Wood's
second marathon, and he
edged Dorothy Jane by
seven seconds.*

University Relations Collection,
Rasmuson Library

ON AUGUST 15, 1967, THE CHENA RIVER CRESTED *about half a dozen feet above its banks. This photo, looking north along Cushman Street towards downtown Fairbanks, was taken about twenty-five hours after the flood waters had peaked.*

(ABOVE) THE FLOOD WATERS REACHED AS HIGH AS
the bottom of the stairs at the foot of College Hill.

University Relations Collection, Rasmuson Library

(RIGHT) TWO OF THE NEARLY 7,000 FLOOD
evacuees stranded at the university in 1967.

University Relations Collection, Rasmuson Library

DR. VERA ALEXANDER, THE FIRST WOMAN
*to earn a Ph.D. at the University of Alaska,
received her doctorate in Marine Science in 1965.*

Mel Lockwood

LAURENCE J. IRVING, FOR WHOM THE IRVING
*Biosciences Building is named, was one of the
pioneers of modern physiology in the arctic. This 1971
Fred Machetanz painting, commissioned by Grace
and Arthur Schaible, hangs in the entrance to the
Irving Building. It shows Irving at age seventy-four*
*on the Bering Sea pack ice, measuring the
temperature of an infant harbor seal. In the
background is the University of Alaska research vessel
Alpha Helix.*

Institute of Arctic Biology

REKNOWNED GEOPHYSICIST AND GEOPHYSICAL
Institute advisor Sydney Chapman (left) inspects the
equipment in a NASA research aircraft that flew to
Alaska in 1968. With Chapman are UA geophysicists
Gerald Romick (center) and Chapman's former
student Syun Akasofu.

T. Neil Davis Collection, Rasmuson Library

SCIENTISTS AT THE GEOPHYSICAL INSTITUTE HOLD
a cable to demonstrate "the verification of conjugate
auroras at the North and South Poles." From left to

right: Neil Davis, Milt Peek, Wallace Murcray, Hans
Nielsen, Russ Beach, Jim Wells, and Eugene Wescott.

Geophysical Institute

UNIVERSITY OF ALASKA ARCHIVIST
Paul McCarthy begins processing a new collection of papers donated to the university by Ernest Gruening following his defeat in the 1968 U.S. Senate campaign.

University Relations Collection,
Rasmuson Library

DON DINKLE, A PROFESSOR OF
plant physiology at the Agricultural Experiment Station, showing a new strain of corn developed for Alaska.

University Relations Collection,
Rasmuson Library

EDNA WILDER TEACHES A CLASS
in the art of skin sewing.

Alumni Services Collection, Rasmuson Library

(BELOW) JIMMY BEDFORD (SECOND FROM
*left), the irrepressible motor scooter-riding
journalism professor (author of* Around the
World on a Nickel) *with four photography
students in the early 1970s.*

University Relations Collection, Rasmuson Library

PHILOSOPHY PROFESSOR RUDY KREJCI *in the early 1960s. Born in central Czechoslovakia, Krejci escaped from the communists in 1951 by hiding in a coal car on a train bound for Austria. After earning his Ph.D., he came to the University of Alaska in 1960 to teach German and Russian, and later helped establish the philosophy department.*

Claus-M. Naske

(BELOW) BRUCE R. GORDON (AT LEFT) *an assistant registered guide and professor of French and Spanish, with Charles J. Keim, a registered guide and dean of the College of Arts and Letters, on a hunting trip in August 1964. Gordon served as the first elected head of the University Assembly in 1968. Dean Keim, a prolific author on Alaskan topics, encouraged and coaxed dozens of young writers to turn their experiences into publishable manuscripts.*

Bruce R. Gordon

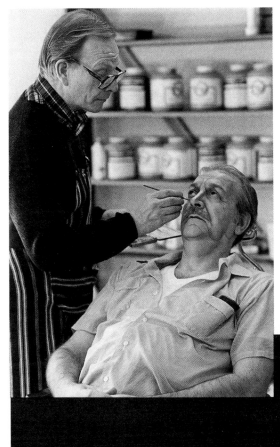

PROFESSOR LEE SALISBURY APPLIES MAKEUP TO *Gene DeWilde for a production of Oscar Wilde's "The Importance of Being Earnest." Salisbury was the founder of the Drama Workshop, and directed at least two plays a year for more than thirty years.*

Sabra McCracken

(BELOW) THE FIRST PRODUCTION IN THE NEW *Fine Arts Theatre in February 1971 was "The Man of La Mancha," directed by Lee Salisbury, with set design by Walter Ensign, Jr. Members of the cast (from left to right) included: Dennis Goff, Tom Butters, Pat Cahill, Melinda Mattson, Steve Burgess, Roy Corral, and Ron Short.*

Lee Salisbury

261

MEMBERS OF THE CREATIVE WRITER'S WORKSHOP
in the old library in the Bunnell Building.

Ed Skellings

HUNDREDS OF *students and faculty crowded the University Commons in February 1968 to hear eight panelists debate the pros and cons of smoking marijuana.*

All-Alaska Weekly

THE 1967 COMMENCEMENT PARADE LED BY
university marshall William Cashen, flanked by
Regent Elmer Rasmuson on the left and Dean Earl
Beistline on the right. Cashen carried the ceremonial
university mace of silver, jade, and rosewood created
by art professor Ron Senungetuk in honor of the
university's 1967 Golden Anniversary.

Alumni Services Collection, Rasmuson Library

(ABOVE) SUMMER MUSIC CAMP AT THE UNIVERSITY OF
*Alaska in 1964, with Professor Charles W. Davis
dishing it out. In the chow line from left to right: Gary
Keskela, George Yeager, Paul Sauer, Bev Taylor, and
Joan Murphy.*

Music Department

(RIGHT) FAITH WILLIAMS DURING FINALS
week outside McIntosh Hall in May 1963.

Sandra Stringer

ANNOUNCER LOUISE KOWALSKI READS THE NEWS
on KUAC-FM, the voice of the University of Alaska.

John Reisinger

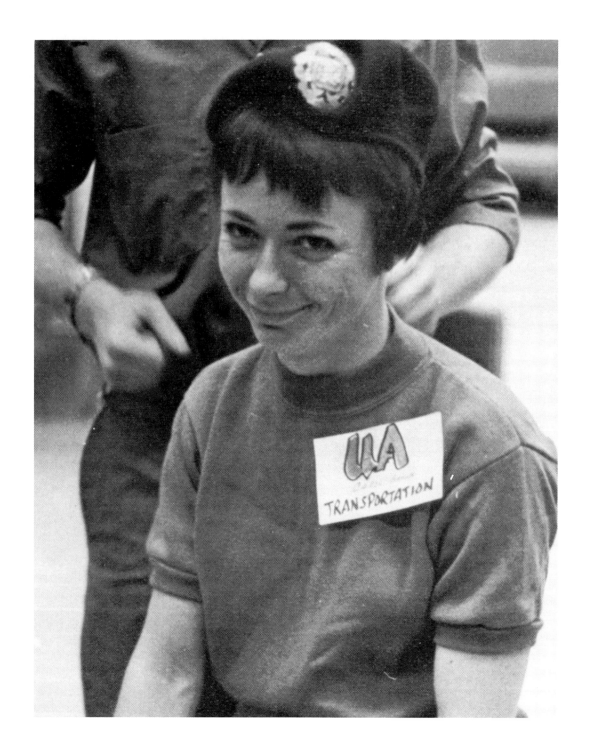

CAROL BROWN HELPS WITH STUDENT
orientation and registration during the 1969 fall
semester. Brown, who worked with Student Affairs for
many years, was a regular fixture of student life at the
university until she died of cancer in 1992.

Rasmuson Library

A PARTY AT CELIA HUNTER'S HOME IN DOGPATCH, *honoring Phil Holland—winner of the 1969 Joel Weigert Award as the outstanding graduating senior man—shortly before he left to join the Peace Corps in India. Standing in back from left to right: Phil Waner, philosophy professor Walter Benesch (holding his baby son Ilya), Phil Holland, and biologist Dave Norton. Seated: Frank Holland (Phil's father), artist Bill Berry, Mark Berry, Renate Benesch, Liz Berry, Carol Norton, and Paul Berry.*

Celia Hunter

(RIGHT) GRADUATE STUDENT AND SKARLAND HALL *resident advisor John Davies carries the bags of Mary Worrall, left, Adran Messer, center, and Carol Muller, as they move into the dorm in September 1968.*

University Relations Collection, Rasmuson Library

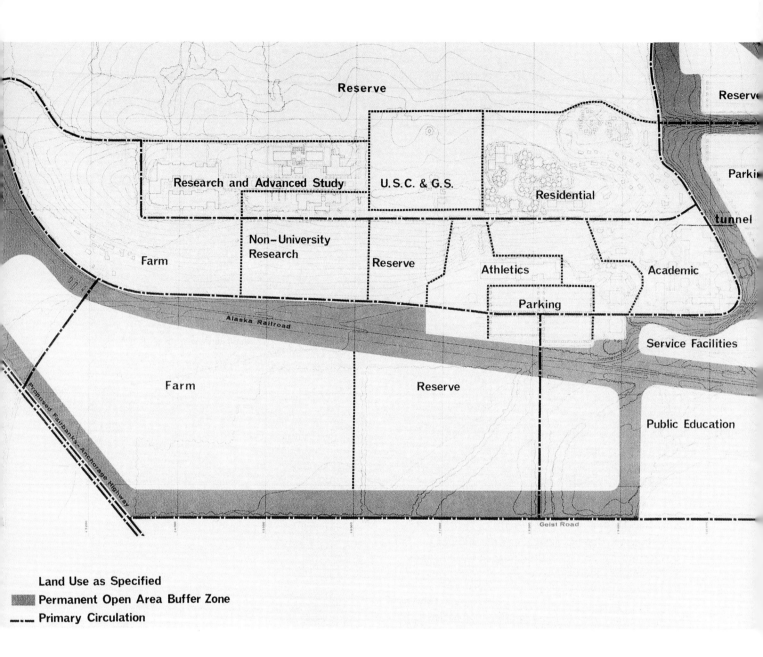

Reserve

Research and Advanced Study

U.S.C. & G.S.

Reserve

Parki

Residential

tunnel

Farm

Non–University Research

Reserve

Athletics

Academic

Parking

Alaska Railroad

Service Facilities

Farm

Reserve

Public Education

Geist Road

Land Use as Specified

Permanent Open Area Buffer Zone

Primary Circulation

THE LONG-RANGE CAMPUS LAND USE PLAN IN THE
1960s. *The area dedicated to "Research and Advanced
Study" is the West Ridge research complex.*

Rasmuson Library

268

PRESIDENT AND MRS. WOOD ON MAY 15, 1970 *wield a two-handled shovel at the ground breaking ceremony for the new student activities center named in honor of Dr. Wood. The* Fairbanks Daily News-Miner *suggested the center should be named the "Woods [plural] Activities Center," since the two of them were an inseparable team. Looking on from the podium is campus historian William Cashen. Among the other spectators are Regents Hugh "Bud" Fate and William A. O'Neill, student Mary Hughes, and Charles Sargent, director of planning and development.*

University Relations Collection, Rasmuson Library

THE "STAIRS TO NOWHERE" *under construction in Wood Center.*

Alumni Services Collection, Rasmuson Library

PAMELIA STEIGER (LEFT) AND KAREN KOWALSKI,
student guides at the University of Alaska Museum,
show off the crowded collection of stuffed bears.

Alumni Services Collection, Rasmuson Library

(RIGHT) ONE BUILDING THAT PRESIDENT WOOD
long dreamed of building—though he never succeeded
in raising the needed funds—was a spectacular
"Museum of the North" to replace the old gymnasium
as the home of the university's invaluable artifacts.
Plans in 1967 called for the new museum to feature
the "Dome of the Barabara," a planetarium "designed
to simulate phenomena of the northern skies."

Rasmuson Library

270

THE LARGEST CONSTRUCTION PROJECT IN UNIVERSITY history up to that time, the fine arts and library complex was built in October 1968 on the site of the old campus power plant. The five-story library, in the upper right hand corner of the photograph, contained floor space approximately equal in area to the combined total square footage of all the academic buildings constructed during the first three decades on College Hill. The entire complex—housing the library, as well as the art, music, and theatre departments—provided more than a quarter of a million square feet. At the time, it was reputed to be the largest structure in Alaska.

University Relations Collection, Rasmuson Library

CONSTRUCTION IN 1969 OF THE PREFABRICATED *Modular Units on the steep hillside between the upper dorms on Rainey Ridge and Lathrop Hall. Called the "train wreck" by some students, the unique apartments accommodated married and graduate students for twenty years until the fire marshal condemned the complex in 1989.*

Rasmuson Library

273

FIREMEN BATTLE THE WORST BLAZE IN UNIVERSITY *history. A $500,000 fire in the commons on June 14, 1968, killed Robyn Aubrey, a twenty-year-old sophomore from Eagle River majoring in biological sciences. Aubrey worked in the commons, and apparently rushed into the office to try to save the cash box. The fire started when six gallons of grease ignited in a deep fat fryer. Attempts to control the blaze were slowed because water pressure had been temporarily turned off in the commons due to campus construction. The fire also destroyed twenty-nine paintings of Alaskan bush pilots by Harvey Goodale, which were a gift from pioneer aviator Bob Reeve. Color photographs of the Goodale paintings were saved and later put on permanent display in the Rasmuson Library.*

University Relations Collection, Rasmuson Library

THE BACKWASH FROM A HOVERING HELICOPTER *was one of several techniques used to remove snow from the Beluga inflatable structure. Accumulated snow caused the first collapse of the Beluga in 1969, only a month after its installation.*

University Relations

(ABOVE) ERNEST AND DOROTHY GRUENING AT THE *dedication of the Gruening Building in May 1972. A hero to many young Americans in the 1960s for his steadfast opposition to the war in Vietnam, Gruening and Wayne Morse of Oregon were the only two members of the U.S. Senate to vote against the 1964 Tonkin Gulf Resolution. During the dedication of the Gruening building the 85-year old former senator looked up at the massive eight-story social science fortress named in his honor and said, "Don't they know I'm a dove?"*

Alumni Services Collection, Rasmuson Library

(UPPER RIGHT) A 1968 ARTIST'S CONCEPTION OF THE *eight-story Gruening Building; the students strolling in the tree-lined plaza are all wearing either sideburns or mini-skirts. The three-story building on the right is Hess Hall, the first concrete dormitory on campus, which was demolished in 1970 to make way for construction of the Gruening Building.*

University Relations Collection, Rasmuson Library

(LOWER RIGHT) CONSTRUCTION OF THE GRUENING *Building in 1971–1972.*

University Relations Collection, Rasmuson Library

To accommodate the record student enrollment in the fall of 1969, the university opened the first four floors of Bartlett Hall, even though contractors had not yet completed the building. Students living in Bartlett that semester protested the lack of laundry facilities and telephones, as well as "intermittent water, erratic elevator service, erratic heating and inadequate janitorial service." During one unexpected water outage on a Sunday night, about 30 Bartlett residents with "bath towels over their shoulders and toothbrushes in their hands" marched to President Wood's house chanting "We want water." Mrs. Wood told the protestors that President Wood was on a trip out of town.

The four students above were staging their own sit-in at the laundry facilities in Bartlett Hall. Left to right: Bruno Caciagli, Bill Evans, Dave Allowan, and Dan Davenport.

Rasmuson Library

(Right) "The Glass Bead Game" was the most versatile and talented musical group in Fairbanks in the early 1970s. Named after a popular Herman Hesse novel, the group played blues, jazz, and rock and roll. The members from left to right, outside the old Howling Dog Saloon in Ester: Sam Levine (flute and sax), Pat Fitzgerald (drums), Donna Stewart—sitting in front (flute and piano), Phil Falkowski (piano), Jim Bartlett (acoustic guitar), Susan McInnis (lead singer), Gary Wescott—leaning over (lead guitar), and Ron "Rif" Rafson (bass). A sometime member of the band (not in the picture) was Al Green, who performed memorable trumpet duets by himself, playing two horns at the same time.

Howard Ringley

A MORATORIUM DAY PROTEST BANNER ON CONSTITUTION HALL. Rasmuson Library

AFTER MARCHING FOUR MILES FROM THE *university campus to downtown Fairbanks, an estimated crowd of about 350 peaceful antiwar protestors cross the Cushman Street Bridge on Moratorium Day, October 15, 1969.*

Polar Star

(**BELOW**) **A FLYER ANNOUNCING THE SCHEDULE OF** *the Moratorium Day March from the university to downtown Fairbanks.*

Rasmuson Library

MORATORIUM DAY MARCH

October 15, 1969

1. Marchers will convene in the University of Alaska Plaza
    at 2:15 p.m. (Please be prompt)

2. The group will proceed east on College Road to Illinois
    Street, and then south to the parking lot of Samson Hard-
    ware (immediately north of Cushman Street Bridge), arriving
    at 3:45 p.m.

3. At that point anti-war airmen and soldiers from Eielson and
    Wainwright, high school students, and concerned townspeople
    will join the demonstration.

4. The enlarged group will then leave at exactly 4:15 p.m. to
    march south on Cushman as far as Airport Road. (The
    Moratorium Day Committee will try to furnish return rides,
    but marchers should attempt to make their own arrangements.)

5. This will be a <u>peaceful demonstration</u>, please cooperate with
    marshals.

THE RETURN OF THE "FULL-COURT PRESS"
The main lobby of Signers' Hall, once a basketball court where athletes raced back and forth, became an arena for registration lines after the building's renovation in 1984–1985.

Sam Winch, University Relations

From UA to UAF 1973–1993

In the mid-1980s, Glen Franklin (class of 1936) organized an alumni campaign to erect a life-size bronze sculpture of former President Charles E. Bunnell on the Bunnell Memorial Plaza. Located near the 1915 concrete cornerstone planted by his rival James Wickersham, Bunnell's statue has become a university landmark. Sculptor Joan Bugbee Jackson cast the former president in midstride with a determined look on his face—on his way perhaps to advise the current chancellor and other administrators in Signers' Hall about the future of the university, or possibly to scold someone parked illegally in the visitor's parking lot.[1]

The bronze Bunnell is a symbol of the origin and heritage of the University of Alaska in Fairbanks at a time when higher education in Alaska requires the same courage and initiative shown by the leaders of the past. In the twenty years since William R. Wood retired in 1973, both the university and the post of president have changed dramatically. No one person could ever again play the dominant role of the first four pioneer presidents. Bunnell and Wood, the two longest-serving University of Alaska chief executives, led the institution for a total of forty-one years. In contrast, there have been seven UA presidents in the last twenty years—including four different presidents in a span of only twelve months in 1977–1978. Even long-time university employees cannot remember all of their names.

In the last two decades, the University of Alaska has evolved from a single entity on College Hill into a system of three separately accredited universities in Fairbanks (University of Alaska Fairbanks), Anchorage (University of Alaska Anchorage), and Juneau (University of Alaska Southeast). The statewide organization is governed by a single board of regents and supervised by a single administration headquartered in Fairbanks. The "University of Alaska" no longer exists as an educational institution with students; the name survives only on the administrative structure of the statewide system. Each of its three units has its own chancellor, catalog, mission statement, student government, alumni organization, and branch campuses. Pointedly, UAA's logo modifies the university seal, replacing the year 1917 with "Anchorage." Among the three units, UAF is designated as the comprehensive institution responsible for statewide research programs, including the Cooperative Extension Service, and is also the only university in the system to grant doctoral degrees.[2]

The evolution of this three-in-one statewide system of higher education has been difficult and complicated, and it is too soon to evaluate fully these

UA's epidemic of local logos

Since the early 1980s, several UA presidents have attempted to develop a new logo to represent the entire University of Alaska statewide system, but like the mystery of the Holy Trinity, no one has yet quite solved the problem of how the three-in-one UA system can be represented.

On February 19, 1982 President Jay Barton explained to the *Sun-Star* that he would like to replace the university system's dozens of different letterheads, which included logos with dogsleds, caribou and even school buses. The president wanted a new unified logo for the entire institution, one that would preserve campus identity but show all were part of one university.

Barton claimed the least inspiring UA symbols were those based on the university seal. "That seal approach is archaic," he told the *Sun-Star*. "It's an old fashioned kind of thing." Barton preferred a logo that was "clean and light. This is a modern young university in a modern young state, and I'd like to go to a more symbolic design." Neither Barton nor later presidents have been able to come up with a satisfactory design, and the university seal is still the only statewide logo.

---

enormous changes. The university's administrative structure has been shuffled and reshuffled countless times. For a while, organizational charts changed almost monthly. "Enough growth, change and controversy has been packed into the last ten years at the University of Alaska," a reporter claimed in 1979, "to make a century at quieter institutions."[3] In the mid-1980s, a student wrote an entire master's thesis on the organizational changes in the community college in Juneau. According to author Kathleen Stewart, the orgy of UA reorganizations began in the 1970s when "the University experienced more expansions, more problems, more conflicts, and more threats . . . than ever before. Reorganizations had solved few . . . difficulties, but would continue to be the solution of choice in the following years of strife and upheaval."[4]

Wood's successor as president was Dr. Robert W. Hiatt, a marine biologist who had spent twenty-six years in various capacities at the University of Hawaii. In 1975, President Hiatt reorganized and decentralized the University of Alaska system, and launched an ambitious plan to expand the community college system throughout rural Alaska. Hiatt's new organizational chart abolished the position of "provost," the chief executive officer slot for the Fairbanks campus. From 1970–1975 this position had been held by Earl Beistline, a 1939 graduate in mining engineering, who had also been dean of the School of Mines since 1949.[5] The 1975 reorganization placed the three large university campuses in Fairbanks, Anchorage, and Juneau under the control of individual chancellors. Hiatt picked Howard Cutler, former academic vice president in the Wood administration in the early 1960s, as the first chancellor of the University of Alaska Fairbanks.[6]

With the 1975 appointment of Chancellor Cutler, the Fairbanks campus, which had for so long been *the* University of Alaska, became the University of Alaska Fairbanks, the primary residential and research unit in a statewide university system. (Over the course of the next thirteen years, the preferred style of the new campus title included first a comma, then a dash, and finally no punctuation at all between "Alaska" and "Fairbanks.") Students and faculty found it strange getting used to the school's new name and identity. Not until the early 1980s did the lettering on the university's Nanook logo officially change from UA to UAF, and it was the middle of the decade before ASUA renamed itself ASUAF.[7]

Even before the 1975 reorganization, Fairbanks students had grown keenly aware of the emergence of other university campuses in the system. In 1974, Governor William A. Egan chose Ronald Wendte, a graduate student at the Juneau campus, to be the first student regent. "News of the governor's appointment met with shock, rage, and disgust from students on this campus," the *Polar Star* reported in February 1974, "for the selection obviously smacks of political tokenism."[8] Fairbanks students had been instrumental in lobbying for the creation of the student regent position. The other campuses—each of which were allowed to submit the names of two nominees—had shown little interest, while Fairbanks had staged a hotly contested four-way election to choose its candidates, Allen Blume and Rusty Walker.[9] The first student regent from Fairbanks, Gerard R. LaParle, was not selected until 1976.

Another touchy symbolic issue arose in late 1975, when the board of regents reserved up to $250,000 to build, lease or purchase a luxury home or condominium in Anchorage for the use of university state-wide administrators. Fairbanks students quickly dubbed it the "Hiatt [sic] House;" the *Polar Star* printed a cartoon that pictured President Hiatt's new "house" as a seven-story hotel. At a time when the university claimed to be under an "austerity budget" and said it could no longer afford to publish a new catalog for students every year, the Hiatt House outraged students and the general public, and further enmeshed university affairs with the bitter regional rivalries that characterize Alaskan politics.[10]

Fairbanksans take pride in disagreeing on almost everything except support for the university, one of the largest employers in the Fairbanks North Star Borough. Interior residents and politicians of all political persuasions have always unanimously resisted any possible signs that the headquarters of the university or any major university programs might be moved to Alaska's largest city. The transition of the Fairbanks campus from the "UA" to "UAF" left many local residents uneasy about the future of the school. Did the 1971 start-up of the Anchorage Senior College, which became the nucleus of UAA, forebode the decline of the Fairbanks campus? Furthermore, in the 1960s and 1970s, boosters such as *Anchorage Daily Times* publisher Bob Atwood nearly succeeded in moving the state capital from Juneau to Southcentral Alaska. Fairbanksans feared the next goal might be an academic version of the capital move, shifting the headquarters of the university from its historic home in Fairbanks to Anchorage. "That Anchorage has grown to be the biggest city in the state" the *Fairbanks Daily News-Miner* noted in 1972, "is no particular qualification to demand . . . headquarters of the Uni-versity of Alaska." The newspaper pointed out that the central campuses of most statewide university systems were seldom in the largest urban areas: for instance, the academic "capitals" of various states were Boulder, not Denver; Lincoln, not Omaha; Baton Rouge, not New Orleans; Berkeley, not San Francisco; Eugene, not Portland; Columbia, not St. Louis, *et cetera*, and therefore the University of Alaska's heart should remain in Fairbanks, not Anchorage.[11]

The Hiatt House was never built, but the proposal was still pending in early 1977 when the

285

Alaska Native Language Center

Michael Krauss has always been attracted to what he calls "underdog languages." When he came to the University of Alaska at age twenty-six, the young linguist had already completed a doctoral dissertation at Harvard on the Inishmaan dialect of Irish Gaelic, and had studied Faroese and Icelandic. But with his arrival in Fairbanks in September 1960 to teach French and linguistics, he adopted as his life's work the investigation and preservation of Alaska's richest but most endangered cultural legacy: its twenty Aleut, Eskimo and Indian languages.

"Every language is as infinitely complex as a living organism," Krauss once wrote. "As such it is surely the most marvelous manifestation of the human mind. A hundred linguists working a hundred years could not fully fathom the mystery of a single language."

Yet in 1960 Krauss was the only academic linguist in the state of Alaska; many of Alaska's languages were on the slide towards extinction and had never been recorded or written down. It was a race against time to document and try to save as many of these languages as possible.

In the spring of 1961 Krauss taught the first college course ever on an Alaska Native language; the course was Yupik Eskimo. Students in the class included Martha Teeluk, a Native speaker from St.

Mary's, and Irene Reed, who subsequently took over the teaching duties and helped write a basic Yupik grammar. Krauss's own research focused on Athabaskan languages and then on compiling a dictionary of the Eyak language of the Copper River Delta area, a missing link between the Tlingit and Athabaskan languages. Only one Native speaker of Eyak is left today: Marie Smith (age seventy-two).

In 1972 the state legislature established the Alaska Native Language Center at UAF to research and document Alaska's Native languages. Under Krauss's direction, the ANLC has been instrumental in the development of Alaska's bilingual education programs, and has preserved a vast literature of Native oral traditions through transcription and translation. Over the last two decades the center has published about 250 titles in nineteen languages, including Inupiaq Eskimo, Central Yupik Eskimo, Siberian Yupik, Alutiiq Eskimo, Aleut Eskimo, Eyak, Tlingit, Haida, and eleven Athabaskan languages.

Despite the impressive work of ANLC scholars such as Krauss, Jeff Leer, Larry Kaplan, James Kari,

university's central administration nearly collapsed. In February, President Hiatt was forced to resign after the university announced it faced an estimated cash shortfall of up to $10 million, and could go broke within two months unless bailed out immediately by the state government. Poor billing and accounting practices, a faulty new computer system, and the failure of a university bond issue in November 1976—the first time that Alaskan voters had ever rejected a university bond request—brought on the fiscal crisis. Evy Walters, the editor of the alumni

magazine, declared in the spring of 1977 that the university had reached "the brink of destruction."[12]

Alaska governor Jay Hammond, the first University of Alaska graduate to occupy the governor's mansion, maintained that the financial crisis began with the university's too-rapid expansion in the late 1960s. A budget shortfall in the early 1970s, which required a legislative appropriation of one million dollars to help the university balance its books, should have been adequate warning. "The university's financial problems really started about ten or twelve

Steve Jacobson, Edna MacLean, Irene Reed, Eliza Jones, James Nageak and others, the future for most of Alaska's Native languages—like so many minority languages around the world—appears bleak. Only two of Alaska's twenty languages are still spoken regularly by children: Central Yupik and Siberian Yupik. Though no Alaska languages have yet become extinct, Krauss estimates that within the next twenty years half of Alaska's languages may decline to the point where it "becomes impossible to retrieve further information about them, or traditional knowledge and wisdom expressed in them."

The Alaska Native Language Center's mission is to avert or delay this impending cultural catastrophe. Whether it succeeds or not, ANLC's attempt to save these languages and literatures from oblivion may well be recognized one day as the University of Alaska's most original contribution to the world of knowledge.

LINGUIST MICHAEL KRAUSS AT THE BLACKBOARD *in the spring of 1961 leads the first college course ever taught in Yupik Eskimo. The sentence on the board reads, "Maybe you will want to be able to hunt seals." Shown around the table from left to right: Annette Bork (face mostly obscured), Bertha Iokienna, Chuck Degnan, Martha Teeluk, Irene Reed, and Ambrose Towarak.*

Rasmuson Library

years ago," Governor Hammond said in 1978. "The whole financial structure was held together with bailing wire, bandaids and paper clips."[13]

Following Hiatt's resignation, Juneau campus chancellor Charles O. Ferguson served as interim president while the regents conducted a nationwide search, finally selecting Dr. Neil Humphrey from the University of Nevada to be the seventh president of the University of Alaska. After four months on the job, Humphrey suddenly announced his resignation on December 19, 1977, claiming that a combination

of "legislative interference" and the university's systemic financial ills made it impossible for him to continue.[14] Humphrey later admitted that the UA's financial affairs were in such a mess that he feared criminal indictments might soon be brought against top university officials. "The scope and extent of the financial debacle which had occurred was overwhelming," Humphrey said.[15]

The regents next offered the presidency to Dr. Donald Schwartz of Indiana University-Purdue University at Fort Wayne, one of the finalists from the search of the previous summer. In mid-January, regents announced they were on the verge of finalizing all the details with Schwartz. "I think he will be our next president," said Hugh Fate, president of the board.[16] However, after mulling over the offer for several weeks, Schwartz turned down the job. Frustrated by the failure to find a permanent president, the board of regents gave a sixteen-month presidential contract to its executive secretary, Foster Diebold, until a new search could be initiated. Not until the summer of 1979, two and a half years after Hiatt's resignation, did the university presidency finally achieve some stability with the hiring of Dr. Jay Barton from West Virginia University who became the fifth president in the six years since William R. Wood's retirement in 1973.[17]

During Jay Barton's five-year tenure as UA president (1979–1984), he gradually restored the confidence of both politicians and the public in the battered university administration. Barton, known for showing up at his office as early as 4:30 in the morning—which led staffers to speculate that he never adjusted to Alaska time when he moved here from the east coast—had a fascination with emerging technologies. His administration oversaw improvements in telecommunications that made the University of Alaska system a leader in long distance delivery education.[18]

Donald O'Dowd from the State University of New York succeeded Barton in office and served six years (1984–1990) as the University of Alaska's chief executive. Under O'Dowd's tenure, statewide administrative staff finally moved from the central UAF campus into the partially completed Butrovich Building—named for long-time Alaskan legislator John Butrovich—built on the old cow pasture on West Ridge below the Geophysical Institute. O'Dowd's longest lasting accomplishment was the 1986–1987 restructuring of the entire university system, a controversial cost-cutting move necessitated by the mid-1980s collapse of world oil prices, which saw state revenues and university appropriations plummet. O'Dowd abolished eleven community colleges and merged their functions into the university system. He consolidated a total of fifteen administrative units into three regionally administered institutions headquartered in Fairbanks, Anchorage and Juneau, which he claimed cut administrative costs by about six million dollars a year. When O'Dowd retired in 1990, the regents selected Dr. Jerome Komisar, also from SUNY, as the eleventh president of the University of Alaska.[19]

Even during the tumultuous days in the 1970s, when a moving van parked perpetually outside the president's house, most UAF students were hardly concerned about the turnover at the top. The UA's financial crisis did not filter down to the classroom directly, since the statewide administration had increasingly placed itself at arm's length from the UAF campus. *Polar Star* editor Dermot Cole had complained in 1976 that President Hiatt and other top UA administrators were "about as well known to most students as . . . local FBI men. Many students would not even recognize Hiatt if they passed him on the paths between Wood Center and the library."[20]

As chief administrator of the Fairbanks campus, the UAF chancellor was far better known to students. Howard Cutler, a personable administrator trained in economics, served as chancellor from 1975 to 1981. He and his wife Enid, a skilled portrait

Taking precautions
in the wake of tragedy

Like all institutions, UAF has felt the impact of rising crime and violence. In UAF's three-quarters of a century there have been two murders on campus: the killing of 18-year-old Jody Stambaugh in Moore Hall in December 1972, and 20-year-old Sophie Sergie in Bartlett Hall in April 1993. The two slayings were tragic reminders that the university is not immune to the violence that pervades modern America. In May 1993, in response to the murder of Sergie, Chancellor Joan Wadlow created a task force chaired by Professor Patricia Kwachka to explore ways to improve student safety.

As in the world at large, safety on a university campus comes at the price of stricter regulations and reduced individual freedom. While no one has advocated a return to the restrictions of the 1950s in the dormitories, when 10:30 P.M. curfews and sign-in and sign-out sheets were the order of the day for female students, new procedures have been established to tighten security in campus housing. Phones have been installed in all dormitory rooms, a measure that students have fought for since the 1970s, and dorm monitors now guard the doors to residence halls.

MEMBERS OF UAF CHANCELLOR JOAN WADLOW'S *safety task force address student concerns at a September 1993 public forum in Wood Center. From left: Victoria Farrell, student; ASUAF president Karlin Itchoak; student services coordinator Mike* *Sfraga; chair of the task force Professor Patricia Kwachka; secretary Chris Bennett; dean of students Carla Kirts; resident assistant Bart Smith; and parent Jeff Cook.*

Wendy Hower

artist, were both actively involved in student and local affairs. Cutler held regular "fireside chats" in Wood Center to keep in touch with student concerns. In 1980–1981, editors Bill Zybach and Polly Walter and other students resurrected the yearbook *Denali*, which had not been published since 1970 due to a lack of student interest, and dedicated the volume to Chancellor Cutler.[21]

In 1981, President Barton replaced Cutler with Patrick J. O'Rourke, former chancellor of the university's ten community colleges. Besides being the youngest chief executive in UAF's history—he turned forty a week before his appointment, making him almost a year and a half younger than President Terris Moore had been in 1949—Chancellor O'Rourke also happened to be the most experienced in Alaskan education, having worked in the field for nearly fifteen years, largely in rural Alaska. Born in New York into a working class Irish immigrant family, O'Rourke graduated from St. John's University in 1964 and came to Alaska two years later as the coordinator of Adult Basic Education in Bethel. In 1970, O'Rourke moved to Fairbanks to direct Upward Bound, but returned to Bethel in 1972 as the first president of Kuskokwim Community College. Five years later, he became chancellor of the entire UA community college system, responsible for higher education in Bethel, Kenai, Ketchikan, Kodiak, Valdez, Palmer, Nome, and Sitka, as well as Anchorage Community College and the Tanana Valley Community College in Fairbanks.[22]

During his decade as UAF chancellor (1981–1991), O'Rourke left his stamp on the Fairbanks campus as surely as any of the pioneer presidents. The only UA chief executives with longer records of service are Charles Bunnell and William Wood. Many long-time faculty claim O'Rourke's insistence on high academic standards for faculty—balancing teaching, research, and public service—brought UAF to a par with other state universities nationwide. To invigorate teaching and take advantage of the campus's wide array of scientific research institutes, he started a policy of joint appointments between the various institutes and their related academic disciplines, trying to bring fresh research directly into the classroom. As part of the national effort to reform higher education, he launched a core curriculum for all undergraduates. Creation of an honors program attracted top students, while the establishment of a new interdisciplinary graduate program in northern studies took advantage of UAF's location in the subarctic circumpolar north. With the support of Native leaders, O'Rourke started the innovative Rural Alaska Honors Institute (RAHI), which offered rural students between their junior and senior high school years an opportunity to take summer school classes at UAF, and to prepare for college life. His instigation of an International Programs Office helped establish UAF's strong position among northern academic institutions and led, for instance, to UAF's designation as the English-language university for students from Greenland.

As a result of the 1987 restructuring, UAF became a multicampus statewide institution with branch campuses in Bethel, Nome, and Kotzebue; learning centers as far flung as Fort Yukon, Galena, McGrath, Tok, and Unalaska; and fisheries programs and extension offices in Southcentral and Southeastern. Altogether, UAF programs reach 113 communities across the state of Alaska. With UAF's expanded mission under the restructured university system, the institution also made a special commitment to "enhancing educational opportunities for Alaska's rural and native populations."[23]

Always mindful of UAF's special status as the oldest institution of higher education in Alaska, O'Rourke ensured the university never forgot its roots. As a measure of this commitment, he decided to save and remodel the oldest major building on campus (the one-time gymnasium-library-museum constructed in 1931–1935) for use as UAF's administrative center. After the museum had moved into the new Otto Geist Museum on West Ridge in 1980, the "old gym," which had never had an official name, seemed as if its last life would be as a run-down storage shed, ready for the wrecking ball. Critics called it a firetrap and an eyesore that should be demolished as university plans had long envisioned.

In its previous lives, President Bunnell's first permanent concrete structure had been the heart of UAF history. As Ann Tremarello noted, for thirty years the "old gym" had been the largest hall on campus and the scene of every imaginable event involving more than a handful of people, including registrations, graduations, guest speakers, presidential inaugurations, theatrical productions, basketball games, funerals, formal dances, campus assemblies, physical education classes, ROTC drills, beauty contests, Engineers' Day, Starvation Gulch, and much more. One of the most notable events in the building's history, the signing of the Alaska

Constitution in February 1956, provided the inspiration for the restored structure's name: Signers' Hall.[24]

Though the ostentatious decor of the restored Signers' Hall bore no resemblance to the building's earlier incarnations, its renovation in 1984–1985 as the focal point of the campus symbolized how UAF was building on its heritage as the University of Alaska's flagship campus. When Pat O'Rourke retired in 1991, Dr. Joan K. Wadlow from the University of Oklahoma moved into the chancellor's office on the top floor of Signers' Hall. Wadlow is the third chancellor of UAF, and the first woman to head the campus in its 75-year history.

As UAF looks ahead to the 21st century, the number of students and the scope of teaching and research on College Hill continues to expand in dozens of fields: research into global change, resource development and the depletion of the ozone layer; work on the preservation of Alaska Native languages and literature; the writing of history, fiction and poetry; the study of art, anthropology, music, mathematics and philosophy. The university's new $25 million supercomputer—nicknamed "Denali"—is one of the fastest and most advanced computers in the world, and will enable scientists to create climate models of unprecedented sophistication. In 1991 NASA selected UAF as a "Space Grant" university, making it one of only five schools in America with a combined land, sea, and space grant mission to explore everything on the earth and beyond, continuing the quest that began in 1915 when Judge James Wickersham laid the concrete cornerstone on College Hill.

Highlights 1972–1993

1972

March Playing *Also Sprach Zarathustra* (the theme from the film *2001: A Space Odyssey*) student-owned KMPS Radio, managed by Rusty Walker, goes on the air. KMPS is the first radio station in Alaska with a "progressive rock" format.

October Led by activist Mike States, "Students for McGovern" sponsors a visit to UA by Leonard Nimoy, the actor who played Mr. Spock in the original *Star Trek* TV series. In his speech at Bartlett Hall Nimoy claims it is not logical for anyone to vote for Richard Nixon.

November For the first time the *Polar Star* endorses a slate of specific candidates, including democratic presidential nominee George McGovern. Editor Brian Rogers explains that with the voting age now lowered to 18, this is the first election in which most college students are eligible to vote.

1973

Spring First publication of *THEATA* (Tlingit, Haida, Eskimo, Athabaskan, Tsimshian, Aleut), a magazine of nonfiction articles by Native students.

March Led by Mike Lessley, Dick Lee, and Mark Beauchamp, the UAF Nanooks win their first intercollegiate basketball championship by defeating Dean Nicholson's Central Washington Wildcats for the NAIA District I title.

May Robert W. Hiatt is inaugurated as the fifth president of the University of Alaska. Among the 428 graduates receiving degrees are Robin C. Kennedy, granddaughter of Dr. Charles E. Bunnell, founding president of the university.

Summer Completion of new $1.3 million Health and Safety Building brings all UAF emergency services under the same roof. The facility includes a computerized alarm system and dispatch center for the fire department. UA's new state of the art ambulance, known as "Uncle Able," was purchased with funds raised by students, alumni, and local residents.

June KUAC-TV provides full coverage of the U.S. Senate Watergate Hearings on a one-day delay basis.

September Protests over newly instituted parking fees rile students and faculty. Bartlett Hall resident Pat Osborne suggests no one buy the $40 decals. "If an individual got caught 16 times a semester and appealed his tickets," Osborne reasons, "at most, he would only end up paying the original $40."

October Former music professor Greeta K. Brown files a $400,000 sex discrimination suit against the UA. Only two of the university's full professors are women. The case would not be concluded until 1978, when the Alaska Supreme Court would rule in Brown's favor.

November Final approval is given for construction of the Trans-Alaska Pipeline.

SHEILA COLE (AT LEFT) AND ANOTHER *ASUA volunteer supervise the University of Alaska's first Student Regent Election (S.R.E.) in November 1973, to choose the names of two nominees to send to the governor. Winners of the hotly contested campaign are Allen Blume and Rusty Walker. To the dismay of Fairbanks students, however, Governor William Egan chooses Ronald Wendte, a graduate student from Juneau, as the first student regent.*

Polar Star

December To save electricity during the 1973 energy crisis, traditional Christmas lights are prohibited.

1974

April The first annual Festival of Native Arts is held at UAF to celebrate Alaska's diverse Native cultural traditions. Official start of construction of Trans-Alaska Pipeline project.

May Under contract from the Alyeska Pipeline Service Co., a team of archaeologists from the University of Alaska Anthropology Department under Dr. John Cook begins archeological surveillance and inspection of the Trans-Alaska Pipeline Project. UA archaeology graduates on the project include Glenn Bacon, Jim Dixon and Dale Slaughter. Under a previous contract university archaeologists had surveyed and mapped about 200 sites along the proposed pipeline route and catalogued about 10,000 prehistoric items.

July Tanana Valley Community College is established.

August Nearly one-third of all the candidates for public office in the state's primary election are graduates or former students of the University of Alaska.

October June Duncan, Mary Slotnick and Anne Sanchez of the English department, and Andrea Helms of the political science department, file sex discrimination charges against the university. The Human Rights Commission finds in their favor in March 1975.

November Jay S. Hammond, class of 1949, is the first University of Alaska graduate elected governor of the State of Alaska. Among the UA graduates appointed to high positions in Hammond's administration are Commissioner of Administration Andy Warwick, Director of the Division of Lands Michael C. T. Smith, and Commissioner of Environmental Conservation Ernst W. Mueller.

1975

July UA statewide system is reorganized. The new position of chancellor is created as the chief executive officer of the Fairbanks campus.

September UAF enrollment falls to 2,497, the lowest since 1967, and nearly one-third below the record year of 1970–1971. Admissions director Ann Tremarello notes the decline is due to the high wages paid on the Trans-Alaska Pipeline, as former students "feel that the time to make money is now, while [the university] is always going to be here." Housing remains tight. To prevent pipeline workers from registering for classes just so they can move into the dorms, Bill Lex, head of residence education, institutes a requirement that all students must complete a minimum of 12 credits per semester to remain eligible for campus housing.

October The *Polar Star* reports that most engineering students now carry pocket calculators, worth on average about $200, instead of slide rules. The bookstore plans to discontinue selling slide rules in 1976.

November Opening of the Wood Center Pub.

December Release of President Hiatt's "Academic Development Plan" intended to chart the future of the university.

1976

January Howard Cutler takes office as the first chancellor of the University of Alaska Fairbanks. The front page headline in the *Polar Star* warns that a "troubled campus" awaits him. "The new chancellor should be forced to live in the dorms, eat in the dining halls and take six hours of courses his first semester," one student claims. UAF men's basketball team closes out the 1975–1976 season with its best mark in intercollegiate history: 22–6. Steve Frank leads the team by averaging 17.4 points a game.

February Purchase of a new Honeywell 66/20 Computer, the university's first interactive computer, which does not require the use of computer punch cards.

July Dedication of Heritage Lamp Park in front of the Lola Tilly Commons. "The main purpose of the lamp is to cheer the Natives who come here to go to school," said Emily Ivanoff Brown, or Ticasuk, an elder, educator, student, and author from Unalakleet. Ticasuk thought the gas-powered lamp, modeled after a traditional Eskimo seal-oil lamp, would serve as a friendly beacon and eternal symbol of Native culture.

September For the first time in the history of the institution, UAF enrollment figures show more female students (53%) than males (47%).

1977

February With disclosure of an imminent financial crisis and an estimated $10 million shortfall, President Hiatt resigns and is replaced on an interim basis by Juneau Chancellor Charles O. Ferguson.

April English department releases inaugural issue of *Permafrost*, a student journal of fiction, poetry, and photography. Faculty advisors are Norma Bowkett and John Morgan.

July First oil reaches Valdez in Trans-Alaska Pipeline.

THE WOMEN'S INTERCOLLEGIATE VOLLEYBALL TEAM is created in 1979, to provide women with athletic opportunities comparable to those available to men. In the same year, the women's basketball team gets its own locker room.

Mike Holman, Student Affairs

August — Regents select Dr. Neil Humphrey as the seventh president of the University of Alaska.

December — After four months on the job, President Humphrey resigns, stating the university's financial ills are not "correctable" under present conditions.

1978

February — Regents appoint their executive secretary Foster Diebold as the eighth president of the University of Alaska until a new search can be initiated.

1979

April — First performance of the Tuma Theater for the Festival of Native Arts.

July — Jay Barton is chosen as the ninth president of the University of Alaska. Barton is the fifth man to hold the position in six years.

October — UAF journalism department begins publication of the *Northern Sun*.

November — Officials in the art department paint over a graphic mural which had been painted on the walls of the art department in 1976–1977 depicting the impact of pipeline construction on Fairbanks. "I didn't like it," one student said of the painting, which depicted among other things a prostitute and a rowdy construction worker. "It was the epitome of the pipeline—all bad." Nevertheless she thought it was a piece of local history and should have been saved for the future.

1980

September — UAF begins offering a degree in Alaska Native Studies; the U.S. Secretary of Commerce officially designates UAF as the 16th sea grant college in the United States. Meanwhile the U.S. Navy decides to discontinue scientific operations at the Naval Arctic Research Laboratory at Point Barrow, which UAF has operated for the federal government for more than a quarter-century.

1981

May President Jay Barton appoints Patrick J. O'Rourke as the second chancellor of the University of Alaska Fairbanks.

November The first publication of the *Sun-Star*, the student paper born of the merger of the *Northern Sun* and the *Polar Star*.

1982

March Georgianna Lincoln of the Tanana Chiefs Conference criticizes UAF for the high dropout rate of Native students.

April UAF announces that due to improved computer publishing, the catalog will resume annual publication in 1983.

September UAF celebrates the 60th anniversary of the enrollment of the first students in 1922. Construction is underway on the Tanana Valley Community College's "Red Building" on Geist Road; TVCC officials hope construction will be complete by August 1983.

October Completion of Constitution Park between Constitution Hall and the Gruening Building. The park replaces the mud hole that had formed in front of the library every spring for the past decade.

1983

January Chancellor O'Rourke's convocation address, in which he looks ahead to "UAF in 1990," suggests that UAF eventually may have to cap its enrollment at about 5,000 full-time equivalent students, a level predicted to be reached in four years. The *Fairbanks Daily News-Miner* calls the enrollment cap "one of the worst ideas we've heard in a long time."

February Grade point averages at UAF are too high, according to Chancellor O'Rourke, who contends that having 55% of students earning A's and B's is too many students above average.

Spring Construction begins on a $13.2 million addition to Rasmuson Library.

June KUAC-TV ranks first nationwide among public television stations with largest per capita audience during prime time.

September Inauguration of the Honors Program.

1984

January Alaska raises legal drinking age from 19 to 21, spurring plans to develop Hess Commons into a social hall in order to provide more nonalcohol-related activities.

May President Ronald Reagan visits UAF on a rest stop during his return trip from China to the United States, and meets Pope John Paul II at the Fairbanks International Airport.

July Donald O'Dowd becomes the tenth president of the University of Alaska.

September Vibration from construction on the new addition to the Rasmuson Library weakens support timbers in the tunnel to the lower parking lot stairs. The tunnel is closed indefinitely.

November Anonymous flyers posted widely around campus criticize the decision to remodel Signers' Hall and state that Chancellor O'Rourke "runs UAF very similar to a Central American republic." The *Sun-Star* defends the chancellor, claiming there are no reports of "rebellious faculty, staff or students being shot at sunrise in Constitution Plaza or tortured in the bowels of Gruening."

December A new Student Apartment Complex (SAC) of 60 units on Rainey Ridge opens and helps relieve a campus housing shortage.

1985

April UAF students protesting large budget cuts stage a "Death of Education" wake in Constitution Park between the Gruening Building and the Rasmuson Library. To dramatize their concern, students carry a black plywood coffin loaded with UAF catalogs. After speeches from protestors, administrators, and politicians, the wake concludes with a drum roll, a salute from a battery of toy rifles, and the closing of the coffin.

October UAF signs a student exchange program with the University of Copenhagen.

November Installation of "Elysian," the $140,000 white tubular steel sculpture 33 feet long and 18 feet high, on the grass south of Wickersham Hall.

1986

February Bartlett Hall director Cam Pollock launches a full-scale campaign to bring David Letterman to UAF. Dave does not respond.

March The Geophysical Institute announces that it has submitted a research proposal to President Reagan's Strategic Defense Initiative (or Star Wars) Office. The GI proposal would fund basic research on a mechanism that could neutralize enemy missiles in outer space.

April The parking problem gets worse, especially since new additions to the Duckering Building and the Rasmuson Library have eliminated two parking lots in the core area. According to Fred Sacco of Safety and Security, UAF sells approximately 5,000 parking decals, more than twice the number of available parking spaces with plug-ins.

August UA narrowly averts declaring "financial exigency" during the financial crisis caused by the collapse of world oil prices.

ON A VISIT TO UAF IN *June 1990, former President Jimmy Carter and his wife Rosalynn are given a brief history of the Permafrost Tunnel by geological engineer Nils Johansen.*

Cal White, University Relations

1987

June   Closure of the WAMI Medical Science Program at UAF.

July   Due to restructuring, UAF becomes a multicampus university with branches in Bethel, Nome, and Kotzebue, and rural education centers in Tok, Fort Yukon, Dillingham, Delta, McGrath, Nenana, and Unalaska.

1988

February   Comparatively low salaries are causing a faculty brain drain from UAF to the Lower 48 in certain disciplines, especially in engineering, computer science, and business.

September   Statistics indicate the average UAF student is age 31.

1989

January   The National Science Foundation's Polar Ice Coring Office opens on the UAF campus, sponsoring research expeditions to Greenland and Antarctica.

February   Fire Marshall orders the Modular Units closed due to numerous fire code violations.

March   Scientists aboard the Institute of Marine Science's *R/V Alpha Helix* are among the first investigators into Prince William Sound following the *Exxon Valdez* Good Friday oil spill.

June   Dedication of the Butrovich Building.

September   In cooperation with the Scandinavian Writers' Association, UAF opens the first Nordic House in the United States on the UAF campus. The residence enables visiting artists and writers to conduct workshops, seminars and lectures.

1990

March   National broadcast on PBS of "Arctic Haze," a half-hour documentary on polar air pollution produced by KUAC-TV. Creation of the Center for Global Change and Arctic System Research.

June   Bradford Washburn, the noted photographer, cartographer, and explorer, donates his collection of photographs and records from more than half a century of exploration to the Rasmuson Library.

August   Ground-breaking ceremonies are held for the new $27.5 million Natural Sciences Facility on Rainey Ridge west of the upper dorm complex; Chancellor O'Rourke, 49, announces his intention to resign in June 1991 after a decade at UAF.

1991

February   NASA designates UAF as a Space Grant Institution.

April   Ribbon-cutting ceremony for the new SAR (Synthetic Aperture Radar) Facility at the Geophysical Institute.

July   Joan K. Wadlow becomes the third chancellor of UAF.

September   New core curriculum is introduced for UAF undergraduates. A new graduate program offering a master's degree in Northern Studies begins.

1992

April   UAF students rally to protest budget cuts and stage a sleep-in at the statewide administration Butrovich Building. Chancellor Wadlow promises to cut UAF administrative costs by 20%.

September   Ground breaking is held for the new Student Recreation Center near the old site of the Beluga. Due to long-deferred maintenance on its old buildings, UAF faces up to 1,200 fire code violations and hundreds of millions of dollars in repairs.

1993

January   UAF completes a ten-page "Strategic Plan" for the year 2000. One goal is to strengthen graduate education and to continue the development of UAF as the leading research center on the circumpolar north.

February   Installation of Dobson spectrometer on the roof of the Geophysical Institute enables UAF scientists to study the earth's shrinking ozone layer.

April   Sponsored by the new Women's Studies program, Anita Hill gives a guest lecture at the Charles W. Davis Concert Hall on the issue of sexual harassment.

May   Start of northern*MOMENTUM*, UAF's first private fundraising campaign, with a goal of raising $10 million.

Portfolio
1973–1993

THE OLDEST CONCRETE BUILDING ON CAMPUS, *the former gym/library/museum, reopened as Signers' Hall in 1984–1985, housing the UAF administration.*

Sam Winch, University Relations

FOUR OF THE UNIVERSITY OF ALASKA'S FIRST FIVE
*presidents and their spouses, at the formal installation
in May 1974 of the fifth, Robert W. Hiatt. From left to
right: Katrina Moore, Terris Moore, Virginia Patty,
Ernest Patty, Dorothy Jane Wood, William R. Wood,
Elizabeth Hiatt, and Robert W. Hiatt. President
Hiatt's inauguration ceremony was broadcast live
across Alaska by KUAC-TV in the station's first live
statewide telecast.*

University Relations Collection, Rasmuson Library

THE LINE WAITING FOR REGISTRATION
in the fall of 1973 outside the Bunnell Building.

University Relations Collection, Rasmuson Library

POLAR STAR

university of alaska fairbanks

Vol. XXXI Issue 28
Friday, May 3, 1974

Kurt Pfitzer, a music student, spoke to some 200 people Wednesday during a rally protesting cuts in courses at the Fairbanks campus. For details, see story on page 2.

inside

</>- Regents eliminate $20 course fee   page 2
- Stambaugh suit hits University   page 3
  Hilliard, Shelton, Egan named

(LEFT) WEARING A BLACK ARM BAND, MUSIC *student Kurt Pfitzer speaks from the steps of the Rasmuson Library to a crowd of about 200 students. Pfitzer and others led the May 1974 student demonstration to protest President Hiatt's rumored proposal to move up to one-third of UAF's programs (allegedly including the music department) from Fairbanks to Anchorage.*

Polar Star

(RIGHT) THE 1977–1978 FINANCIAL CRISIS, *which forced the resignation of President Hiatt, inspired this gruesome cartoon in the* Alaska Advocate *in February 1977.*

(BELOW) CARTOONIST MARJORIE KOWALSKI'S *rendering of the "Hiatt House," the 1975 plan of the Board of Regents to reserve up to $250,000 to build a residence in Anchorage for President Hiatt (on left with a Gladstone bag) and other top university administrators. The controversial proposal was still pending when President Hiatt was forced to resign in February 1977.*

Polar Star

Opening the University closet

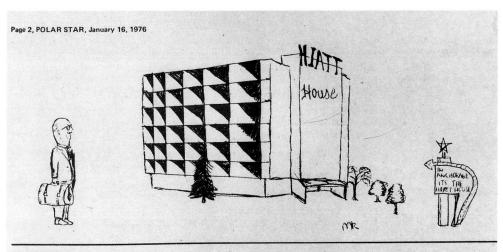

Page 2, POLAR STAR, January 16, 1976

Editorial

New 'austerity budget' provides for 'Hiatt House' in Anchorage

PRESIDENT HIATT ENJOYS A JOKE ON HIMSELF.
*In early 1976, to cultivate an identity for the UA
statewide administration separate from the UAF
campus administration, he installed a barrier in the
Bunnell Building east corridor leading to his office.
The "Please Do Not Feed" sign on the fence of the
"statewide zoo" was one response.*

University of Alaska Public Affairs

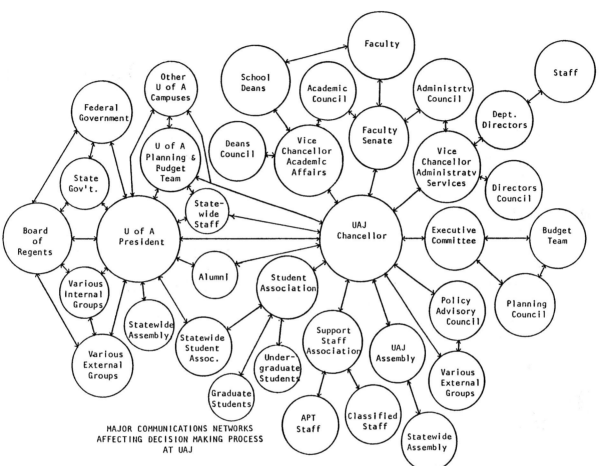

MAJOR COMMUNICATIONS NETWORKS
AFFECTING DECISION MAKING PROCESS
AT UAJ

Figure 61. UAJ's Decision-making Process, 21 June 1982 (359)

DEMONSTRATING HOW COMPLEX THE UA STATEWIDE
*system became in the 1970s and 1980s, and why it
was sometimes so hard for the university
administrators to make a decision, is this 1982 flow
chart supposedly showing the "decision-making
process" at the University of Alaska Juneau.*

MUSICAL PRESIDENTS

The combined tenure of the University of Alaska's first four presidents had lasted 52 years, but the financial crisis of 1977–1978 caused an unprecedented turnover at the top in administrators. In the space of only 12 months, four men held the post of president:

Robert Hiatt, Charles Ferguson, Neil Humphrey, and Foster Diebold, while another man, Donald Schwartz, was offered the job and turned it down.

All photos this page: University of Alaska Public Affairs

ROBERT HIATT
Resigned in February 1977.

CHARLES FERGUSON
Interim president, February 1977–August 1977.

NEIL HUMPHREY
Hired in August 1977, resigned in December 1977.

FOSTER DIEBOLD
Board of regents executive secretary, promoted to president for 18 months, February 1978–July 1979.

(ABOVE) JAY BARTON, UNIVERSITY OF ALASKA
president from 1979 to 1984, at the fountain in the
Bunnell Memorial Plaza. Barton helped restore a
sense of stability to the top level of UA administration.

University of Alaska Public Affairs

(UPPER RIGHT) PRESIDENT DONALD O'DOWD
marches for United Way in September 1986. O'Dowd
initiated the massive restructuring of the university
system in 1986–1987, which eliminated the
community colleges and reorganized
the entire university.

Charles Mason, University of Alaska Public Affairs

(LOWER RIGHT) JEROME KOMISAR TOOK OFFICE
in 1990 as the 11th president of the University of
Alaska system.

Annemarie Kuhn, University of Alaska Public Affairs

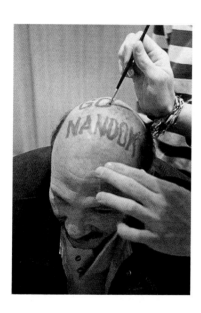

AN ADMINISTRATOR USES HIS HEAD
Harris Shelton, long-time dean of students and vice chancellor for student affairs, shows his support for the Nanooks during the 1990 Homecoming ceremonies.

Student Affairs

(ABOVE) IN 1975–1976, THE UAF NANOOKS POSTED *their all-time winningest season in intercollegiate play with a record of 22–6. Forward Steve Frank (second from the right) led the team in scoring and averaged 17.4 points a game. Back row, left to right: Kavik Hahn, Bill Kilgore, Lloyd Burns, Rick Garcia, Jim Burton, Willie Easton, Jeff Hutton, Lester Caril, Steve Frank, and Randy Small. Front row, left to right: Mike Engeldinger, head coach Al Svenningson, assistant coach Al Silver, and Ricky Terrell.*

UAF Athletic Department

(RIGHT) UAF BASKETBALL COACH GEORGE *Roderick cuts down the net in a wild celebration in Patty Center on March 4, 1989, after the Nanooks defeated the University of Alaska Anchorage Seawolves. The victory earned UAF its first Great Northwest Conference Championship, and a spot in the NCAA Division II tournament, as one of the 32 best teams in the country for 1988–1989.*

Sun-Star

(ABOVE) CHANCELLOR HOWARD CUTLER AND HIS
*wife Enid, with a group of faculty, staff, and students,
cut the University of Alaska's 60th anniversary cake
in the spring of 1977, sixty years after the
incorporation of the institution in 1917. Confusion
over the genuine birthdate of the university
continued, however, as five years later in 1982, the
university again claimed to celebrate its 60th
birthday. The second birthday party marked sixty*

*years since the admission of the first students in 1922.
Between Mr. and Mrs. Cutler is Foster Diebold, the
executive secretary of the board of regents, who
became the eighth president of the University of
Alaska in 1978.*

University Relations

(RIGHT) HOWARD AND ENID CUTLER
*receive season tickets No. 1 and No. 2
upon his retirement as UAF
chancellor in 1981.*

Sabra McCracken, University Relations

(ABOVE) CHANCELLOR PAT O'ROURKE FLIPS *hamburgers at the annual chancellor's barbecue during the beginning of the fall semester.*

Student Affairs

(LEFT) UAF CHANCELLOR PATRICK J. O'ROURKE ON *an "I Want You to Register" poster in 1982. O'Rourke replaced Howard Cutler in 1981. At age forty, he was the youngest chief executive in the history of UAF.*

Rasmuson Library

GRACEFUL DANCERS FROM THE VILLAGE OF
*Wainwright—from left to right, Mary Ellen, Yaaki
and Maasak— perform in the Davis Concert Hall at
UAF's annual Festival of Native Arts. The festival was
first held in March 1974 to celebrate the rich cultural
heritage of all of Alaska's Native peoples, including
Yupik, Inupiaq, Haida, Tsimpshean, Aleut, Tlingit,
and Athasbaskan. Today the festival has grown to*

*become one of the most important events of the year,
drawing hundreds of performers and thousands of
visitors, to enjoy original dancing, drama, music,
native crafts, the blanket toss, fiddling, and story
telling.*

Festival of Native Arts

(ABOVE) WILLIE HENSLEY (AT CENTER), A DEMO-
cratic candidate for the U.S. House of Representatives
in 1974, speaks to students on the Bunnell Memorial
Plaza. Hensley attended the university for two years
in the early 1960s, and later returned as a graduate
student in 1966, at which time he became one of the
leading activists in the Alaska Native land claims
movement. He was one of the chief architects of the
historic 1971 Alaska Native Claims Settlement Act,
which established thirteen Alaska Native regional
corporations and gave them title to nearly forty-four
million acres of land. The students facing the camera
and listening to Hensley are 1974–1975 ASUA
president Ric Davidge (left) and ASUA senate
president Bob Williams.

Sandra Stringer

(RIGHT) THE "LOON WOMAN"
of Spirit Theater, performing at
the 1990 Festival of Native Arts.

Cal White, University Relations

NATIVE STUDENTS TOSS THEIR ART PROFESSOR,
*Glenn Dasher, in the air in front of the Gruening
Building during the 1985 Festival of Native Arts. The
origin of the Inupiaq blanket toss or "nalukatuq" has
been much debated. Some authorities claim it was to
spot whales, while others maintain it was primarily*

*entertainment. Still a regular tradition at Barrow, the
goal is to go as high as possible in the air and land on
your feet.*

Sam Winch, University Relations

316

(ABOVE) "DOC SOUTH" (PLAYING THE FIDDLE) AND *his string band lead an April 1975 All Campus Day hoe-down in Wood Center.*

University Relations Collection, Rasmuson Library

(RIGHT) OUTSIDE MCINTOSH HALL, A SPRING *Carnival snow sculpture caricatures a regular sight during the 1974–1977 construction of the Trans-Alaska Pipeline: a Texas oil field worker riding into town. During the pipeline era some "students" enrolled at UAF merely to live in a dorm, because they could not find accommodations in over-crowded Fairbanks. Overall, however, enrollment dropped sharply during pipeline construction to less than 2,500 students in 1975–1976, almost 30% less than the peak year of 1970–1971, as hundreds of former students decided to earn pipeline wages instead of college credit.*

University Relations Collection, Rasmuson Library

A TREE TRIES TO GROW ON CAMPUS, THANKS TO *the green thumb of Vice Chancellor Bill Phillips, who helped plant the 1984 Arbor Day tree in front of the Wood Center. Assisting in the operation were Jim Matthews (left), director of Cooperative Extension, and Jim Drew, dean of the School of Agriculture and Land Resources Management.*

Kurt Savikko, University Relations

JO SCOTT (CENTER), THE FOUNDING AND *producing director of the Fairbanks Summer Arts Festival, with music director and conductor Myron Romanul (left) from Karlsruhe, Germany, and artistic director Fred Buda (right), a percussionist with the Boston Symphony and the Boston Pops. Created in 1980, the annual summer arts festival has become one of Alaska's most notable cultural events of the year, featuring jazz, classical and vocal music, ballet, modern dance, landscape painting, drawing, theatre, figure skating and ice dancing. Produced by Jo Scott in cooperation with the theatre, art, music and athletic departments of UAF, the two-week-long "study-performance" festival attracts more than 500 registrants and 12,000 spectators to UAF each summer from around the world.*

Ken Kollodge

KUAC-TV PROGRAM MANAGER MYRON TISDEL,
*giving the thumbs up sign, and KUAC-FM station
manager Kit Jensen during Festival '79, the first on-
air fundraiser to support public radio and television
in Fairbanks. KUAC's goal that first year was only
$20,000, but listeners and viewers pledged more than
$54,000. Over the years, the March festivals have
become community-wide celebrations for KUAC and
the people it serves, raising several hundred thousand
dollars each year for public broadcasting.*

KUAC

KLONDIKE

(LEFT) THE ARCTIC CHAMBER ORCHESTRA POSES IN *the fall of 1984 on the old sternwheeler* Klondike *in Whitehorse, Yukon Territory. Other communities on the tour that year were Cordova, Yakutat, Petersburg, Wrangell, Hydaburg, Ketchikan and Juneau.*

Seated (left to right) in front:
1. Kaari (Wennen) Parrish
2. Eric Toskey
3. Dori (Irish) Olsen
4. Gina Betts-Harvey
5. Laura (LaSalle) Bergh
6. Karen Toland
7. Nan Butler
8. John Aspnes
9. Jane Aspnes

Middle row (left to right):
10. Kathleen DeCorso
11. Jo Roberts
12. John Frey
13. Donna Matschke
14. Kathleen Butler-Hopkins
15. Erik Kokborg
16. Judith Schwartz
17. Celeste (Eubank) Goering
18. Irene Price

19. Cheryl Saupe-Frey
20. Dorli McWayne
21. Judy Gill
23. Heidi Senungetuk
26. Nancy Morgan
27. Bruno DiCecco
29. Terry Chapin
30. Sandra Chaffin
31. Charles "Chip" Davis
32. Dan Osterback
33. Annamarie Schutter
34. Peggy Schwartz
36. Caryn Wiegand
38. Nic Larter

Back row (left to right):
22. James Kowalsky
24. Libby Neeley
25. Bruce Walling
28. Sandra (Serdehley) Clark
35. Marcus Thompson, viola soloist
37. Gordon Wright, conductor

Not pictured
39. Marty Getz

Barry McWayne

321

GEOGRAPHY PROFESSOR DON LYNCH
with the whole world in his hands.

Rasmuson Library

IN 1988, THIRTY YEARS AFTER HE
graduated from UAF, noted
mathematician Ronald Graham of Bell
Laboratories returned to Fairbanks as
the commencement speaker. During
the course of his memorable speech, he
dazzled the audience with his juggling
ability.

Sam Winch, University Relations

EMERITUS HISTORY PROFESSOR WILLIAM R. HUNT
always taught his students that historians had to be
good detectives. A prolific scholar and an expert on
murder mysteries, the occult, and exploration
literature, Hunt is a recognized authority on Alaskan
and polar history. During the twelve years he taught
at UAF (from 1967 to 1979), he wrote numerous
books, including A Dictionary of Rogues, North of 53,
Arctic Passage *and the official 1976 bicentennial*
history of Alaska. Since then, he has gone on to
publish more than half a dozen other titles, including
a history of law enforcement in Alaska, an account of
the Frederick Cook–Robert Peary North Pole
controversy, and biographies of characters as diverse
as explorer Vilhjalmur Stefansson, whiskey peddler
John J. Healy, muscle magazine king Bernarr
MacFadden and detective William J. Burns.

Seattle-Post Intelligencer

UPON HIS RETIREMENT IN 1988, PROFESSOR *Emeritus Lee Salisbury carried the university mace and led the commencement processional, with Chancellor Pat O'Rourke at his side. In 1993 the* *university officially named the UAF theatre in Salisbury's honor.*

Sam Winch, University Relations

A SUN-STAR IS BORN

From its first crudely-produced mimeographed sheet in October 1946, to its final issue thirty-five years later in the spring of 1981, the Polar Star created controversy. Founded as a mild voice of student protest, the Polar Star was always unpredictable. Some years it was quite good and others it was downright unreadable.

With the creation of a full-fledged journalism department in 1966 headed by Jimmy Bedford, which offered a major in journalism for the first time, the Polar Star became a natural outlet for aspiring reporters. In the 1960s and 1970s, the Polar Star was a training ground for many professional journalists including Kent Sturgis, Phil Deischer, Jean Kizer, Kim Elton, Dermot Cole, Susan McInnis, Brian Rogers, Howard Ringley, Julie Hart, Craig Medred, Carl Sampson, and many others.

Any good newspaper is bound to offend on occasion, but depending on the personality of the editor, the Polar Star sometimes read like the Polar Enquirer, libeling its way through the news. In 1979
the journalism department created a rival paper with a synonymous name to do battle with the Polar Star: the Northern Sun. Even though the Sun was supervised by members of the journalism department, not all readers thought it any better than its student-directed competition. "As a matter of fact," one writer complained in February 1980, "except for the lack of typos and the name of the paper, the Northern Sun and the Polar Star are practically identical."

In the fall of 1980, ASUA President Jason Kuehn started "impeachment" proceedings against Polar Star editor Mark Springer, claiming the paper was misusing ASUA funds. The following year the Polar Star, the university's oldest publication, merged with the Northern Sun, creating a new paper with a double-twin bill for a name: the Sun-Star. The editorial staff assured readers Sun-Star was merely an "interim name" until a better one could be found. Apparently they could not think of another name, as Sun-Star still shines from the top of the front page every week.

The masthead of the first issue of the Northern Sun/Polar Star *on November 13, 1981.*   Rasmuson Library

(ABOVE) A COLD WALK BACK THROUGH TIME IN THE *Permafrost Tunnel, led by Earl Beistline. The Permafrost Tunnel—not to be confused with the old College Mine tunnel directly underneath College Hill—is located in Fox, about a dozen miles from campus. Excavated in 1964 by the U.S. Army CRREL (Cold Regions Research and Engineering Lab), the Permafrost Tunnel is a unique laboratory used jointly by UAF and CRREL. The tunnel extends 360 feet into the permanently frozen hillside, and drops 100 feet below the surface to bedrock, which is at least 40,000 years old and perhaps much older. Descending through the tunnel, a visitor can see various layers through time, including a lower silt accumulation 30,000 years old that was on the tundra surface when the mastodon roamed in the last ice age. The temperature inside the tunnel is 26 degrees Fahrenheit year round.*

Sabra McCracken, University Relations

(LEFT) ELMER E. AND MARY LOUISE RASMUSON *at the dedication of the expansion of the Rasmuson Library in 1985.*

Sabra McCracken, University Relations

325

THE CONSTRUCTION OF CONSTITUTION PARK IN *the fall of 1982 eliminated the mudhole that had formed every spring for nearly a decade between Constitution Hall, the Gruening Building and the Rasmuson Library. Completion of the landscaping, long delayed due to lack of funds, provided the finishing touches to the large structures built at the center of campus in the late 1960s and early 1970s.*

Sabra McCracken, University Relations

(ABOVE) TWO DECADES AFTER IT WAS FOUNDED IN 1962, *the West Ridge research complex had grown into the largest arctic research park in North America. The West Ridge includes the College Observatory, the Otto Geist Museum, the Arctic Health Research Center, the Irving Building, the O'Neill Building (with its distinctive silos), and the Elvey Building.*

Sabra McCracken, University Relations

(LEFT) THE SIGNPOST IN FRONT OF THE *Geophysical Institute's Elvey Building on West Ridge is a symbol of the global reach of GI's research program. Installed in 1973 by then-director Keith Mather, distances on the brown and blue directional signs were calculated precisely by computer.*

Sabra McCracken, University Relations

DR. ROBERT ELSNER OF THE INSTITUTE OF MARINE *Science in 1981. His research on the diving physiology of marine mammals uncovered a naturally occurring intense constriction of coronary circulation, somewhat similar to the constriction of coronary arteries in human heart attack victims.*

Sabra McCracken, University Relations

(BELOW) GRADUATE STUDENTS GEORGE HOLMES, *Mike Kennedy (standing, left to right) and Jackie Grebmeier confer with Professor Peter McRoy (left) and technician Norma Haubenstock (right) aboard the research vessel* Thomas G. Thompson *(University of Washington) during a 1988 study of the seas between Alaska and Russia.*

Carla Helfferich

PROFESSOR OF MARINE SCIENCE DON K. BUTTON *of the Institute of Marine Science checks samples from an incubation experiment at IMS's Seward Marine Center in 1983.*

IMS Publications

(ABOVE) CAPTAIN TOM CALLAHAN, SKIPPER OF THE R/V Alpha Helix, *relaxes on the dock of the UAF Seward Marine Center, the ship's home port. The 133-foot research vessel is owned by the National Science Foundation but operated by the Institute of Marine Science. In 1980, the Alpha Helix replaced the smaller Acona, which had supported UAF marine studies since 1964. The larger ship enabled scientists to expand their research in the rough water of the Bering Sea and the Gulf of Alaska. The Alpha Helix carries a crew of nine and can provide accommodations for up to fifteen scientists. The vessel has a cruising speed of 9.5 knots and a range of 6,500 miles, and provides a year-round platform for oceanographic research on the open ocean and in Alaska's shelf and coastal waters. With its specially strengthened hull, the Alpha Helix is equipped to perform limited surveys in zones of seasonal ice.*

Institute of Marine Science

(OPPOSITE) WITH THE STATE'S RELATIVELY SPARSE *population, Alaska provides UAF professors and students in geology, paleontology, glaciology, archaeology, and other fields with an unparalleled natural outdoor laboratory. (Top) Geology student Peter Frantz surveys an outcrop near Isabelle Pass in the Alaska Range during a 1985 summer field camp. (Bottom) A group of archaeology students excavate a site in 1991 on Panguingue Creek near Healy, in the northern foothills of the Alaska Range.*

Sam Winch (top) and Cal White (bottom), University Relations

(ABOVE) TERRY CHAPIN (AT LEFT) AND KEITH *Van Cleve examine a spruce tree in Bonanza Creek Experimental Forest, one of the university's long-term ecological research projects supported by the National Science Foundation.*

Sam Winch, University Relations

NOT ALL OF THE ANIMALS AT THE INSTITUTE OF
*Arctic Biology's Large Animal Research Station
(popularly known as the "Musk Ox Farm") are large.
In this 1981 picture, Norma Mosso hand feeds a baby
musk ox calf.*

Don Borchert, Institute of Arctic Biology

LAB ASSISTANT HEATHER MCINTYRE *cuts roses growing in the Agricultural Experiment Station greenhouse on West Ridge. Agricultural experiments under northern conditions are still a vital part of UAF's land grant mission.*

Sam Winch, University Relations

(ABOVE) DR. BRIAN BARNES OF THE INSTITUTE OF *Arctic Biology explains his research on arctic ground squirrels to a visiting group of students. Barnes made one of the most startling biological findings of recent years in 1987–1989, when he discovered that arctic ground squirrels hibernate with a core body temperature of 27 degrees Fahrenheit, the first known mammals capable of naturally lowering their body temperatures below the freezing point of water. Discovery of exactly how the squirrels supercool themselves could have an enormous impact on human medicine. "Right now, the obvious area of interest is in maintaining donor organs," Barnes says. "Kidneys and hearts can only be kept competent for a matter of a few days, or even hours, and still be transplanted with a chance of success." The squirrels equipped with radio transmitters hibernating in the woods on West Ridge may someday provide the solution to such problems.*

University Relations

(ABOVE) STUDENTS STROLL
*through the ice fog on
campus in January 1983.*

Sabra McCracken, University Relations

(RIGHT) TWO WARM-BOOTED
*UAF students try to grin at 60
below on January 8, 1983: Larry
Klein (at left) and Mike Sfraga.*

Student Affairs

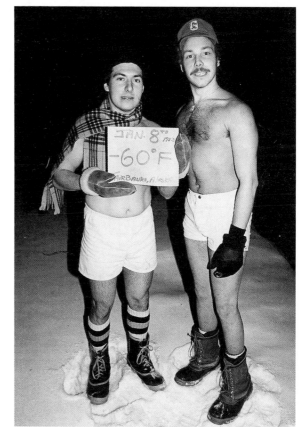

(LEFT) CHRISTMAS LIGHTS
*atop the metal roof of
Wood Center.*

Student Services

DURING A RECORD-BREAKING COLD SNAP IN
*January-February 1989, a group of students, faculty
and staff took time out for a UAF beach party outside
Wood Center at 50 below zero. The party animals
from left to right include:*

1. *Thomas Henry*
2. *Tom Betz*
3. *Greg Snoddy*
4. *Steve McKinley*
5. *Joe Beach*
6. *unidentified*
7. *Gail Adams*
8. *Lynn Lashbrook*
9. *Nancy Hill*
10. *Tim McConnell*
11. *Doug Desorcie*
12. *John Harding*
13. *Curtis Beavers*
14. *Jackie Debevec*
15. *Chris Tilly*

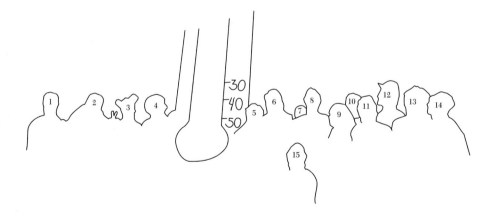

Genezaret Barron

336

AMERICAN SOCIETY of
CIVIL ENGINEERS
UAF CHAPTER
presents

DOUBOLA

"A Double curving
thin shell of unrein-
forced sintered
snow and water. This
design is based on
the intersection of
two hyperbolic
paraboloids."

we would
like to
Thank
the following
contributors

R+M CONSULTANTS
SPENARD BUILDER SUPPLY
DENALI FENCEWORKS
NORTHLAND WOOD
PAY 'N' PAK
UAF PHYSICAL PLANT
CAMPUS SECURITY
HOWARD FRUWIRTH

THE BUILDING OF THE ENGINEERS' SNOW AND ICE *bridge has been an annual UAF rite of spring for more than three decades. Most years the ice structure is a relatively simple arch of some form, but the 1991 "Doubola" was a graceful and elaborate creation by student engineers "based on the intersection of two hyperbolic paraboloids." The tradition of UAF ice engineering began in December 1960 when Jerry Rosenberger and other student engineers created a 19-foot ice obelisk across the street from Wickersham Hall. The university had ruled out their original plan of building the obelisk next to the entrance to the*

university, fearing that "the tower might collapse and smash a vehicle in the vicinity." At that time the engineers knew relatively little about the strength of ice as a building material. They experimented by adding sawdust to water before freezing. "On one occasion the mixture spoiled," the Polar Star *noted in February 1961, "and the odor of fermenting sawdust permeated the entire first floor of the Eielson Memorial Building . . . ."*

Cal White, University Relations

(ABOVE) NERD NIGHT, IN THE WOOD CENTER PUB
in 1987–1988, joined other memorable traditional pub
events such as Beach Party, Casino Night, Rocky

Horror Night, Flasher Night, Cheapo-Sleazo, the Toga
Party, and the Marie Osmond Birthday Party.

Student Affairs

(RIGHT) OVER THE YEARS, THE
*tradition of the Freshman Bonfire
that began in 1923 has evolved into
the annual Starvation Gulch bonfire
contest, in which each dormitory
tries to build the biggest structure of
scrap wood. The builders of this
1987 masterpiece were proud of
their creation.*

Scott Wallace

LIKE A PRESIDENT THROWING OUT THE FIRST PITCH, *Vice Chancellor for Student Affairs Harris Shelton opens UAF's All Campus Day or "Spring MeltDown" in the early 1980s with the ceremonial dropping of the first rotten watermelon of the season from the roof of the Gruening Building.*

Student Affairs

RONALD REAGAN—WHO AS A MOVIE ACTOR ONCE *played opposite a chimp named Bonzo—as president shares a photo opportunity with a polar bear named Nanook. The UAF mascot gave Reagan a UAF hockey sweatshirt at the welcoming ceremonies in the Patty Center during the president's 1984 visit to the Fairbanks campus. On his way back to Washington, D.C. from a trip to China, the president stopped in Fairbanks to meet with Pope John Paul II.*

Richard Veazey, Media Services

CAM POLLOCK, RESIDENCE HALL DIRECTOR OF
*Bartlett Hall, and a dedicated fan of "Late Night with
David Letterman," launched a letter writing campaign
in January 1986 to bring Dave Letterman and his
show to UAF. Pollock sent hundreds of letters and
petitions, but Dave never responded with even a
single reason—let alone his top ten—why he would
not come to Fairbanks. According to Pollock the
number one reason probably was: "He's chicken."*

Student Affairs

(RIGHT) "GETTING SOME RAYS"
*on the south-facing wall of
the Rasmuson Library
in the early 1980s.*

Sun-Star

(ABOVE) STUDENTS FROM WICKERSHAM
Hall clean up on All Campus Day, April 1983.

Sun-Star

Dissecting "Joe" Student

What makes the UAF student different from his collegiate peers across the country? It's hard to pin down some of the intangibles—how can you measure a college community on a scale of "mellow" or "laid back"? How do you identify the average student at a university whose diversity is a hallmark?

Well, we couldn't do it without sponsoring an essay contest on the topic, and who would want to wade through all those papers anyway? But we did send reporter Paul Gruba out to identify some of the characteristics of that elusive creature, the average UAF student. Here are a few.

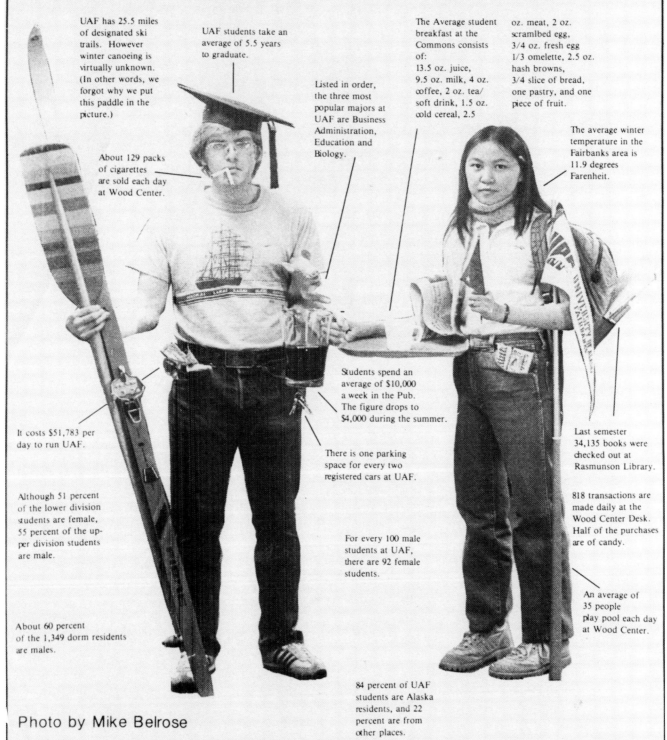

UAF has 25.5 miles of designated ski trails. However winter canoeing is virtually unknown. (In other words, we forgot why we put this paddle in the picture.)

UAF students take an average of 5.5 years to graduate.

Listed in order, the three most popular majors at UAF are Business Administration, Education and Biology.

The Average student breakfast at the Commons consists of: 13.5 oz. juice, 9.5 oz. milk, 4 oz. coffee, 2 oz. tea/soft drink, 1.5 oz. cold cereal, 2.5 oz. meat, 2 oz. scramlbed egg, 3/4 oz. fresh egg 1/3 omelette, 2.5 oz. hash browns, 3/4 slice of bread, one pastry, and one piece of fruit.

About 129 packs of cigarettes are sold each day at Wood Center.

The average winter temperature in the Fairbanks area is 11.9 degrees Farenheit.

It costs $51,783 per day to run UAF.

Students spend an average of $10,000 a week in the Pub. The figure drops to $4,000 during the summer.

Last semester 34,135 books were checked out at Rasmunson Library.

There is one parking space for every two registered cars at UAF.

818 transactions are made daily at the Wood Center Desk. Half of the purchases are of candy.

Although 51 percent of the lower division students are female, 55 percent of the upper division students are male.

For every 100 male students at UAF, there are 92 female students.

An average of 35 people play pool each day at Wood Center.

About 60 percent of the 1,349 dorm residents are males.

84 percent of UAF students are Alaska residents, and 22 percent are from other places.

Photo by Mike Belrose

(LEFT) A PROFILE OF SUPPOSEDLY TYPICAL
UAF students which ran in the 1983 Denali.

Rasmuson Library

(ABOVE) KRISTI KNAPP RAPPELS OFF THE ROOF
of the Gruening Building in the early 1980s. Every
year ROTC students practice rappelling techniques
down the sides of the eight-story structure.

Sabra McCracken, University Relations

(Right) Under the gaze of Albert Einstein, *Agatha "Gustie" John (at left) tutors Roseanne "Tami" Levi in the math lab in Rural Students Services.*

(Below) A potluck at the Rural Student *Services lounge on the fifth floor of the Gruening Building, the home away from home for many UAF Native students who come to Fairbanks from the villages. Known as Student Orientation Services (SOS) until 1982, RSS helps students make the transition from village to university life. Kneeling and eating in the center of the photo is James Nageak, a professor of Inupiaq Eskimo.*

EMILY IVANOFF BROWN, TICASUK, A YUP'IK ESKIMO
*from Unalakleet, is applauded by her fellow graduates
at commencement in 1980, when she received her
third UA degree at age 76. An inspiring teacher and
writer, Ticasuk was the author of "Grandfather of
Unalakleet" (later published as* Roots of Ticasuk). *She
founded the Alaska Native Heritage Writers
Association, and raised the funds to erect the Heritage
Lamp and Park across from McIntosh Hall on the
UAF campus in 1976. Modeled after a traditional
Eskimo seal-oil lamp, the propane light is lit at
commencement every spring. Ticasuk said the main
purpose of the lamp was to "cheer the Natives who
come here to go to school," by reminding them of
"their home life, their heritage, their background."*

Alumni Services Collections, Rasmuson Library

BANNERS HANGING FROM THE STAIRWAY IN WOOD *Center announce a full slate of upcoming campus events in mid-March 1982.*

Sabra McCracken, University Relations

(ABOVE) A LIGHT-HEARTED MOMENT AT A MEETING *of the board of directors of the University of Alaska Alumni Association in the early 1980s, when the UA went to their heads. From left to right: Bob Williams; Bill Coghill; Mike Tinker (president); Ted Cox; Jim Brown (vice president); Walt Phillips; Nancy* *Mendenhall; Ken Bell; Katrina Smathers (seated); Jan Brewer (administrative assistant); Jana Blakestad (executive director); Ed Anders.*

University Relations

(RIGHT) LEONA ALLRIDGE, A 1981 GRADUATE, displays the blue and gold UAF license plates first available in February 1991 from the Alaska Department of Motor Vehicles. UAF receives a portion of the $50 fee for each personalized UAF plate.

Cal White, University Relations

HONOR CLASS ALUMNI GATHER FOR THE SUMMER
1992 reunion during the celebration of UAF's 75th anniversary.

1. *Douglas B. Colp '40*
2. *Albert C. Visca '29*
3. *Elizabeth "Betty" (Wilcox) Magnuson '62*
4. *Rodger C. Hughes '62*
5. *E. L. "Ozzie" Oszustowski '87*
6. *Dale G. Fox '72*
7. *Leo F. Rhode '40*
8. *Michael L. Musick '67/'72*
9. *Robert H. Saunders '42*
10. *Gnell I. (Gregory) Saunders (matric)*
11. *David R. Dobberpuhl '72*
12. *Jennifer M. (Risch) Nelson '72*
13. *George E. Gordon '62*
14. *Sally R. (O'Neill) Wien '62*
15. *Ruthelyn (Elliot) Kulm '42*
16. *Kim B. (Griffin) Zonge 'x59*
17. *Donald MacDonald III '32*
18. *Florence (Allen) Holmes '39*
19. *Kenneth L. Zonge '62*
20. *Elsa R. (Lundell) Mahan '39*

21. *Helen (Arndt) McCain 'x43*
22. *Richard O. Mahan '39*
23. *Pamelia (Adair) Steiger '67*
24. *Earl H. Beistline '39*
25. *Gerald A. Ottem '42*
26. *Oliver V. Kola '38/'39*
27. *Mary E. (Eagan) Cook '40*
28. *Joseph T. Flakne '34*
29. *William "Hank" Ullrich '42*
30. *Robert B. Duncan 'x39*
31. *Theodore A. Loftus '27/'28*
32. *George Karabelnikoff '38*
33. *Glen D. Franklin '36*
34. *Earl L. Fosse '42*
35. *William G. Stroecker '42*
36. *Helen L. (Linck) Atkinson '36*
37. *Vera Alexander '65*
38. *John W. Kessel '42*
39. *Hilja I. (Reinikka) Bolyan '36*
40. *James P. Doogan '37*

Cal White, University Relations

350

A LOT OF TALK AND A LITTLE DIRT RESULTED FROM *the August 1990 ground breaking ceremonies for the $27.5 million Natural Science Facility on Rainey Ridge west of Moore Hall. Among the politicians with shovels and hard hats were three UAF graduates who were instrumental in getting the appropriation for the facility: Rep. Niilo Koponen, Rep. Bert Sharp, and Sen. Steve Frank. The ground breaking party includes*

from left: UA President Jerome Komisar, Rep. Niilo Koponen, Sen. Bettye Fahrenkamp, Rep. Mark Boyer, Rep. Bert Sharp, Sen. Steve Frank, Gov. Steve Cowper, chemistry professor and natural sciences dean Paul Reichardt, and Chancellor Pat O'Rourke.

Cal White, University Relations

JOAN WADLOW, THE THIRD
*chancellor of the University
of Alaska Fairbanks.*

Cal White, University Relations

UAF CHANCELLOR JOAN WADLOW AND FORMER
*UA vice-president Art Buswell with UAF's 1965 twin
engine Beechcraft King Air. Students studying
airframe and powerplant mechanics in the trades and
industry department use the plane for instruction in
the repair of turbine-powered aircraft and
complex aircraft systems, such as hydraulics,
pressurization and de-icing.*

Cal White, University Relations

A CARTOON IN THE NOVEMBER 1992 *Fairbanks Daily News-Miner lampoons a plan to build a multi-million dollar escalator from the Taku parking lot, near Farmers Loop Road, up to the Fine Arts Complex. In the face of strong opposition from students, faculty, and the public—marked by constant puns about "escalating costs of higher education" and references to "golden stairs"—UAF administrators abandoned the escalator idea, and the stairs were simply remodeled.*

Fairbanks Daily News-Miner

FACED WITH RISING COSTS, DECLINING REVENUES *and more than one hundred million dollars in deferred maintenance costs, UA officials tried a new tack to raise money: leasing the farm. In the summer of 1993 the public learned that some UA administrators wished to lease the agricultural fields on the UAF campus to Carr-Gottstein Foods and the huge Wal-Mart discount chain to build a shopping center. Local residents fiercely defended the farm— which was the original* raison d'être *for the college itself—as a treasured green belt, a research park and a sanctuary for migrating birds every spring and fall. In the face of nearly unanimous public opposition from the Fairbanks community, which agreed campus lands should be preserved for educational and environmental reasons, UAF chancellor Joan Wadlow vetoed the proposed shopping mall.*

Genezaret Barron

354

THE DEATH OF TRADITION? IN OCTOBER 1992,
an ironic twist occurred in the history of the UAF Tradition Stone, the grave marker that students erected in 1957 to protest President Patty's ban on alcohol. Campus police seized the 400-pound stone, which had been stolen countless times, as possible evidence in a fraud and forgery investigation. Alumni and students were outraged at the attempt to keep the Tradition Stone in jail. Buttons were circulated reading "Free the Stone."

At the time of its capture, the stone was in four pieces, allegedly from falling off the back of a truck during a "getaway attempt about six years ago." According to the Sun-Star, campus police recovered only three of the four pieces. During its captivity, the stone was restored and repaired, and there was some

discussion (just as there had been in 1975 when the Wood Center Pub opened) of burying the tradition of the Tradition Stone by placing it on permanent display. However, few thought it a good idea to let any organized group—even the student government—control the stone. ASUAF tried to establish a Tradition Stone Scholarship Fund, and offered students and others the chance to have their picture taken with the stone for five or ten dollars. No one showed up at the photo opportunity.

Anxious to get rid of the stone, the university looked the other way in early 1993 when it was stolen once again, enabling the tradition to live on.

Cal White, University Relations

(OVERLEAF) STUDENT BOB MITCHELL
dances with Bunnell.

Sam Winch, University Relations

355

Appendices
Notes
Sources
Index

Student Body Presidents

Research by Karl Thoennes
(ASUAF president, '83–'84 and '85–'86)

1922–23   Jack Shanly

1924–25   Clifford Smith

1925–26   Arthur W. Loftus

1926–27   John Calvin Boswell

1927–28   Albert C. Visca

1928–29   Aldwin David Roberts

1929–30   Larry C. Doheny

1930–31   Alvin Polet

1931–32   Charles Herbert
Harold Bently, Herbert's vice president, drowned in the Chena River before finishing the term.

1932–33   Joe Flakne

1934–35   John Baldwin
"Polls were watched during open hours by three husky undergrads, who saw that all voting was done peacefully, legally, and honestly."

1935–36   Glen Franklin
AAC&SM became the University of Alaska during Franklin's term; the student association was officially renamed ASUA on September 25, 1935.

1936–37   John O'Shea

1937–38   Leo Rhode

1938–39   Earl Beistline

1939–40   Kenneth Kyger
Kyger was killed by a falling tree immediately after the expiration of his term in 1940.

1940–41   Al Ehrensing
Balance in ASUA treasury: $30.00.

1941–42   William Race
Race left Alaska before the election of a successor—his wife convened the meeting for the election of new officers in the fall, and then left to join her husband.

1942–43   Donald Wilcox

1943–45   Elizabeth Crites
First female president. Crites served for two years, apparently unopposed at the end of the her first year; no elections were found for the second year.

1945–46   James "Skip" MacKinnon

1946–47   Stanley Lefond

1947–48   Frederick Brusher

1948–49   Fred Schikora
Schikora was the first president of ASUA, Inc., which was disincorporated in 1964.

1949–50   Donald Eyinck

1950–51   Louis Reebs

1951–52   Howard Park

1952–53   Dean Hughes

1953–54   Loyal Burkett

1954–55   Dean Hughes *(resigned in March)*
David Hoopes

1955–56   Kenneth W. Carson *(resigned in December)*
Dorothy Ferguson

1956–57   Stewart Butler

1957–58	Gerald Hook *(resigned in October)* John Reed 　　*Reed was elected in a special election held* 　　*in October.*
1958–59	James Boyd *(resigned in December)* Henry W. Hanson III
1959–60	Henry W. Hanson III
1960–61	Kenneth Kareen
1961–62	James Nankervis 　　*Nankervis died in an auto accident on his* 　　*way back to school in September.* Kenneth Gain *(resigned in October)* Ronald Rizzi *(resigned in February)* Richard Stock
1962–63	Patrick L. Sharrock *(resigned in February)* John Neilsen
1963–64	Gerald Smetzer
1964–66	Patty Jo Anderson 　　*ASUA was disincorporated; Anderson re-* 　　*signed in January.* Stanley Thorsheim *(resigned in February)* Phillip Holland 　　*New ASUA Constitution.*
1966–67	Frank Flavin
1967–68	Michael Platt
1968–69	Steven Snyder 　　*Resigned in January to take a job with the* 　　*American Student Association.* Glenn Bacon
1969–70	Patrick Rice *(resigned in October)* William Hao
1970–71	Dennis Dooley 　　*Ran three times due to low voter turnout.*
1971–72	Chip Wagoner
1972–73	Karl Sopp 　　*Sopp was Senate president; when Dick* 　　*Hertz, a fictitious person, won the election,* 　　*Sopp served as president. Three elections* 　　*were held before the summer, with no win-* 　　*ners. Sopp resigned in September, and an-* 　　*other election was held in October.* Timothy Martin *(resigned in February)* Craig Forrest
1973–74	George Utermohle *(resigned in February)* George Weiss 　　*Four streakers ran through a Senate meet-* 　　*ing this year.*
1974–75	Ric Davidge
1975–76	Patrick Osborne *(resigned in February)* David Slemmons
1976–77	Timothy White *(resigned in January)* Mark Rippy
1977–78	Angela Liston
1978–79	Ronald Mesler
1979–80	Roy Hale Geiersbach 　　*Near the end of his term, Geiersbach was* 　　*impeached. He vetoed the impeachment;* 　　*the Senate did not recognize his veto;* 　　*Geiersbach resigned. President-Elect Kuehn* 　　*refused to assume office early—Geiersbach's* 　　*VP had resigned earlier—and Senate Presi-* 　　*dent Bill Zybach served as temporary presi-* 　　*dent.*
1980–81	Jason Kuehn
1981–82	Jason Kuehn 　　*The first two-consecutive-term elected presi-* 　　*dent to finish both terms.*
1982–83	John DiBene
1983–84	Karl E. Thoennes III
1984–85	James Roth 　　*Resigned in January, went to work in Wash-* 　　*ington.* Tom Van Flein
1985–86	Karl E. Thoennes III
1986–87	Curtis R. Tindall 　　*Tindall was impeached in January.* Earle Williams
1987–88	John Foster Wallace
1988–89	John Foster Wallace
1989–90	Tom Brice
1990–91	Tim Lamkin
1991–92	Sue Thompson
1992–93	Henrik Wessel
1993–94	Karlin Itchoak

Honorary Degree Recipients

1932   Steese, James Gordon, *D. Sc.*

1935   Wickersham, James, *LL. D.*

1940   Anderson, Jacob P., *D. Sc.*

1946   Brandt, Herbert, *D. Sc.*

1949   Duckering, William Elmhirst, *D. Eng.*
       Jackson, Henry M., *LL. D.*
       Seaton, Stuart Lyman, *D. Sc.*

1950   Dimond, Anthony J., *LL. D.*
       Larsen, Helge, *D. Sc.*

1951   Twining, Nathan Farrague, *LL. D.*
       Warren, Hon. Earl, *D. P. Sc.*
       Washburn, Henry Bradford, Jr., *Ph. D.*

1952   Nerland, Andrew, *LL. D.*
       Reed, John C., *D. Sc.*

1953   Patty, Ernest N., *D. Eng.*
       Tuve, Merle A., *D. Sc.*

1954   Balchen, Bernt, *D. Sc.*
       Schmitz, Henry, *D. Sc.*

1955   Gasser, George, *D. Sc.*
       Gruening, Ernest, *LL. D.*
       Knowland, William Fife, *LL. D.*
       Wilkins, Hubert A., *D. Sc.*
       Wood, Walter A., *D. Sc.*

1956   Green, Edith S., *LL. D.*
       Loussac, Zachariah J., *LL. D.*

1957   Geist, Otto William, *D. Sc.*
       Grosvenor, Elsie May Bell, *LL. D.*
       Grosvenor, Gilbert, *LL. D.*
       MacKenzie, Norman A. M., *LL. D.*

1958   Chapman, Sydney, *D. Sc.*
       Drake, C. Marie, *D. Lit.*
       Fry, Franklin C., *D. Lit.*
       Seaton, Fred A., *LL. D.*
       Walsh, Michael J., *LL. D.*

1959   Fohn-Hansen, Lydia, *D. Hum.*
       Irwin, Don, *D. Hum.*
       Lehleitner, George, *LL. D.*
       O'Brien, Leo W., *LL. D.*
       Teller, Edward, *D. Sc.*

1960   Bartlett, E. L. "Bob," *LL. D.*
       FitzGerald, Gerald, *D. Sc.*

1961   Bunche, Ralph J., *LL. D.*
       Field, William O., *D. Sc.*
       Keller, William, *LL. D.*
       Snodgrass, Milton D., *D. Sc.*

1962   Armstrong, R. Rolland, *D. Hum.*
       Aspinall, Wayne N., *LL. D.*
       Thomas, Lowell J., Sr., *LL. D.*
       Wien, Noel, *D. Sc.*

1963   Doolittle, James H., *D. Sc.*
       Reeve, Robert, *D. Sc.*
       Shaw, Robert, *D. F. A.*
       Tilly, Lola Cremeans, *D. Hum.*

1964   Albrecht, C. Earl, *D. Sc.*
       Sasayama, Tadao, *LL. D.*
       Terry, Luther L., *LL. D.*

1965   Anderson, Clinton P., *LL. D.*
       Brewer, Max C., *D. Sc.*

1966   Hale, Mary, *D. F. A.*
       Kimpton, Lawrence, *LL. D.*
       McCracken, Harold, *D. Lit.*
       Trippe, Juan, *LL. D.*

1967   Atwood, Evangeline, *D. Lit.*
       McGinnis, Frederick P., *D. Hum.*
       Miller, Henry L., *LL. D.*
       Moore, Philip H., *D. Sc.*
       Moore, Terris, *LL. D.*
       Snedden, C. W., *LL. D.*

1968   FitzGerald, Joseph H., *LL. D.*
       Goding, M. Wilfred, *LL. D.*
       Herrington, William C., *LL. D.*
       Irving, Laurence, *D. Sc.*
       Mather, Keith B., *D. Sc.*
       Soboleff, Walter A., *D. Hum.*

1969   Anderson, Robert O. *LL. D.*
        Baker, Joel W., *LL. D.*
        Beistline, Earl H., *LL. D.*
        Bingle, Bert J., *D. Hum.*
        Boyd, Louise Arner, *D. Sc.*
        Elvey, Christian T., *D. Sc.*

1970   Bell, Margaret, *D. Lit.*
        Bronk, Detlev Wulf, *D. Sc.*
        Demmert, Archie, *D. Hum.*
        Hanna, G. Dallas, *D. Sc.*
        Rasmuson, Elmer E., *LL. D.*

1971   Gould, Laurence M., *D. Sc.*
        Heurlin, M. C. "Rusty," *D. F. A.*
        Jovanovich, William, *D. Laws*
        Redfield, Alfred C., *D. Sc.*

1972   Egan, William A., *LL. D.*
        Monserud, Sally, *D. Hum.*
        Rae, Kenneth, *LL. D.*
        Schaible, Arthur J., *D. Sc.*
        Smith, Paul A., *D. Sc.*

1973   Bentley, Helen D., *D. Laws*
        Hiebert, A. G., *D. Public Service*
        Kerr, Clark, *D. Laws*
        Machetanz, Fred, *D. F. A.*
        Magnuson, Warren G., *D. Laws*
        Maurer, Paul, *D. Humane Letters*
        Michener, James A., *D. Laws*
        Peratrovich, Frank, *D. Public Service*
        Scholander, Per F., *D. Sc.*

1974   Commager, Henry S., *L. H. D.*
        Hearst, William R., Jr., *LL. D.*
        Rivers, Ralph J., *LL. D.*
        Rock, Howard, *L. H. D.*
        Sarnoff, Robert, *LL. D.*

1975   Degnan, Frank A., *D. Public Service*
        Roberts, Walter Orr, *D. Public Service*
        Stevens, Theodore F., *D. Laws*

1976   Marchand, Leslie A., *D. Humane Letters*
        Murie, Margaret E., *D. Humane Letters*
        O'Neill, Patrick H., *D. Sc.*

1977   Gravel, Mike, *D. Laws*
        Handler, Philip, *D. Sci.*
        McFarland, Robert E., *D. Public Service*

1978   Oliver, Ethel Ross, *D. Public Service*
        Ostar, Allan, *D. Laws*

1979   Fletcher, Joseph O., *D. Sc.*
        Isaac, Andrew T., *D. Hum.*
        Wold, JoAnne, *D. Humane Letters*

1980   Armstrong, Terence E., *D. Sc.*
        Butrovich, John, *D. Laws*
        Nordale, Ladessa, *D. Laws*

1981   Berry, William, *D. Hum.*
        Nerland, Leslie, *D. Public Service*
        Washburn, Albert Lincoln, *D. Sc.*

1982   Brown, Emily I., *D. Hum.*
        Fejes, Claire, *D. Hum.*
        Sheldon, Robert, *D. Public Service*

1983   Dementi, Jean, *D. Hum.*
        Haines, John, *D. Letters*
        Randolph, Carl, *D. Public Service*

1984   Barton, Jay, *D. Sc.*
        Belon, Al, *D. Sc.*
        Berton, Pierre, *D. F. A.*
        Goodale, Ellen, *D. F. A.*
        Goodale, Harvey, *D. F. A.*

1985   Cogo, Robert, *D. Letters*
        Motzfeldt, Jonathan, *D. Laws*
        Weller, Rosamond, *D. Hum.*
        Young, Donald E., *D. Laws*

1986   Demientieff, Mary, *D. Hum.*
        Martin, Fredericka, *D. Hum.*
        Press, Frank, *D. Sc.*

1987   Kaveolook, Harold, *D. Education*
        Neakok, Sadie, *D. Laws*
        Rausch, Robert, *D. Public Service*
        Teeland, Walter, *D. Sc.*
        Weber, Florence, *D. Sc.*

1988   Connelly, Hugh, *D. Laws*
        Fate, Hugh B., *D. Public Service*
        Graham, Ron, *D. Sc.*
        Quam, Louis, *D. Sc.*

1989   Brooks, James, *D. Sc.*
        Fanning, Kay, *D. Letters*
        Huntington, Sidney, *D. Public Service*
        Ott, Charlie, *D. Letters*

1990   Hammond, Jay, *Medal of Merit*
        Heiner, Lawrence, *D. Sc.*
        Jones, Eliza, *D. Letters*
        Lee, Richard, *D. Letters*
        Nelson, George, *D. Laws*
        Scott, Josephine Ryman, *D. Humane Letters*

1991   Gottstein, Barnard Jacob (B. J.), *D. Laws*
        Péwé, Troy L., *D. Sc.*
        Schaible, Grace Berg, *D. Laws*

1992   Fate, Mary Jane, *D. Laws*
        McCann, Sgt. James, *D. Laws*
        Schaller, George, *D. Sc.*
        Southall, Doris, *D. Laws*

1993   Boorstin, Daniel J., *D. Letters*
        Pruitt, William O., Jr., *D. Sc.*
        Ray, Dorothy Jean, *D. Letters*
        Viereck, Leslie A., *D. Sc.*

Notes

Preface

1. James B. Meigs, "Out of the Ivory Tower," *Outside Magazine*, January 1988, 59-60. For a detailed explanation of what is known about the prehistory of the UAF campus see Charles M. Mobley's *The Campus Site: A Prehistoric Camp at Fairbanks, Alaska* (Fairbanks: University of Alaska Press, 1991).

2. Transcript of interview with Patrick H. O'Neill, Living History Program, Columbia University, 1976, 124.

3. *New York Times*, 6 February 1990, c4.

4. Dale L. Walker, *C. L. Sonnichsen: Grassroots Historian* (El Paso: Texas Western Press, 1972), 85.

Chapter 1

1. The only in-depth biography of James Wickersham is Evangeline Atwood's *Frontier Politics: Alaska's James Wickersham* (Portland: Binford and Mort, 1979). Wickersham's personal memoir is *Old Yukon: Tales-Trails-Trials* (St. Paul: West Publishing Co., 1938). His unpublished diaries are on microfilm in the Rasmuson Library, University of Alaska Archives, while many of his papers are at the Alaska State Library in Juneau.

2. *Fairbanks Daily News-Miner*, 28 April 1917.

3. Terrence Cole, *Crooked Past: The History of a Frontier Mining Camp, Fairbanks, Alaska* (Fairbanks: University of Alaska Press, 1991), 58.

4. Department of the Interior, *Report of the Governor of Alaska to the Secretary of the Interior 1915* (Washington: Government Printing Office, 1915), 68.

5. *Fairbanks Evening News*, 1 August 1905.

6. C. C. Georgeson, *Report on Agricultural Investigations in Alaska, 1905*, Office of Experiment Stations, Bulletin No. 169, (Washington: Government Print-

ing Office, 1906), 17. The story that Joslin suggested the site for the Experiment Station is in "Building the Tanana Railroad," *Farthest North Collegian*, December 1927, 13. For general information about the Tanana Mines (later the Tanana Valley) Railroad, see Cole, *Crooked Past*, 82-87; and Duane Koenig, "Ghost Railway in Alaska: The Story of the Tanana Valley Railroad," *Pacific Northwest Quarterly*, January 1954, 8-12.

7. *Annual Report of Alaska Agricultural Experiment Stations for 1908* (Washington: Government Printing Office, 1909), 15, 43-47.

8. *Annual Report of Alaska Agricultural Experiment Stations for 1909* (Washington: Government Printing Office, 1910), 22.

9. James Wickersham, *An Address Delivered at the Laying of the Cornerstone of the Alaska Agricultural College and School of Mines on July 4th, 1915, by Hon. James Wickersham, Delegate to Congress from Alaska* (Fairbanks: Printed by the author, 1915), 1.

10. *Ibid.*, 4.

11. *Congressional Record*, Vol. 52, 63rd Congress, 3rd Session, February-March 4th, 1915, 4544.

12. *Fairbanks Daily News-Miner*, 28 April 1917.

13. *Ibid.* Arguments given by opponents and supporters of the college are summarized by Harriet Hess, "In the Beginning," *Farthest North Collegian*, June 1925, 15-16.

14. Wickersham Diary, 21 June 1915.

15. For the name "Birch hill" see "Club Looking for College on Birch Hill," *Fairbanks Daily News-Miner*, 21 November 1916; 16 February 1917; James Kari, *Lower Tanana Athabaskan Listening and Writing Exercises* (Fairbanks: Alaska Native Language Center, 1991), 24.

16. Harriet Hess, "In the Beginning," 14.

17. Wickersham, *Old Yukon*, 180.

18. Donald Orth, *Dictionary of Alaska Place Names* (Washington: Government Printing Office, 1971), 262, 1046; Atwood, *Frontier Politics*, 108-109.

19. Wickersham Diary, 25 June 1915; 10 July 1915.

20. *Ibid.*, 30 June 1915; William R. Cashen, *Farthest North College President: Charles E. Bunnell and the*

early history of the University of Alaska (Fairbanks: University of Alaska Press, 1972), 109.

21. Wickersham Diary, 24 June 1915.

22. Atwood, *Frontier Politics*, 274.

23. Wickersham, *An Address Delivered at the Laying of the Cornerstone . . .* , 2, 6-7.

24. Department of the Interior, *Report of the Governor of Alaska to the Secretary of the Interior 1919* (Washington: Government Printing Office, 1919), 74.

25. *Fairbanks Daily News-Miner*, 29 December 1915.

26. A. H. Brooks, et. al., *Mineral Resources of Alaska: Report on Progress of Investigations in 1920*, U.S. Geological Survey Bull. No. 722 (Washington: Government Printing Office, 1922), 8-9; Philip S. Smith, et. al., *Mineral Resources of Alaska: Report on Progress of Investigations in 1931*, U.S. Geological Survey Bull. No. 844 (Washington: Government Printing Office, 1934), 14.

27. Department of the Interior, *Report of the Governor of Alaska to the Secretary of the Interior 1918* (Washington: Government Printing Office, 1919), 7, 10.

28. *Fairbanks Daily News-Miner*, 16 February 1917.

29. Quoted in *Fairbanks Daily News-Miner*, 15 May 1917.

30. *Fairbanks Daily News-Miner*, 29 May 1917.

31. *Ibid.*, 26 April 1917.

32. *Ibid.*, 29 April 1917.

33. *Ibid.*, 11 August 1917; Cashen, *Farthest North College President*, 135; *Alaska Alumnus*, April 1958, 4; for a complete list of UAF regents from 1917 to 1974 and analysis of how and why they were chosen see: Evangeline Atwood, "Custodians of Alaska's Academia," *Alaska Journal*, Autumn 1974, 214-216.

34. "Erceg Gives Historical Information," *Alaska Alumnus*, July 1958, 4; Hess, "In the Beginning," 16.

35. Wickersham to Hess, 16 November 1917, abstract in "Notes on the Early History of the University of Alaska 1915–1937," Bunnell Papers, Rasmuson Library, University of Alaska Archives.

36. Hess, "In the Beginning," 16-17.

37. Cashen, *Farthest North College President*, 118.

38. *Ibid., 10.*

39. *Ibid., 17.*

40. *Ibid., 49.*

41. *Fairbanks Daily News-Miner*, 5 October 1916; Atwood, *Frontier Politics*, 286.

42. Cashen, *Farthest North College President, 136.*

43. *Ibid., 79.*

44. *Fairbanks Daily News-Miner*, 14 September 1922; *Nenana News*, 14 September 1922.

45. Department of Interior, *Report of the Governor of Alaska to the Secretary of the Interior 1922* (Washington: Government Printing Office, 1922), 65-66.

46. *Fairbanks Daily News-Miner*, 14 September 1922.

Chapter 2

1. Cashen, *Farthest North College President, 114.*

2. *Fairbanks Daily News-Miner*, 18 September 1922; "First Registration at College," *Alaska Alumnus*, 3-4; LarVern (Borell) Keys, "The First Years at College: Memoirs of July 1922 to July 1935," 9, unpublished manuscript in Keys Collection, Rasmuson Library, University of Alaska Archives.

3. For the list of courses see *Bulletin of the Alaska Agricultural College and School of Mines* (1922); Cashen, *Farthest North College President*, 143-144.

4. *Ibid.*

5. University Relations, University of Alaska Fairbanks, Margaret Murie Press Release, 5 May 1976, 3-4.

6. Keys, "The First Years at College," 6.

7. Cashen, *Farthest North College President*, 147; Ernest Patty, *North Country Challenge* (New York: David McKay Co., 1969), 49.

8. *Bulletin of the Alaska Agricultural College and School of Mines* (1922), 11; Keys, "The First Years at College," 6-7.

9. *Polar Star* 1 November 1957; William R. Cashen, "Cashen's Corner," *Alaska Alumnus*, Fall 1966, 10-11. For an early description of the college library see Leslie A. Marchand, "Among the Five Thousand," *Farthest North Collegian*, June 1925, 20-22; "Alaska Agricultural College and School of Mines," n.d., n.p.

10. Cashen, *Farthest North College President*, 164; "First Registration at College," *Alaska Alumnus*, 3-4; Audrey Loftus to Althea St. Martin, Alumni Relations, University of Alaska Fairbanks, January 1992.

11. Dorothy (Roth) Loftus, "The Pedro Monument Speech 1988: 'Dorothy Remembers,'" 14.

12. Audrey Loftus to Althea St. Martin, Alumni Relations, University of Alaska Fairbanks, January 1992; *Alaska Agricultural College and School of Mines, Catalogue No. 1* (Fairbanks: Tanana Publishing Co., April 1923), 54-55; *Farthest North Collegian*, February 1923, 12.

13. Cashen, *Farthest North College President*, 154; William R. Cashen, "Cashen's Corner," *Alaska Alumnus*, Summer 1972, 6-7; Patty, *North Country Challenge*, 27. Thanks to Dan Nielsen, whose father was a long-time resident of College, for the chance to see his manuscript, "A Brief History of College," and his copy of Jack Shanly's homestead file #01062.

14. Keys, "The First Years at College," 16-17; Patty, *North Country Challenge*, 28.

15. Arthur W. Loftus, "A Homestead 'Frat' House," *Farthest North Collegian*, June 1924, 9-10.

16. Cashen, *Farthest North College President*, 158.

17. *Ibid.*, 218, 279; "Undergrad Builds Cabin on Russian Plan Near Campus," *Farthest North Collegian*, 1 April 1934; *Denali 1935*, 77, 79; "Bungalows and Bachelors," *Farthest North Collegian*, December 1924, 17-19; interview with Lola Tilly, 16 March 1992; telephone interview with Ted Loftus, 26 March 1992.

18. William H. Wilson, *Railroad in the Clouds: The Alaska Railroad in the Age of Steam, 1914–1945* (Boulder: Pruett Publishing, 1977), 86, 190-191; *Alaska Agricultural College and School of Mines, Catalogue No. 4*, 10; *Biennial Report of the Board of Trustees of the Alaska Agricultural College and School of Mines 1929–1931* (n.d.), 22; "Student Affairs," *Farthest North Collegian*, December 1924, 16.

19. William R. Cashen, "Where Did You Say the University is Located?," *Alaska Alumnus*, Winter 1971–72, 6-7; "College Post Office," *Alaska Alumnus*, January 1962, 12.

20. Loftus, "The Pedro Monument Speech 1988," 14.

21. Keys, "The First Years at College," 15.

22. *Alaska Agricultural College and School of Mines, Catalogue No. 2*, 10.

23. *Alaska Agricultural College and School of Mines, Catalogue No. 3*, 8.

24. For accounts of the annual freshman bonfire see the following articles in the *Farthest North Collegian*: "In a Social Way," February 1924, 22; "By the Light of a Bonfire," December 1925, 16-22; "The Crackling Blaze," December 1926, 26-31.

25. Robert McCombe, "The Fastest Game in the World," *Farthest North Collegian*, March 1926, 17-18; "Winners of the Keen Trophy," *Farthest North Collegian*, June 1926, 21.

26. Cashen, *Farthest North College President*, 157.

27. "College Athletics," *Farthest North Collegian*, February 1923, 13.

28. Quoted in K. W. Abell and John C. Boswell, "The College Goes South," *Farthest North Collegian*, December 1926, 16.

29. *Denali 1934*, 47-48.

30. *Farthest North Collegian*, February 1923, 13.

31. "Ad Summum," *Farthest North Collegian*, February 1923, 3.

32. *Polar Star*, 16 February 1955.

33. "Ad Summum," *Farthest North Collegian*, February 1923, 3.

34. For general information about land-grant colleges see: *Land-Grant Fact Book: Centennial Edition* (Washington: American Association of Land-Grant Colleges and State Universities, n.d.); G. Lester Anderson, ed., *Land-Grant Universities and Their Continuing Challenge* (Michigan State University Press, 1976).

35. *Alaska Agricultural College and School of Mines, Catalogue No. 4*, 63.

36. Patty, *North Country Challenge*, 23-24; "Playing the Game," *Farthest North Collegian*, June 1926, 21.

37. Interview with Lola Tilly, 16 March 1992.

38. William R. Cashen, "Cashen's Corner," *Alaska Alumnus*, Winter 1966, 7-9.

39. Cashen, *Farthest North College President*, 202; the *Biennial Report of the Board of Trustees of the*

Alaska Agricultural College and School of Mines 1929–1931 (n.d.), 23, lists 32 student employees.

40. William R. Cashen, "Cashen's Corner," *Alaska Alumnus*, Fall 1971, 4-7.

41. William R. Cashen, "Cashen's Corner," *Alaska Alumnus*, Fall 1966, 10-11.

42. *University of Alaska* (College: December 1936).

43. For information about the importance of the gold dredging industry to Fairbanks and the college see John C. Boswell, *History of Alaskan Operations of United States Smelting, Refining and Mining Company* (Fairbanks: Mineral Industries Research Laboratory, 1979).

44. For information on the expansion of the campus see: "The New Campus," *Farthest North Collegian*, December 1925, 21; "Revamping the Campus," *Farthest North Collegian*, December 1926; "Buildings and Grounds," *Farthest North Collegian*, December 1927, 14; *Alaska Agricultural College and School of Mines, Catalogue No. 6*, 911.

45. *Biennial Report of the Board of Trustees of the Alaska Agricultural College and School of Mines 1929–1931* (n.d.), 23.

46. Ann Tremarello, "'Signers' Hall' Reopened," *Alaska Alumnus*, June 1985, 4; "Signers' Hall," *Faculty and Staff Newsletter*, 29 October 1984, 31.

47. *Fairbanks Daily News-Miner*, 14 May 1934; *Farthest North Collegian*, 1 September 1931.

48. *Farthest North Collegian*, 1 September 1930.

49. Wickersham Diary, 19 June 1922.

50. Atwood, *Frontier Politics*, 49.

51. Wickersham Diary, 20 May 1934.

52. William Cashen, "Cashen's Corner," *Alaska Alumnus*, Summer 1971, 6-7.

53. Wickersham Diary, 18 May 1935.

54. *Farthest North Collegian*, 1 May 1934.

55. *Ibid.*, 1 November 1934; 1 July 1935; William R. Cashen, "Cashen's Corner Revisited," *Alaska Alumnus*, June 1985, 5.

Chapter 3

1. William Cashen, "Cashen's Corner Revisited," *Alaska Alumnus*, June 1985, 5.

2. *Farthest North Collegian*, 1 July 1935.

3. *Ibid.*, 1 April 1935.

4. *University of Alaska Bulletin, General Catalogue 1936–1937*, 25.

5. Patty, *North Country Challenge*, 94; Cashen, *Farthest North College President*, 237-238.

6. Cashen, *Farthest North College President*, 255; *University of Alaska Bulletin, General Catalogue 1936–1937*, 6-7

7. *Polar Star*, 1 November 1957.

8. *Farthest North Collegian*, 1 December 1935; Minutes of the Board of Regents, 5 October 1936. The regents' minutes are on microfilm in the archives of the Rasmuson Library.

9. *Farthest North Collegian*, 1 April 1935; 1 October 1935; 1 December 1935; 1 January 1936; *Biennial Report of the Board of Trustees of the Alaska Agricultural College and School of Mines 1929–1931* (n.d.), 26.

10. Atwood, *Frontier Politics*, 387, 394; Wickersham Diary, 9 March 1935.

11. Wickersham Diary, 9 March 1935.

12. Atwood, *Frontier Politics*, 395.

13. *Farthest North Collegian*, 1 May 1939.

14. Atwood, *Frontier Politics*, 397.

15. *Ibid.*, 385.

16. Terrence Cole, *Ghosts of the Gold Rush* (Fairbanks: Tanana-Yukon Historical Society, 1977), 23.

17. For a biography of Otto Geist see: Charles J. Keim, *Aghvook, White Eskimo: Otto Geist and Alaskan Archaeology* (Fairbanks: University of Alaska Press, 1969). William Cashen, "Cashen's Corner," *Alaska Alumnus*, Winter 1970, 6-7.

18. *Biennial Report of the Board of Trustees of the Alaska Agricultural College and School of Mines 1929–1931* (n.d.), 20.

19. For an account of Geist's work on St. Lawrence Island see: Otto William Geist and Froelich G. Rainey, *Archaeological Excavations at Kukulik* (Washington: Government Printing Office, 1936).

20. *Farthest North Collegian*, 1 March 1942.

21. *Biennial Report of the Board of Trustees of the Alaska Agricultural College and School of Mines 1929–1931* (n.d.), 19.

22. *Farthest North Collegian*, 1 March 1941.

23. Keim, *Aghvook, White Eskimo*, 241, 286.

24. *Farthest North Collegian*, 30 November 1929.

25. *Farthest North Collegian*, 1 November 1946.

26. Minutes of the Board of Regents, 5 October 1936.

27. Mobley, *The Campus Site*, 5-6; *Farthest North Collegian*, 1 November 1946.

28. William Cashen, "Cashen's Corner," *Alaska Alumnus*, Fall 1968, 7-9; Patty, *North Country Challenge*, 83-84.

29. *Ibid.*; *Farthest North Collegian*, 1 December 1930; 1 March 1936; 1 July 1936; 1 April 1947.

30. *Denali 1934*, 28.

31. Stanley P. Young, "The Return of the Musk Ox," from the Smithsonian Report for 1942, Publication 3720, 317-322. Reprinted in *Congressional Record*, Vol. 87, Part 13, A3897-A3899.

32. Vilhjalmur Stefansson, *The Northward Course of Empire* (New York: Harcourt, Brace and Co., 1922), 140.

33. *Fairbanks Daily News-Miner*, 18 February 1935; *Farthest North Collegian*, 1 March 1936.

34. Stanley Young, "The Return of the Musk Ox," 317-322.

35. John W. Coady and Robert A. Hinman, "Management of Muskoxen in Alaska," 47-51, in David R. Klein, et. al., *Proceedings of the First International Muskox Symposium*, Biological Papers of the University of Alaska, Special Report No. 4, December 1984.

36. Timothy E. Smith, "Status of Muskoxen in Alaska," 15-18, in David R. Klein, et. al., *Proceedings of the First International Muskox Symposium*, Biological Papers of the University of Alaska, Special Report No. 4, December 1984; Alaska Legislature, Division of Legislative Audit, "A Special Report on the Dept. of Fish and Game and the University of Alaska Management of State Muskoxen," 10 February 1988.

37. *Farthest North Collegian*, 1 June 1935.

38. *Ibid.*, 1 February 1938; Veryl R. Fuller and Ervin H. Bramhall, *Auroral Research at the University of Alaska 1930–1934* (College: Misc. Publications of the University of Alaska, 1937), 130.

39. On the role of gold mining see: Terrence Cole, "Golden Years: The Decline of Gold Mining in Alaska," *Pacific Northwest Quarterly*, April 1989, 62-71.

40. *Farthest North Collegian*, 1 February 1939; *University of Alaska Bulletin, General Catalogue 1943–1944*, 91-98.

41. *Alaska Agricultural College and School of Mines, Catalogue No. 9*, 60; Boswell, *History of Alaskan Operations of U.S.S.R. & M. Co.*, 25; *Farthest North Collegian*, 1 May 1938; 1 June 1939.

42. *Farthest North Collegian*, 1 March 1935.

43. *Ibid.*; *Fairbanks Daily News-Miner*, 30 June 1944.

44. *Farthest North Collegian*, 1 November 1936.

45. Atwood, "Custodians of Alaska's Academia," *Alaska Journal*, Autumn 1974, 216; *Farthest North Collegian*, 1 January 1947.

46. *Farthest North Collegian*, 1 October 1938.

47. *Ibid.*, 1 October 1940; 1 September 1940.

48. *University of Alaska Bulletin, General Catalogue 1940–1941*, 19.

49. *Farthest North Collegian*, 1 July 1943.

50. *Ibid.*, 1 March 1947.

51. *Ibid.*, 1 July 1943.

52. *Farthest North Collegian*, 1 August 1935; William Cashen, "Cashen's Corner," *Alaska Alumnus*, Spring 1970, 7-8.

53. *Farthest North Collegian*, 1 November 1940; 1 April 1941; Minutes of the Board of Regents, 14 October 1940.

54. *Farthest North Collegian*, 1 January 1942.

55. *Ibid.*, 1 May 1942.

56. *Denali 1943/1944*, 71; *University of Alaska Bulletin, General Catalogue 1945–1946*, 99; *University of Alaska Bulletin, General Catalogue 1946–1947*, 101.

57. Cole, "Golden Years," 66; *University of Alaska Bulletin, General Catalogue 1943–1944*.

58. Minutes of the Board of Regents, 5 September 1942.

59. *Fairbanks Daily News-Miner,* 20 July 1944; 8 September 1944; *Farthest North Collegian,* 1 May 1945; 1 October 1943.

60. *Farthest North Collegian,* 1 May 1944; 1 February 1945.

61. *Ibid.,* 1 November 1943.

62. *Ibid.,* 1 April 1944; 1 September 1945; 1 November 1945.

63. *University of Alaska Bulletin, General Catalogue 1947–1948,* 117. Among the other former UA students who returned after the war to complete their education were Gil Monroe, Donald Cook, and Edwin Brenner. *Farthest North Collegian,* 1 October 1945.

Chapter 4

1. *Farthest North Collegian,* 1 September 1945; *Jessen's Weekly* (Fairbanks), 23 December 1949, 1; Danny Nielsen's research notes on the history of College were helpful with background information.

2. "Governor Recalls Days on Fairbanks Campus," *Alaska Alumnus,* Spring 1975, 3.

3. Manuscript of an article written by Charles E. Bunnell in November 1945 for *Army Times,* Univ. of Alaska President's Papers, Box 1, 1943/48, file 14, University of Alaska Archives, Rasmuson Library.

4. *Alaska Agricultural College and School of Mines, Catalogue No. 8,* 7-8.

5. *University of Alaska Bulletin, General Catalogue 1946–1947,* 17.

6. *Polar Star,* 13 May 1960.

7. *Farthest North Collegian,* 1 November 1946; November 1948.

8. Cashen, *Farthest North College President,* 275.

9. *Farthest North Collegian,* 1 May 1938; *Denali 1938,* 44.

10. Kati Marton, *The Polk Conspiracy: Murder and Cover-up in the Case of CBS News Correspondent George Polk* (New York: Farrar, Straus, and Giroux, 1990). For news of Polk's death see *New York Times,* 16 May 1948, 43; 17 May 1948, 1; for Murrow's reaction see Edward Bliss, Jr., ed., *In Search of Light: The Broadcasts of Edward R. Murrow* (New York: Alfred A. Knopf, 1967), 133; and A. M. Sperber, *Murrow: His Life and Times,* (New York: Freundlich Books, 1986), 302-314. For the Polk award see *New York Times,* 27 October 1948, 25.

11. *Farthest North Collegian,* 1 January 1947.

12. *Ibid.,* 1 December 1947.

13. Gruening Diary, December 30-31, 1939, Gruening Collection, University of Alaska Archives, Rasmuson Library.

14. Ernest Gruening, *Many Battles: The Autobiography of Ernest Gruening* (New York: Liveright, 1973).

15. *Farthest North Collegian,* 1 March 1945.

16. Gruening, *Many Battles,* 347.

17. *Farthest North Collegian,* 1 May 1946.

18. Gruening, *Many Battles,* 347.

19. *Farthest North Collegian,* 1 December 1947.

20. *Ibid.*

21. *Farthest North Collegian,* July 1948.

22. *Jessen's Weekly,* 14 October 1949, 25.

23. Ernest Gruening, *The State of Alaska* (New York: Random House, 1954), 317-318.

24. *Farthest North Collegian,* 1 February 1945; untitled manuscript written for V. Stefansson in President's Papers, Box 5, 1943/48, File #107, University of Alaska Archives, Rasmuson Library.

25. *Farthest North Collegian,* 1 September 1948.

26. Cashen, *Farthest North College President,* 360.

27. *Jessen's Weekly,* 8 July 1949, 30.

28. *Farthest North Collegian,* October 1948.

29. *Jessen's Weekly,* 1 July 1949, 7.

30. Donald Orth, *Dictionary of Alaska Place Names* (Washington: Government Printing Office, 1971), 1011.

31. T. Neil Davis, *The College Hill Chronicles,* is a valuable in-depth look at Terris Moore and his presidency (University of Alaska Foundation, 1993). For other information about Moore see: Terris Moore, *Mt. McKinley: The Pioneer Climbs* (College: University of Alaska Press, 1967); Richard L. Burdsall

and Arthur B. Emmons, (with contributions by Terris Moore and Jack T. Young) *Men Against the Clouds: The Conquest of Minya Konka* (Seattle: The Mountaineers, 1980).

32. For information about the craters named for Chapman and Elvey see: University of Alaska News Release, 23 November 1970, Davis Collection, University of Alaska Archives, Rasmuson Library. For the history of the Geophysical Institute see: Doreen Fitzgerald, "Institute History: The Elvey-Chapman Years," *The Geophysical Institute Quarterly*, Vol. 7, No. 4, Summer 1989, 4-10; *Farthest North Collegian*, December 1957.

33. *Farthest North Collegian*, October 1952; *Polar Star*, 15 September 1954; Fitzgerald, "The Elvey-Chapman Years," 7.

34. *Farthest North Collegian*, December 1949, 15.

35. *Ibid.*, 6.

36. *University of Alaska Bulletin, General Catalogue 1948–1949*, 12; Cashen, *Farthest North College President*, 311-312.

37. *Biennial Report, University of Alaska 1950–1952*, 2.

38. Prentiss French, "Report to Accompany the Master Plan for the University of Alaska," 5.

39. *Ibid.*, 10-11.

40. *Farthest North Collegian*, October 1952; October 1953.

41. Gruening Diary, 1947, undated.

42. *University of Alaska Bulletin, General Catalogue 1947–1948*, 6.

43. Ernest Patty to Elmer Rasmuson, President's Papers, 26 June 1959.

44. Minutes of the Board of Regents, 13 January 1951; *Annual Report of the Governor of the Territory of Alaska for 1951*, 27.

45. William Cashen, "A Survey of Alaska Students Who Have Attended the University of Washington 1933–1948," (M.A. Thesis, Univ. of Washington, 1948), 35.

46. See Terris Moore, "Some Problems of Higher Education in Alaska," President's Papers, Box 1, 1951/52, File 34.

47. Terris Moore to the Board of Regents, President's Papers, 23 October 1953.

48. Elmer Rasmuson to author.

49. *Polar Star*, 13 May 1960.

50. Patty to Frank Heintzleman, President's Papers, 14 July 1955.

51. Patty, *North Country Challenge*, 213.

52. Patty to Board of Regents, President's Papers, 14 September 1959.

53. *Polar Star*, 6 February 1976.

54. Patty to Board of Regents, President's Papers, 16 March 1956.

55. *Polar Star*, 10 March 1954; 22 March 1954.

56. *Biennial Report of the President, University of Alaska, 1957–1959*, 12.

57. *Farthest North Collegian*, March 1957; Patty, *North Country Challenge*, 209; *Polar Star*, 9 February 1955.

58. *Biennial Report of the President, University of Alaska, 1957–1959*, 23; *Farthest North Collegian*, June 1957.

59. "Charles E. Bunnell Memorial Building Dedicated," *Alaska Alumnus*, July 1960, 2.

60. *Polar Star*, 2 November 1956.

61. *Farthest North Collegian*, November 1956; *Alaska Alumnus*, January 1957, 2. For a copy of Bunnell's will, see President's Papers 1960–61, Box 12, file 172.

62. *Fairbanks Daily News-Miner*, 17 August 1992.

63. *Polar Star*, 22 March 1954.

64. *Ibid.*, 13 October 1954.

65. Patty, *North Country Challenge*, 205-206.

66. "Upgrading in Alaska," *Time Magazine*, 2 May 1960, 42-44. See Audrey Loftus, "*Time* Maligns University of Alaska," *Alaska Alumnus*, July 1960, 6.

67. *Polar Star*, 7 April 1954.

68. *Farthest North Collegian*, November 1956; *Polar Star*, 19 October 1956.

69. *Fairbanks Daily News-Miner*, 19 November 1957.

70. *Polar Star*, 19 October 1956; Butler to Board of Regents, President's Papers, 5 March 1957; *Our*

Schools: A History of Elementary and Secondary Public Education in the Fairbanks Area (Fairbanks: Fairbanks North Star Borough School District, 1990), 33-35.

71. *Polar Star,* 30 November 1956.

72. *Ibid.*; 25 January 1957.

73. Patty to the Board of Regents, President's Papers, 10 December 1956.

74. For information on the Tradition Stone see for example: Patty, *North Country Challenge,* 239-242; *Polar Star,* 31 October 1975; and the file on the Tradition Stone in the Alumni Association Office.

Chapter 5

1. *Time,* 4 February 1957.

2. *Fairbanks Daily News-Miner,* 12 March 1957.

3. Minutes of the Board of Regents, 14 May 1959; *University of Alaska Catalog 1960–1961,* 10-11.

4. Ernest Patty, *"Our Product Is People": President's Report to the Board of Regents, The Governor, the Legislature and the Citizens of the State of Alaska* (Fairbanks: University of Alaska, 1959.)

5. Rasmuson to Patty, President's Papers, 24 March 1958.

6. *Alaska Alumnus,* January 1961, 11; Patty to Members of the Board of Regents, President's Papers, 23 September 1959.

7. Minutes of the Board of Regents, 20 October 1960.

8. James D. MacConnell, et. al., *Planning for Action: Progress Report No. 3* (College: University of Alaska, 1960), 5.

9. For information about Wood see: Scott Yates, "Making Light of the Dark," *Alaska Magazine,* July 1985, 10-11; *Alaska Alumnus,* April 1960, 3; *Polar Star,* 12 January 1962; "In Appreciation of William R. Wood," by E. E. Rasmuson, President's Papers, 6 October 1971; *Fairbanks Daily News-Miner,* 9-10 June 1989.

10. *Alaska Alumnus,* January 1961, 5.

11. William R. Wood, *Not From Stone* (Fairbanks: University of Alaska Foundation, 1983), 12, 24.

12. *Denali 1968* (Vol. 2), 6-7.

13. *Alaska Alumnus,* January 1961, 6.

14. *Ibid.,* 14.

15. "Wood Presidency Draws to Close," *Now in the North,* May 1973; "Trend of Enrollment and Degrees Awarded," UAF Office of Institutional Research.

16. James D. MacConnell, et. al., *A Plan for Action: A Working Guide* (College: University of Alaska, 1959), 6.

17. George W. Rogers, *The Future of Alaska: Economic Consequences of Statehood* (Baltimore: Johns Hopkins Press, 1962), 293.

18. *Alaska Alumnus,* July 1965, 3; John C. Reed and Andreas G. Ronhovde, *Arctic Laboratory: A History (1947–1966) of the Naval Arctic Research Laboratory at Point Barrow, Alaska* (Washington: Arctic Institute of North America, 1971), 729-730.

19. Peter A. Coates, *The Trans-Alaska Pipeline Controversy* (Bethlehem: Lehigh University Press, 1991), 114.

20. Dan O'Neill, comp., *Project Chariot: A Collection of Oral Histories,* Vol. 1 (Fairbanks: Rasmuson Library, 1989), 351, 377-383, 419. O'Neill's two-volume collection of oral histories on Chariot offers a comprehensive look at how participants viewed the project. In 1993, UAF awarded honorary degrees to Pruitt and Viereck in recognition of their contributions to science and their opposition to Project Chariot.

21. *Ibid.,* 284.

22. *New York Times,* 11 November 1963.

23. *Alaska Alumnus,* October 1960, 2-3; January 1961, 2; "Wood Presidency Draws to Close," *Now in the North,* May 1973.

24. *Fairbanks Daily News-Miner,* 19 October 1962; *Anchorage Daily News,* 30 October 1962; speech of E. E. Rasmuson at the Anchorage Chamber of Commerce, 29 October 1962.

25. *University of Alaska Catalog 1970–71,* 33

26. *University of Alaska Catalog 1964–65,* 57; *Alaska Alumnus,* July 1965, 2.

27. "Wood Presidency Draws to Close," *Now in the North,* May 1973; *University of Alaska Northern Region Self-Study,* September 1974, 17-18.

28. *Fairbanks Daily News-Miner*, 19 May 1970, 4; *Summer News*, (University of Alaska Bulletin), 10 August 1967; *Nanook News*, 3 March 1966.

29. *Fairbanks Daily-News Miner*, 30 October 1969.

30. *Polar Star*, 28 October 1960; Audrey Loftus to Alaska State Legislators, 14 February 1959, Alumni Association.

31. *Polar Star*, 7 December 1962.

32. *Alaska Alumnus*, July 1962, 7; *Denali 1964*, 366; *Denali 1965*, 227.

33. *University of Alaska Basketball Guide* 1968–1969; UAF Sports Information Director, Karen Jones.

34. *Polar Star*, 5 March 1969; 19 March 1969.

35. *Ibid.*, 7 December 1970; 7 December 1973.

36. *Ibid.*, 2 April 1969; 3 December 1971.

37. O'Neill, *Project Chariot: A Collection of Oral Histories*, Vol. 1, 437; *Polar Star*, 13 March 1968; *Alaska Alumnus*, Fall 1969, 13.

38. *Polar Star*, 24 September 1967. A succinct description of the university during the flood appears in *Now in the North*, July-August 1967 and *Alaska Alumnus*, Fall/Winter 1967/68, 4-8. A wide variety of documents relating to the flood are in the President's Papers, 1967/68, Box 42. See also the *Fairbanks Daily News-Miner*, 6 August 1977.

39. *Polar Star*, 23 November 1962.

40. *Now in the North*, July-August 1967; *Polar Star*, 26 March 1971.

41. *High Water News*, 22 August 1967; issues of the *High Water News* can be found in President's Papers, 1967–68, Box 42.

42. *Now in the North*, July-August 1967.

43. *Polar Star*, 2 November 1966; 5 October 1973; 15 March 1974.

44. *A Tribute to 30 Years! UAF Drama Workshop 1956–1986*.

45. *Ibid.*

46. *Polar Star*, 16 November 1955.

47. *Polar Star*, 17 February 1961; Terrence Cole, "KUAC: A Public Service of the University of Alaska Fairbanks," March 1992 Program Guide.

48. KUAC files contain two large scrapbooks with many clippings relating to the history of the radio and television station.

49. *The Fairbanks Symphony Orchestra: Twenty-five Years: A Celebration*.

50. *Polar Star*, 5 February 1971.

51. Interview with history professor Claus-M. Naske.

52. *Polar Star*, 1 October 1971; 2 February 1973.

53. *Ibid.*, 28 September 1973; 4 December 1968.

54. *Ibid.*, 5 October 1973.

55. *Ibid.*, 28 September 1973; 9 March 1973.

56. Interview with UA Vice President Brian Rogers; *Northern Sun*, 29 February 1980.

57. *Polar Star*, 7 May 1969; 10 December 1971; *Fairbanks Daily News-Miner*, 30 October 1969, 7.

58. *Fairbanks Daily News-Miner*, 16 May 1970, 3.

59. *Ibid.*, 19 May 1970, 4.

60. *Polar Star*, 2 October 1970; 14 April 1972.

61. *Alaska Alumnus*, Spring 1970, 6; *Polar Star*, 5 March 1971; 26 March 1971.

62. *Alaska Alumnus*, Summer 1966, 8-9; *Polar Star*, 15 January 1965.

63. *Denali 1934*, 51; *Polar Star*, 21 September 1956; 29 January 1965; 16 October 1968.

64. *Jessen's Weekly*, 26 June 1963; *Polar Star*, 4 October 1963.

65. *Polar Star*, 26 February 1971.

66. David R. Klein, "Misplaced Values in Landscape Architecture," *Northern Engineer*, Vol. 3, No. 1, Spring 1971, 13-15.

67. Tape of Mailer-Ellison Lecture, Oral History Collection, Rasmuson Library; *Fairbanks Daily News-Miner*, 5 April 1965, 1; *Polar Star*, 9 April 1965.

68. Hilary Mills, *Mailer: A Biography* (New York: Empire Books, 1982), 300.

69. *Polar Star*, 2 December 1966; 6 May 1968. At Skellings' suggestion, fellow Flying Poet Donald Kaufmann wrote his doctoral dissertation on Mailer's career up to 1966. Published in 1969 by Southern

Illinois University Press, *Norman Mailer: The Count-down* begins with Chapter 10 and ends with Chapter 1, an arrangement which Kaufmann claimed enabled him to "zero in on where literature, milieu, and personality converge, at the heart of the controversy that sticks to Mailer." (xvi) In his acknowledgments Kaufmann credits Skellings as "one of the few who can wrestle with Mailer in elevators without ever coming down," referring to the bear hugs Mailer and Skellings exchanged in an elevator at the Anchorage airport, when Mailer arrived in Alaska. (viii)

70. *Ibid.*, 17 April 1968.

71. William M. Ullom to W. R. Wood, President's Papers, 1966–67, English Dept., July-Sept 1966, 28 August 1966.

72. *Denali 1968* (Vol. 1), 18-23; Press release 6 June 1967, from files of Ed Skellings.

73. *Denali 1968* (Vol. 4), 53-55; *Polar Star*, 8 May 1968.

74. *Fairbanks Daily News-Miner*, 9 June 1970; *Polar Star*, 25 September 1970.

75. *Polar Star*, 19 February 1971; 26 March 1971.

76. For information about the SAF controversy see President's Papers, 1970–71, "Students for Academic Freedom," Box 8; *Polar Star*, 9 April 1971; 4 May 1971; 11 February 1972; *Fairbanks Daily News-Miner*, 7 April 1971; 8 April 1971; 10 April 1971; 14 April 1971; 16 April 1971.

77. *Polar Star*, 5 May 1972; 28 April 1972.

78. *Fairbanks Daily News-Miner*, 19 May 1971, 4. For the controversy over student evaluations of teaching see: *Polar Star*, 3 April 1968; 7 December 1970; 12 November 1971; 28 January 1972; 4 February 1972; 24 March 1972.

79. *Polar Star*, 15 October 1971; 14 April 1972. For information on the founding of the University Assembly see the minutes of the Faculty Council and the Board of Regents, as well as *Polar Star*, 24 February 1967; 22 October 1967; 3 April 1968; 3 April 1972.

80. Phil Holland to Rasmuson, President's Papers, 1964/65, Box 25, File 313, 9 May 1965; *Polar Star*, 9 October 1964; 7 December 1964; *The University of Alaska, Self-Evaluation Report I* (College, Alaska, Prepared for the Higher Commission of the Northwest Assoc. of Secondary and Higher Schools, September 1964), 110-111; *Alaska Alumnus*, October 1964, 8-9.

81. *Polar Star*, 3 April 1972; 13 April 1973; 4 May 1971; 13 October 1972; 15 October 1971; 23 February 1973; 9 February 1973.

82. *Alaska Alumnus*, Fall 1966, 12; *Polar Star*, 30 September 1966; 10 December 1967; 4 May 1971; 24 September 1971.

83. *Polar Star*, 10 December 1967.

84. *Ibid.*, 26 November 1971.

85. *A Book: University of Alaska 1971–1972*, 39; *A Book: University of Alaska 1972–1973*, 30; *Polar Star*, 7 December 1970.

86. *Newsweek*, 24 July 1967, 46.

87. *Polar Star*, 3 May 1967. For Sackett's activities as a student see the interview with him in 1968 *Denali* (Vol. 1), 44-46; *Polar Star*, 11 November 1966; 15 September 1967. At the time of his election to the legislature in 1966, Sackett was ASUA Treasurer. "Campaigning and going to school is hard work," he said, "and I wouldn't wish it on any student." In the 1980s Sackett briefly served on the University of Alaska Board of Regents.

88. *Fairbanks Daily News-Miner*, 20 February 1968; *Polar Star*, 21 February 1968.

89. *Fairbanks Daily News-Miner*, 23 February 1968.

90. *Polar Star*, 2 October 1968.

91. *Ibid.*, 7 October 1967.

92. *Ibid.*, 26 March 1971.

93. *Ibid.*, 10 March 1972.

94. *Polar Star*, 30 October 1970.

95. Memo to "Director, FBI" from "SAC, Anchorage," re "Protest of United States Policy in Viet Nam, University of Alaska, College, Alaska, Information Concerning (IS)." The memo, partially declassified in 1990 at the request of researcher Dan O'Neill, lists the "complete names and positions at the University of Alaska, College, Alaska," of half a dozen war protestors. The name of the FBI informant is still classified, as are the names of the individuals listed in the memorandum.

96. *Fairbanks Daily News-Miner*, 11 May 1970, 3; 16 May 1970, 4.

97. *Polar Star*, 12 November 1971.

98. William L. O'Neill, *Coming Apart: An Informal History of America in the 1960's* (Chicago: Quadrangle Books, 1971), 405.

99. Undated memo to University of Alaska Faculty and Administration from University of Alaska Viet Nam Moratorium Committee, in President's Papers, 1969/70, "Students, General."

100. *Polar Star*, 23 October 1969; *Fairbanks Daily News-Miner*, 20 October 1969, 4.

101. *Fairbanks Daily News-Miner*, 20 October 1969, 2.

102. *Polar Star*, 6 November 1969.

103. *University of Alaska Catalog 1963–64*, 71; *Polar Star*, 18 December 1963.

104. *Polar Star*, 8 February 1963.

105. Minutes of the Board of Regents, 18-20 May 1967; *Polar Star*, 27 March 1968; "History of R.O.T.C. at the University of Alaska," courtesy of Major Terrance Hall.

106. *Polar Star*, 1 May 1968.

107. Gruening, *Many Battles*, 467-468.

108. *Polar Star*, 6 November 1968.

109. Edwin W. Webking, Jr., "The 1968 Gruening Write-In Campaign," (Ph.D. Dissertation, Claremont Graduate School, 1972), 185, 193-194.

110. *Ibid.*, 195.

111. *Ibid.*, 172.

112. *Polar Star*, 16 April 1970.

113. The best history of the construction of the pipeline is Coates' *The Trans-Alaska Pipeline Controversy*.

114. *Fairbanks Daily News-Miner*, 26 September 1969.

115. *Polar Star*, 9 October 1969; 2 April 1970.

116. Coates, *The Trans-Alaska Pipeline Controversy*, 203.

117. *Polar Star*, 2 April 1971.

Epilogue

1. "Alumni Tribute to Bunnell Unveiled at UAF," *UAF Alumnus*, October 1988.

2. *Fact Book 1992 University of Alaska Fairbanks*. In 1986–1987 the old University of Alaska Alumni Association ceased to exist, and was replaced by campus-specific alumni groups in Fairbanks, Anchorage and Juneau. *Alaska Alumnus*, the voice of the alumni association since 1956, ceased publication in the summer of 1986. In the final issue UA President Donald O'Dowd addressed an open letter to UA alumni: "I believe the time has come, when alumni should begin to identify specifically with the campus at which they studied, and with which their memories are most closely associated."
   Original directors of the UAF Alumni Association elected in 1986 included: President Bob Williams, Vice President Cynthia Klepaski, Pete Eagan, Jeanne Kohler, Sally Wien, Nancy Ferko, Jim Moody, Bruce Staser, Tom Tunley, Sheila Zagars and T. D. Dumas. *Alaska Alumnus*, Summer 1986, 1.

3. *Anchorage Times*, 30 December 1979.

4. J. Kathleen Stewart, "Chronology of Organizational Structure Changes in a Community College," (M.A. Thesis, Alaska Pacific University, April 1984), 34.

5. University of Alaska Northern Region Self-Study, September 1974; *Polar Star*, 15 October 1971; 27 September 1974.

6. *Polar Star*, 8 October 1980; *Fairbanks Daily News-Miner*, 7 October 1980.

7. After restructuring in the late 1980s President O'Dowd ordered the dashes to be removed from the names of the individual units in Fairbanks, Anchorage and Juneau. At that time the People's Endowment, a UAF fund-raising group associated with the University Foundation, raised hundreds of dollars in the Wood Center Pub by auctioning off the large wooden dash which the Physical Plant had removed from the sign on the entrance to campus. Winning bidders Marsha Wendt and Pat Schmidt ran the price of the dash up so high, they cut it in half and turned it into two dots.
   When President O'Dowd banished the "nuisance" hyphens from the names of the regional units of the university, UAF English professor Russell Tabbert, author of the definitive *Dictionary of Alaskan English*, pointed out the flaw of the punctuation-less titles.
   "The problem is that they aren't grammatical," Tabbert wrote. "In English a locational noun is linked to a preceding noun with a preposition such as *at* or *in*: for example, 'the University of Alaska at Fairbanks.' When the preposition is elided, the boundary be-

tween the two syntactic groups is marked in writing with punctuation: for example, 'the University of Alaska–Fairbanks.' Apparently, the intent behind removing the punctuation is to try to convey that these are separate institutions and not mere branch campuses."

8. *Polar Star*, 1 February 1974.

9. *Ibid.*, 2 November 1973; 16 November 1973.

10. *Ibid.*, 16 January 1976.

11. *Fairbanks Daily News-Miner*, 13 January 1972.

12. *Alaska Alumnus*, Spring 1977, 3. For a review of the events in 1977–1978 see the *Alaska Advocate*, 9-15 February, 1978.

13. *Fairbanks Daily News-Miner*, 8 April 1978.

14. *Ibid.*, 19 December 1977.

15. *Ibid.*, 6 April 1978.

16. *Ibid.*, 13 January 1978.

17. *Ibid.*, 12 May 1979.

18. *Ibid.*, 16 September 1983; Edee Rhode, "Farewell President Barton," *Alaska Alumnus*, June 1984, 3.

19. In November 1988 Alaska voters rejected a controversial ballot proposition that would have required the breakup of the restructured university into two new and independent systems: a university system and a community college system. O'Dowd said the initiative was "the most significant higher education issue ever placed before the Alaska public." See *Anchorage Daily News*, 4 November 1988, C15.

20. *Polar Star*, 16 January 1976.

21. *Denali 1971–1981.*

22. *Fairbanks Daily News-Miner*, 15 May 1981, 1.

23. *University of Alaska Fairbanks 1988–1989 Catalog*, 9.

24. "Signer's Hall," *Faculty and Staff Newsletter*, 29 October 1984; Ann Tremarello, "'Signers' Hall' Reopened," *Alaska Alumnus*, June 1985, 4. For the controversy over the remodeling of Signers' Hall see: *Sun-Star*, 9 November 1984; 30 November 1984; 7 December 1984.

Sources

Archival Records

With few exceptions, the primary sources for this study are available in the Alaska and Polar Regions (APR) Collection at UAF's Elmer E. Rasmuson Library. The photograph collections of APR are voluminous, and provided the bulk of the images used in this book.

Several manuscript collections contain valuable material, especially the University of Alaska President's Papers, the E. L. "Bob" Bartlett Collection and the Ernest Gruening Collection. Charles Bunnell's personal papers are also quite extensive. Lavern (Borell) Keys, Bunnell's first secretary, donated two short memoirs she wrote about the origins of the college. Chip Wagoner and Ric Davidge, two former ASUA presidents in the 1970s, both had the foresight to save their presidential papers and donate them to the UAF archives. Other long-time figures associated with the university who have donated large collections of materials related to the history of the university are Earl Beistline, William Cashen, Neil Davis, Otto Geist, Dorothy Loftus and Lola Tilly.

James Wickersham's diary is on microfilm in the archives, as are the minutes of the board of regents, and the papers of the territorial governors of Alaska.

In the oral history department of APR there are numerous taped reminiscences of early university history, with anecdotes about prominent figures such as Charles Bunnell, Otto Geist, etc. The oral history program also has the tapes of the 1965 debate between Norman Mailer and Ralph Ellison.

Periodicals

The Rasmuson Library has complete files of the numerous periodicals published at the university over the years, which contain much valuable information. These include: *Farthest North Collegian*, *Alaska Alumnus*, *Now In the North*, *Nanook News*, the *Northern Engineer*, the *Polar Star*, the *Northern Sun*, and the *Sun-Star*. Other regularly published volumes, such as the *"A" Book* (the annual guide to student life), the *Denali* (the annual student yearbook), and the annual college and university catalogs, proved to be invaluable.

Jessen's Weekly (Fairbanks) and the *Fairbanks Daily News-Miner* were also helpful; both are available at the Rasmuson Library on microfilm.

University Publications

Alaska. University. Academic Development Plan Committee. *Academic Development Plan for the University of Alaska*. Fairbanks: University of Alaska, 1975.

Alaska. University. Assembly. University Policies and Curriculum Committee. *Goals and Planning at the University of Alaska*. Fairbanks: University of Alaska, 1970.

Alaska. University. *Faculty Council Minutes, 1963–1967.*

Alaska. University. *University of Alaska Northern Region Self-Study: A report for the Commission on Higher Schools of the Northwest Association of Secondary and Higher Schools, September 1974*. Fairbanks: University of Alaska, 1974.

Alaska-Fairbanks. University. *University of Alaska-Fairbanks Institutional Self-Study 1983/84*. Submitted to the Northwest Association of Schools and Colleges, Commission on Colleges. Fairbanks, July 1984.

Biennial Report of the Board of Trustees of the Alaska Agricultural College and School of Mines, 1929–1931. College, n.d.

Cashen, William R. *Farthest North College President*. Fairbanks: University of Alaska Press, 1972.

Davis, Neil. *The College Hill Chronicles: How the University of Alaska Came of Age*. Fairbanks: University of Alaska Foundation, 1993.

Fact Book 1992: University of Alaska Fairbanks. Fairbanks: UAF Planning, Computing & Information Systems, 1992.

Fairbanks Symphony Orchestra. *Fairbanks Symphony Orchestra: Twenty-Five Years: A Celebration*. Fairbanks, 1982.

Fitzgerald, Doreen. "The Elvey-Chapman Years," *The Geophysical Institute Quarterly*, Summer 1989, 4-10.

Fuller, Veryl R., and Ervin H. Bramhall. *Auroral Research at the University of Alaska 1930–1934*. College: University of Alaska, 1937.

Geist, Otto W. and Froelich G. Rainey. *Archaeological Excavations at Kukulik, St. Lawrence Island, Alaska.* Washington: U.S. Government Printing Office, 1936.

Helfferich, Carla. "1963–1973: Decade of Expansion," (History of Geophysical Institute), *The Geophysical Institute Quarterly*, Winter 1990, 8-14.

Kari, James. *Lower Tanana Athabaskan Listening and Writing Exercises.* Fairbanks: Alaska Native Language Center, 1991.

Keim, Charles J. *Aghvook, White Eskimo: Otto Geist and Alaskan Archaeology.* College: University of Alaska Press, 1969.

Klein, David R., et. al. *Proceedings of the First International Muskox Symposium.* Special Report No. 4. Fairbanks: Biological Papers of the University of Alaska. 1984.

Klein, David R. "Misplaced Values in Landscape Architecture," *Northern Engineer*, Spring 1971, 13-15.

Lackey, Lawrence. *University of Alaska Long Range Development Plan: 1964.* San Francisco: Lackey and Associates, 1964.

——. *Long Range Development Plan: 1968.* San Francisco: Lackey and Associates, 1968.

——. *A Library, Humanities and Fine Arts Facility for the University of Alaska.* San Francisco: Lackey and Associates, 1963.

MacConnell, James D. et. al. *A Plan for Action.* (A single bound volume of the complete "Stanford Plan.")

Mobley, Charles M. *The Campus Site: A Prehistoric Camp at Fairbanks, Alaska.* Fairbanks: University of Alaska Press, 1991.

Moore, Terris. *Mt. McKinley: The Pioneer Climbs.* College: University of Alaska Press, 1967.

——. "Prospects for Community Colleges with Status of Branches of the University of Alaska at Anchorage, Juneau, Ketchikan, and Palmer." College: University of Alaska, 1951.

Northwest Association of Secondary and Higher Schools. *The Commission on Higher Schools Evaluation Committee Report: The University of Alaska Northern Region, October 8-10, 1974.*

O'Neill, Dan. *Project Chariot: A Collection of Oral Histories*, Vol. 1 and Vol. 2. Fairbanks: Rasmuson Library, University of Alaska Fairbanks, 1989.

O'Rourke, Patrick J. "Students—Our teaching, their learning," UAF Convocation Address, Fall 1989.

Patty, Ernest. *North Country Challenge.* New York: David McKay Co., 1969.

——. *This is Your University of Alaska* (Biennial Report of the President of the University, 1955–1957). College: University of Alaska, 1955.

——. *Biennial Report of the President, University of Alaska, 1957–1959.* College: University of Alaska, 1957.

Reed, John C. *Arctic Laboratory: A History (1947–1966) of the Naval Arctic Research Laboratory at Point Barrow, Alaska.* Washington: Arctic Institute of North America, 1971.

Triplehorn, Julia H., and Lee E. Johnson. *Muskox Bibliography.* Fairbanks: Institute of Arctic Biology, 1980.

Wickersham, James. *An Address Delivered at the Laying of the Cornerstone of the Alaska Agricultural College and School of Mines on July 4th, 1915, by Hon. James Wickersham, Delegate to Congress from Alaska.* Fairbanks: Printed by the author, 1915.

——. *A Bibliography of Alaskan Literature 1724–1924.* College: Alaska Agricultural College and School of Mines, 1927.

Wood, William R. *Not From Stone.* Fairbanks: University of Alaska Foundation, 1983.

Government Publications

Alaska. Governor. *Annual Report of the Governor of Alaska to the Secretary of the Interior.* (Various Years.)

Alaska. Legislature. Division of Legislative Audit. *A Special Report on the Dept. of Fish and Game and the University of Alaska Management of State Muskoxen.* Juneau: State of Alaska, 1988.

Fairbanks North Star Borough School District. *Our Schools: A History of Elementary and Secondary Public Education in the Fairbanks Area.* Fairbanks, 1990.

Georgeson, C.C. *Report on Agricultural Investigations in Alaska, 1905*, Office of Experiment Stations, Bulletin No. 169. Washington: Government Printing Office, 1906.

McLean, E. Lee and Associates. *Higher Education in Alaska: A Statewide Study with Recommendations to the Seventh Legislature, Second Session.* McLean and Associates, Consultants, January 1972.

————. *Higher Education in Alaska: A Report With Special Reference to the Community Colleges.* McLean and and Associates, Consultants, 1974.

————. *Higher Education in Alaska: 1974–1975.* McLean and Associates, Consultants, 1975.

Orth, Donald J. *Dictionary of Alaska Place Names.* Washington: U.S. Government Printing Office, 1971.

Smith, Timothy E. *Status and Dispersal of an Introduced Muskox Population on the Seward Peninsula.* Juneau: Alaska Dept. of Fish and Game, 1987.

Stein, Gary C. *Promised Land: A History of Alaska's Selection of its Congressional Land Grants.* Anchorage: Alaska Department of Natural Resources,1987.

U.S. Congress. *Congressional Record.* (Debate on Alaska College land grant.) Vol. 52, Part 5, 63rd Congress, 3rd Session, 4543–4545; 5485-5487.

U.S. Department of Agriculture. *Annual Reports of Alaska Agricultural Experiment Stations* (various years). Washington: Government Printing Office.

Young, Stanley P. *The Return of the Musk Ox.* Smithsonian Publication No. 3720 (reprinted from *Smithsonian Report for 1942,* pp. 317-322). Washington: Smithsonian Institution, 1943.

Theses and Dissertations

Cashen, William R. "A Survey of Alaska Students Who Have Attended the University of Washington, 1933–1948." M.A. Thesis, University of Washington, 1948.

Herreid, Janet. "Alaskan Natives at the University of Alaska: Analysis of Selected Test Results and Academic Achievement." M.E. Thesis, University of Alaska, 1964.

Jacquot, Louis Fred. "Alaska Natives and Alaska Higher Education, 1960–1972: A Descriptive Study." Ph.D. Dissertation, University of Oregon, 1974.

Koponen, Niilo E. "The History of Education in Alaska . . ." Ph.D. Dissertation, Harvard University, 1964.

Stewart, J. Kathleen. "Chronology of Organizational Structure Changes in a Community College." M.A. Thesis, Alaska Pacific University, April 1984.

Tilton, William Tyson. "Initial Attitude Profile of Faculty and Professional Staff Toward Certain Distinctive Elements of Their Professional and Local Environment, University of Alaska, Spring Semester, 1969." M.B.A. Thesis, University of Alaska, 1969.

Webking, Edwin. W. "The 1968 Gruening Write-In Campaign." Ph.D. Dissertation, Claremont Graduate School, 1972.

Books

Anderson, G. Lester. *Land-Grant Universities and Their Continuing Challenge.* East Lansing: Michigan State University Press, 1976.

Arnold, Robert D. *Alaska Native Land Claims.* Anchorage: Alaska Native Foundation, 1976.

Atwood, Evangeline. *Frontier Politics: Alaska's James Wickersham.* Portland: Binford and Mort, 1979.

Atwood, Evangeline, and Robert N. DeArmond. *Who's Who in Alaskan Politics.* Anchorage: Alaska Historical Commission 1977.

Bliss, Edward Jr. *In Search of Light: The Broadcasts of Edward R. Murrow, 1938–1961.* New York: Alfred A. Knopf, 1967.

Boswell, John C. *History of Alaskan Operations of United States Smelting, Refining and Mining Company.* Fairbanks: Mineral Industries Research Laboratory, 1979.

Brooks, Alfred H. *Blazing Alaska's Trails.* Fairbanks: University of Alaska Press, 1973.

Bowkett, Gerald E. *Reaching for a Star: The Final Campaign for Alaska Statehood.* Fairbanks: Epicenter Press, 1989.

Burdsall, Richard L., and A. B. Emmons, Terris Moore and Jack Young. *Men Against The Clouds: The Conquest of Minya Konka.* Seattle: The Mountaineers. 1980.

Coates, Peter. *The Trans-Alaska Pipeline Controversy: Technology, Conservation, and the Frontier.* Bethlehem: Lehigh University Press, 1991 and Fairbanks: University of Alaska Press, 1993.

Cole, Terrence. *Crooked Past: The History of a Frontier Mining Camp: Fairbanks, Alaska.* Fairbanks: University of Alaska Press, 1991.

——. *Ghosts of the Gold Rush*. Fairbanks: Tanana-Yukon Historical Society, 1977.

Collins, Henry B. *Archeology of St. Lawrence Island, Alaska*. Washington: Smithsonian Institution, 1937.

Davis, Neil. *The Aurora Watcher's Handbook*. Fairbanks: University of Alaska Press, 1992.

The Development of the Land-Grant Colleges and Universities and their Influence on the Economic and Social Life of the People. Morgantown: West Virginia University Bulletin, 1963.

Gruening, Ernest. *Many Battles: The Autobiography of Ernest Gruening*. New York: Liveright, 1973.

——. *The State of Alaska*. New York: Random House, 1954.

Hunt, William R. *North of 53*. New York: Macmillan, 1974.

——. *Alaska: A Bicentennial History*. New York: Norton, 1976.

——. *Stef: A Biography of Explorer Vilhjalmur Stefansson*. Vancouver: University of British Columbia Press, 1986.

Kaufmann, Donald L. *Norman Mailer: The Countdown (The First Twenty Years)*. Carbondale: Southern Illinois University Press, 1969.

Mailer, Norman. *Why Are We In Vietnam?* New York: Holt, Rinehart Winston, 1982.

Manso, Peter. *Mailer: His Life and Times*. New York: Simon and Schuster, 1985.

Mead, Robert Douglas. *Journeys Down the Line: Building the Trans-Alaska Pipeline*. New York: Doubleday, 1978.

Miller, Orlando W. *The Frontier in Alaska and the Matanuska Colony*. New Haven: Yale University Press, 1975.

Mills, Hilary. *Mailer: A Biography*. New York: Empire Books, 1982.

Murie, Margaret E. *Two In the Far North*. Anchorage: Alaska Northwest Publishing Co., 1978.

Naske, Claus-M. *Bob Bartlett of Alaska: A Life in Politics*. Fairbanks: University of Alaska Press, 1979.

Naske, Claus-M., and Herman Slotnick. *Alaska: A History of the 49th State*. Norman: University of Oklahoma Press, 1987.

O'Neill, William L. *Coming Apart: An Informal History of America in the 1960's*. Chicago: Quadrangle Books, 1971.

Potter, Jean. *The Flying North*. New York: Ballantine Books, 1972.

——. *Alaska Under Arms*. New York: Macmillan Co., 1943.

Rivenburgh, Viola. *Alaska On the Threshold: Adventures in a Year of Change*. Port Angeles: CP Publications, 1986.

Rogers, George W. *The Future of Alaska: Economic Consequences of Statehood*. Baltimore: Johns Hopkins Press, 1962.

Satterfield, Archie. *The Alaska Airlines Story*. Anchorage: Alaska Northwest Publishing Co., 1981.

Skellings, Edmund. *Heart Attacks*. Gainesville: Florida Technological University, 1976.

——. *Showing My Age*. Miami: Florida International University, 1978.

Sperber, A. M. *Murrow: His Life and Times*. New York: Freundlich Books, 1986.

Stefansson, Vilhjalmur. *The Northward Course of Empire*. New York: Harcourt, Brace and Co., 1922.

Walker, Dale L. *C. L. Sonnichsen: Grassroots Historian*. El Paso: Texas Western Press, 1972.

Wickersham, James. *Old Yukon: Tales-Trails-and Trials*. St. Paul: West Publishing Co., 1938.

Works, George A. and Barton Morgan. *The Land-Grant Colleges*. Washington: Government Printing Office, 1939.

Articles

Cole, Terrence. "Golden Years: The Decline of Gold Mining in Alaska," *Pacific Northwest Quarterly*, April 1989, 62-71.

Koenig, Duane. "Ghost Railway in Alaska: The Story of the Tanana Valley Railroad," *Pacific Northwest Quarterly*, January 1954, 812.

Meigs, James B. "Out of the Ivory Tower," *Outside Magazine*, January 1988, 59-60.

Yates, Scott. "Making Light of the Dark," *Alaska Magazine*, July 1985, 10-11.

Index

Clare Hill

Terrence Cole graduated from the University of Alaska Fairbanks with a bachelor's degree in geography and northern studies in 1976, and a master's degree in history in 1978. After earning a Ph.D. in American history at the University of Washington in 1983, he went on to edit the *Alaska Journal* for four years, before returning to UAF as a history professor in 1988. He is the author of numerous works on Alaskan history, including *Crooked Past*, a history of early day Fairbanks, and *Nome: City of the Golden Beaches*, a history of the Nome gold rush. Dr. Cole has written for *American Heritage*, *Alaska Magazine*, *Pacific Northwest Quarterly*, *Western Historical Quarterly*, *Journal of the West*, and other publications. He and his wife Marjorie (class of '76) live in Fairbanks with their two sons, Henry and Desmond.